# PRAISE FOR *THE*

"*The Big Nine* is provocative, readable, and relatable. Amy Webb demonstrates her extensive knowledge of the science driving AI and the geopolitical tensions that could result between the US and China in particular. She offers deep insights into how AI could reshape our economies and the current world order, and she details a plan to help humanity chart a better course."

—Anja Manuel, Stanford University, cofounder and
partner, RiceHadleyGates

"*The Big Nine* is an important and intellectually crisp work that illuminates the promise and peril of AI. Will AI serve its three current American masters in Washington, Silicon Valley, and Wall Street, or will it serve the interests of the broader public? Will it concentrate or disperse economic and geopolitical power? We can thank Amy Webb for helping us understand the questions and how to arrive at answers that will better serve humanity than our current path. *The Big Nine* should be discussed in classrooms and boardrooms around the world."

—Alec Ross, author of *The Industries of the Future*

"*The Big Nine* makes bold predictions regarding the future of AI. But unlike many other prognosticators, Webb sets sensationalism aside in favor of careful arguments, deep historical context, and a frightening degree of plausibility."

—Jonathan Zittrain, George Bemis Professor of International
Law and professor of computer science, Harvard University

"*The Big Nine* is thoughtful and provocative, taking the long view and most of all raising the right issues around AI and providing a road map for an optimistic future with AI."

—Peter Schwartz, author of *The Art of the Long View*

"*The Big Nine* provides seminal arguments on eschewing 'nowist' mindsets to avoid allocating human agency to the corporations developing AI. Webb's potential scenarios for specific futures are superb, providing detailed visions for society to avoid as well as achieve."

—John C. Havens, executive director, IEEE Global Initiative
on Ethics of Autonomous and Intelligent Systems, and
author of *Heartificial Intelligence: Embracing
Our Humanity to Maximize Machines*

"We need to get Amy Webb to campus. This is one of those cases where organizing discussions of the book would be great—but not enough. We would be wise to engage with Webb directly.... We need more books like *The Big Nine* that are critical of higher education for reasons beyond politics (liberal bias) or costs.... *The Big Nine* is an essential book for anyone interested in a global perspective around the role of companies and governmental policies in determining technological change."

—*InsideHigherEd*

"Amy Webb's guidance and insight on these issues are equally important to every business owner and entrepreneur in understanding and marketing the principles of artificial intelligence to their business solutions and their customers."

—Martin Zwilling, *Alley Watch*

"It is Amy Webb's curiosity and courage to face hard problems that distinguishes her work from the growing stack of other books analyzing AI."

—Law.com

"Amy Webb has written one of the most important books of the year and everyone should read it."

—John Noonan, national security expert and
former nuclear launch officer

# THE BIG NINE

How the Tech Titans
and Their Thinking Machines
Could Warp Humanity

AMY WEBB

**PUBLIC**AFFAIRS

NEW YORK

PublicAffairs
Hachette Book Group
1290 Avenue of the Americas, New York, NY 10104
www.publicaffairsbooks.com
@Public_Affairs

Printed in the United States of America

Originally published in hardcover and ebook by PublicAffairs in March 2019
First Trade Paperback Edition: March 2020

Published by PublicAffairs, an imprint of Perseus Books, LLC, a subsidiary of Hachette Book Group, Inc. The PublicAffairs name and logo is a trademark of the Hachette Book Group.

The Hachette Speakers Bureau provides a wide range of authors for speaking events. To find out more, go to www.hachettespeakersbureau.com or call (866) 376-6591.

The publisher is not responsible for websites (or their content) that are not owned by the publisher.

The Library of Congress has cataloged the hardcover edition as follows:

Names: Webb, Amy, 1974- author.
Title: The Big Nine : how the tech titans and their thinking machines could warp humanity / Amy Webb.
Description: New York : PublicAffairs, [2019] | Includes bibliographical references and index.
Identifiers: LCCN 2018048107| ISBN 9781541773752 (hardcover) | ISBN 9781541773745 (ebook)
Subjects: LCSH: Artificial intelligence—Social aspects. | Artificial intelligence—Economic aspects. | Internet industry—Social aspects. | Social responsibility of business.
Classification: LCC Q334.7 .W43 2019 | DDC 006.301—dc23
LC record available at https://lccn.loc.gov/2018048107
ISBNs: 978-1-5417-7375-2 (hardcover); 978-1-5417-7374-5 (ebook); 978-1-5417-2441-9 (international); 978-1-5417-7373-8 (trade paperback)

LSC-C

10  9  8  7  6  5  4  3  2  1

*To my father, Don Webb,*
*the most authentically intelligent person*
*I've ever known.*

# CONTENTS

# BEFORE IT'S TOO LATE

A rtificial intelligence is already here, but it didn't show up as we all expected. It is the quiet backbone of our financial systems, the power grid, and the retail supply chain. It is the invisible infrastructure that directs us through traffic, finds the right meaning in our mistyped words, and determines what we should buy, watch, listen to, and read. It is technology upon which our future is being built because it intersects with every aspect of our lives: health and medicine, housing, agriculture, transportation, sports, and even love, sex, and death.

AI isn't a tech trend, a buzzword, or a temporary distraction—it is the third era of computing. We are in the midst of significant transformation, not unlike the generation who lived through the Industrial Revolution. At the beginning, no one recognized the transition they were in because the change happened gradually, relative to their lifespans. By the end, the world looked different: Great Britain and the United States had become the world's two dominant powers, with enough industrial, military, and political capital to shape the course of the next century.

Everyone is debating AI and what it will mean for our futures ad nauseam. You're already familiar with the usual arguments: the robots are coming to take our jobs, the robots will upend the economy, the robots will end up killing humans. Substitute "machine" for "robot," and we're cycling back to the same debates people had 200 years ago. It's natural to think about the impact of new technology on our jobs and our ability to earn money, since we've seen disruption across so many industries. It's understandable that when thinking about AI, our minds inevitably wander to HAL 9000 from *2001: A Space Odyssey*, WOPR from *War Games*, Skynet from *The Terminator*, Rosie from *The Jetsons*, Delores from *Westworld*, or any of the other hundreds of anthropomorphized AIs from popular culture. If you're not working directly inside of the AI ecosystem, the future seems either fantastical or frightening, and for all the wrong reasons.

Those who aren't steeped in the day-to-day research and development of AI can't see signals clearly, which is why public debate about AI references the robot overlords you've seen in recent movies. Or it reflects a kind of manic, unbridled optimism. The lack of nuance is one part of AI's genesis problem: some dramatically overestimate the applicability of AI, while others argue it will become an unstoppable weapon.

I know this because I've spent much of the past decade researching AI and meeting with people and organizations both inside and outside of the AI ecosystem. I've advised a wide variety of companies at the epicenter of artificial intelligence, which include Microsoft and IBM. I've met with and advised stakeholders on the outside: venture capitalists and private equity managers, leaders within the Department of Defense and State Department, and various lawmakers who think regulation is the only way forward. I've also had hundreds of meetings with academic researchers and technologists working directly in the trenches. Rarely do those working directly in AI share the extreme apocalyptic or utopian visions of the future we tend to hear about in the news.

That's because, like researchers in other areas of science, those actually building the future of AI want to temper expectations. Achieving huge milestones takes patience, time, money, and resilience—this is something we repeatedly forget. They are slogging away, working bit by bit on wildly complicated problems, sometimes making very little progress. These people are smart, worldly, and, in my experience, compassionate and thoughtful.

Overwhelmingly, they work at nine tech giants—Google, Amazon, Apple, IBM, Microsoft, and Facebook in the United States and Baidu, Alibaba, and Tencent in China—that are building AI in order to usher in a better, brighter future for us all. This isn't to say that other companies like NVIDIA, which develops and innovates in graphics processors, or telecommunications giant Huawei, aren't important parts of the AI ecosystem. They are vitally important and worthy of our attention, but they operate in relatively specific, narrow areas. The big nine tech giants are far more comprehensive in scope. I firmly believe that the leaders of these nine companies are driven by a profound sense of altruism and a desire to serve the greater good: they clearly see he potential of AI to improve health care and longevity, to solve our impending climate issues, and to lift millions of people out of poverty. We are already seeing the positive and tangible benefits of their work across all industries and everyday life.

The problem is that external forces pressuring the nine big tech giants—and by extension, those working inside the ecosystem—are conspiring against their best intentions for our futures. In the United States, Google, Amazon, Apple, IBM, Microsoft and Facebook are hamstrung by the relentless short-term demands of capitalistic society, while in China, Baidu, Alibaba and Tencent are fueling the government's authoritarian ambitions. There's a lot of blame to pass around.

In the US, relentless market demands and unrealistic expectations for new products and services have made long-term planning impossible. We expect Google, Amazon, Apple, Facebook, Microsoft, and IBM to make bold new AI product announcements at their annual conferences, as though R&D breakthroughs can be scheduled. If these companies don't present us with shinier products than the previous year, we talk about them as if they're failures. Or we question whether

AI is over. Or we question their leadership. Not once have we given these companies a few years to hunker down and work without requiring them to dazzle us at regular intervals. God forbid one of these companies decides not to make any official announcements for a few months—we assume that their silence implies a skunkworks project that will invariably upset us.

The US government has no grand strategy for AI nor for our longer-term futures. Unlike China, the American government has not pushed a top-down agenda. While President Donald Trump signed an executive order on AI, it does not elucidate a well-honed plan for deep collaboration between the public and private sectors. It makes no mention of the interplay between AI and other areas of technology, and it does not call for significant investment in AI as a public good. Instead, the US government has assumed the commercial sector would drive all progress.

So in place of coordinated national strategies to build organizational capacity inside the government, to build and strengthen our international alliances, and to prepare our military for the future of warfare, the United States has subjugated AI to the revolving door of politics. Instead of funding basic research into AI, the federal government has effectively outsourced R&D to the commercial sector and the whims of Wall Street. Rather than treating AI as an opportunity for new job creation and growth, American lawmakers see only widespread technological unemployment. In turn they blame US tech giants, when they could invite these companies to participate in the uppermost levels of strategic planning (such as it exists) within the government.

On the one hand, we have asked and allowed the big tech companies to make serious and significant decisions that impact the future of our workforce, our national security, our economic growth and our individual opportunities. On the other hand, individual city governments, well-capitalized advisory groups, and presidential candidates for the 2020 election have published their own punitive and, arguably, unenforceable guidelines on recommended AI ethics, values and rules. In every case, these groups are imposing their narrow ideas and worldviews on the big tech giants without asking for their input. How could this possibly set the backdrop for our tech giants to create positive change? Our AI pioneers have no choice but to constantly compete with each other for a trusted, direct connection with you, me, our schools, our hospitals, our cities, and our businesses.

In the United States, we suffer from a tragic lack of foresight. We operate with a "nowist" mindset, planning for the next few years of our lives more than any other timeframe. Nowist thinking champions short-term technological achievements, but it absolves us from taking responsibility for how technology might evolve and for the next-order implications and outcomes of our actions. We too easily forget that what we do in the present could have serious consequences in the future. Is it any wonder, therefore, that we've effectively outsourced the future development of AI to six publicly traded companies whose achievements are remarkable but whose financial interests do not always align with what's best for our individual liberties, our communities, and our democratic ideals?

Meanwhile, in China, AI's developmental track is tethered to the grand ambitions of government. China is quickly laying the groundwork to become the world's unchallenged AI hegemon. In July 2017, the Chinese government unveiled its Next Generation Artificial Intelligence Development Plan to become the global leader in AI by the year 2030 with a domestic industry worth at least $150 billion,[1] which involved devoting part of its sovereign wealth fund to new labs and startups, as well as new schools launching specifically to train China's next generation of AI talent.[2] In October of that same year, China's President Xi Jinping explained his plans for AI and big data during a detailed speech to thousands of party officials. AI, he said, would help China transition into one of the most advanced economies in the world. Already, China's economy is 30 times larger than it was just three decades ago. Baidu, Tencent, and Alibaba may be publicly traded giants, but typical of all large Chinese companies, they must bend to the will of Beijing.

China's massive population of 1.4 billion citizens puts it in control of the largest, and possibly most important, natural resource in the era of AI: human data. Voluminous amounts of data are required to refine pattern recognition algorithms—which is why Chinese face recognition systems like Megvii and SenseTime are so attractive to investors. All the data that China's citizens are generating as they make phone calls, buy things online, and post photos to social networks are helping Baidu, Alibaba, and Tencent to create best-in-class AI systems. One big advantage for China: it doesn't have the privacy and security restrictions that might hinder progress in the United States.

We must consider the developmental track of AI within the broader context of China's grand plans for the future. In April 2018, Xi gave a major speech outlining his vision of China as the global cyber superpower. China's state-run Xinhua news service published portions of the speech, in which he described a new cyberspace governance network and an internet that would "spread positive information, uphold the correct political direction, and guide public opinion and values towards the right direction."[3] The authoritarian rules China would have us all live by are a divergence from the free speech, market-driven economy, and distributed control that we cherish in the West.

China has been working to exert leadership on the global stage. Between 2017 and 2019, the Chinese Communist Party positioned officials to lead several key agencies within the United Nations, including the Food and Agriculture Organization, the International Civil Aviation Administration, the Industrial Development Organization and the International Telecommunications Union. The party advanced dozens of official memorandums of understanding with UN member nations in support of its economic expansion initiatives. All the while,

China has been working smartly to supply the UN with well-educated civil servants and to fund various UN initiatives. While some at the UN might see this moment an opportunity to shape China's future, what they fail to understand is that Beijing is endeavoring to reshape the UN for its own purposes.

AI is part of a series of national edicts and laws that aim to control all information generated within China and to monitor the data of its residents as well as the citizens of its various strategic partners. One of those edicts requires all foreign companies to store Chinese citizens' data on servers within Chinese borders. This allows government security agencies to access personal data as they wish. Another initiative— China's Police Cloud—was designed to monitor and track people with mental health problems, those who have publicly criticized the government, and a Muslim ethnic minority called the Uighurs. In August 2018, the United Nations said that it had credible reports that China had been holding millions of Uighurs in secret camps in the far western region of China.[4] China's Integrated Joint Operations Program uses AI to detect pattern deviations—to learn whether someone has been late paying bills. An AI-powered Social Credit System, according to a slogan in official planning documents, was developed to engineer a problem-free society by "allow(ing) the trustworthy to roam everywhere under heaven while making it hard for the discredited to take a single step."[5] To promote "trustworthiness," citizens are rated on a number of different data points, like heroic acts (points earned) or traffic tickets (points deducted). Those with lower scores face hurdles applying for jobs, buying a home, or getting kids into schools. In some cities, high-scoring residents have their pictures on display.[6] In other cities, such as Shandong, citizens who jaywalk have their faces publicly shared on digital billboards and sent automatically to Weibo, a popular social network.[7] If all this seems too fantastical to believe, keep in mind that China once successfully instituted a one-child policy to forcibly cull its population.

These policies and initiatives are the brainchild of President Xi Jinping's inner circle, which for the past decade has been singularly focused on rebranding and rebuilding China into our predominant global superpower. China is more authoritarian today than under any previous leaders since Chairman Mao Zedong, and advancing and leveraging AI are fundamental to the cause. The Belt and Road Initiative is a massive geoeconomic strategy masquerading as an infrastructure plan following the old Silk Road routes that connected China with Europe via the Middle East and Africa. China isn't just building bridges and highways—it's exporting surveillance technology and collecting data in the process as it increases the CCP's influence around the world in opposition to our current liberal democratic order. The Global Energy Interconnection is yet another national strategy championed by Xi that aims to create the world's first global electricity grid, which it would manage. China has already figured out how to scale a new kind of ultra-high-voltage cable technology that can deliver power from the far western regions to Shanghai—and it's striking deals to become a power provider to neighboring countries.

These initiatives, along with many others, are clever ways to gain soft power over a long period of time. It's a brilliant move by Xi, whose political party voted in March 2018 to abolish term limits and effectively allowed him to remain president for life. Xi's endgame is abundantly clear: to create a new world order in which China is the de facto leader. And yet during this time of Chinese diplomatic expansion, the United States inextricably turned its back on longstanding global alliances and agreements as President Trump erected a new bamboo curtain.

The future of AI is currently moving along two developmental tracks that are often at odds with what's best for humanity. China's AI push is part of a coordinated attempt to create a new world order led by President Xi, while market forces and consumerism are the primary drivers in America. This dichotomy is a serious blind spot for us all. Resolving it is the crux of our looming AI problem, and it is the purpose of this book. The Big Nine companies may be after the same noble goals—cracking the code of machine intelligence to build systems capable of humanlike thought—but the eventual outcome of that work could irrevocably harm humanity.

Fundamentally, I believe that AI is a positive force, one that will elevate the next generations of humankind and help us to achieve our most idealistic visions of the future.

But I'm a pragmatist. We all know that even the best-intentioned people can inadvertently cause great harm. Within technology, and especially when it comes to AI, we must continually remember to plan for both intended use and unintended misuse. This is especially important today and for the foreseeable future, as AI intersects with everything: the global economy, the workforce, agriculture, transportation, banking, environmental monitoring, education, the military, and national security. This is why if AI stays on its current developmental tracks in the United States and China, the year 2069 could look vastly different than it does in the year 2019. As the structures and systems that govern society come to rely on AI, we will find that decisions being made on our behalf make perfect sense to machines—just not to us.

We humans are rapidly losing our awareness just as machines are waking up. We've started to pass some major milestones in the technical and geopolitical development of AI, yet with every new advancement, AI becomes more invisible to us. The ways in which our data is being mined and refined is less obvious, while our ability to understand how autonomous systems make decisions grows less transparent.

This is particularly bad because at the moment there is no singular entity that can be held accountable for AI's development. In the United States, we have three epicenters of power: our federal government in Washington DC, the financial markets in New York City, and the West Coast between San Jose and Redmond at companies and universities where critical decisions about technology are being made. Each nexus of power believes itself to be dominant. To wit: Microsoft has developed a corporate foreign policy and has departments like "Law Enforcement and National Security" and "Digital Diplomacy." Meanwhile, many governments, including the UK and Denmark, have staffed diplomatic offices in Silicon Valley to operate as "tech embassies."

We have, therefore, a chasm in understanding of how AI is impacting daily life in the present, one growing exponentially as we move years and decades into the future. Shrinking that distance as much as possible through a critique of the developmental track that AI is currently on is my mission for this book. My goal is to democratize the conversations about artificial intelligence and make you smarter about what's ahead—and to make the real-world future implications of AI tangible and relevant to you personally, before it's too late.

Humanity is facing an existential crisis in a very literal sense, because no one is addressing a simple question that has been fundamental to AI since its very inception: What happens to society when we transfer power to a system built by a small group of people that is designed to make decisions for everyone? What happens when those decisions are biased toward market forces or an ambitious political party? The answer is reflected in the future opportunities we have, the ways in which we are denied access, the social conventions within our societies, the rules by which our economies operate, and even the way we relate to other people.

This is not a book about the usual AI debates. It is both a warning and a blueprint for a better future. It questions our aversion to long-term planning in the US and highlights the lack of AI preparedness within our businesses, schools, and government. It paints a stark picture of China's interconnected geopolitical, economic, and diplomatic strategies as it marches on toward its grand vision for a new world order. And it asks for heroic leadership under extremely challenging circumstances. Because, as you're about to find out, our futures need a hero.

What follows is a call to action written in three parts. In the first, you'll learn what AI is and the role the Big Nine have played in developing it. We will also take a deep dive into the unique situations faced by America's Big Nine members and by Baidu, Alibaba, and Tencent in China. In Part II, you'll see detailed, plausible futures over the next 50 years as AI advances. The three scenarios you'll read range from optimistic to pragmatic and catastrophic, and they will reveal both opportunity and risk as we advance from artificial narrow intelligence to artificial general intelligence to artificial superintelligence. These scenarios are intense—they are the result of data-driven models, and they will give you a visceral glimpse at how AI might evolve and how our lives will change as a result. In Part III, I will offer tactical and strategic solutions to all the problems identified in the scenarios along with a concrete plan to reboot the present. Part III is intended to jolt us into action, so there are specific recommendations for our governments, the leaders of the Big Nine, and even for you.

\* \* \*

Every person alive today can play a critical role in the future of artificial intelligence. The decisions we make about AI now—even the seemingly small ones—will forever change the course of human history. As the machines awaken, we may realize that in spite of our hopes and altruistic ambitions, our AI systems turned out to be catastrophically bad for humanity.

But they don't have to be.

The Big Nine aren't the villains in this story. In fact, they are our best hope for the future.

Turn the page. We can't sit around waiting for whatever might come next. AI is already here.

# CHAPTER ONE

# MIND AND MACHINE:
# A VERY BRIEF HISTORY OF AI

The roots of modern artificial intelligence extend back hundreds of years, long before the Big Nine were building AI agents with names like Siri, Alexa, and their Chinese counterpart Tiān Māo. Throughout that time, there has been no singular definition for AI, like there is for other technologies. When it comes to AI, describing it concretely isn't as easy, and that's because AI represents many things, even as the field continues to grow. What passed as AI in the 1950s—a calculator capable of long division—hardly seems like an advanced piece of technology today. This is what's known as the "odd paradox"—as soon as new techniques are invented and move into the mainstream, they become invisible to us. We no longer think of that technology as AI.

In its most basic form, artificial intelligence is a system that makes autonomous decisions. The tasks AI performs duplicate or mimic acts of human intelligence, like recognizing sounds and objects, solving problems, understanding language, and using strategy to meet goals. Some AI systems are enormous and perform millions of computations quickly—while others are narrow and intended for a single task, like catching foul language in emails.

We've always circled back to the same set of questions: Can machines think? What would it mean for a machine to think? What does it mean for us to think? What is thought? How could we know—definitively, and without question—that we are actually thinking original thoughts? These questions have been with us for centuries, and they are central to both AI's history and future.

The problem with investigating how both machines and humans think is that the word "think" is inextricably connected to "mind." The *Merriam-Webster Dictionary* defines "think" as "to form or have in the mind," while the *Oxford Dictionary* explains that it means to "use one's mind actively to form connected ideas." If we look up "mind," both *Merriam-Webster* and *Oxford* define it within the context of "consciousness." But what is consciousness? According to both, it's the quality or state of being aware and responsive. Various groups—psychologists, neuroscientists, philosophers, theologians, ethicists, and computer scientists—all approach the concept of thinking using different approaches.

When you use Alexa to find a table at your favorite restaurant, you and she are both aware and responsive as you discuss eating, even though Alexa has never felt the texture of a crunchy apple against her teeth, the effervescent prickles of sparkling water against her tongue, or the gooey pull of peanut butter against the roof of her mouth. Ask Alexa to describe the qualities of these foods, and she'll offer you details that mirror your own experiences. Alexa doesn't have a mouth—so how could she perceive food the way that you do?

You are a biologically unique person whose salivary glands and taste buds aren't arranged in exactly the same order as mine. Yet we've both learned what an apple is and the general characteristics of how an apple tastes, what its texture is, and how it smells. During our lifetimes, we've learned to recognize what an apple is through reinforcement learning—someone taught us what an apple looked like, its purpose, and what differentiates it from other fruit. Then, over time and without conscious awareness, our autonomous biological pattern recognition systems got really good at determining something was an apple, even if we only had a few of the necessary data points. If you see a black-and-white, two-dimensional outline of an apple, you know what it is—even though you're missing the taste, smell, crunch, and all the other data that signals to your brain *this is an apple.* The way you and Alexa both learned about apples is more similar than you might realize.

Alexa is competent, but is she *intelligent?* Must her machine perception meet all the qualities of human perception for us to accept her way of "thinking" as an equal mirror to our own? Educational psychologist Dr. Benjamin Bloom spent the bulk of his academic career researching and classifying the states of thinking. In 1956, he published what became known as Bloom's Taxonomy, which outlined learning objectives and levels of achievement observed in education. The foundational layer is remembering facts and basic concepts, followed in order by understanding ideas; applying knowledge in new situations; analyzing information by experimenting and making connections; evaluating, defending, and judging information; and finally, creating original work. As very young children, we are focused first on remembering and understanding. For example, we first need to learn that a bottle holds milk before we understand that that bottle has a front and back, even if we can't see it.

This hierarchy is present in the way that computers learn, too. In 2017, an AI system called Amper composed and produced original music for an album called *I AM AI.* The chord structures, instrumentation, and percussion were developed by Amper, which used initial parameters like genre, mood, and length to generate a full-length song in just a few minutes. Taryn Southern, a human artist, collaborated with Amper to create the album—and the result included a moody, soulful ballad called "Break Free" that counted more than 1.6 million YouTube views and was a hit on traditional radio. Before Amper could create that song, it had to first learn the qualitative elements of a big ballad, along with quantitative data, like how to calculate the value of notes and beats and how to recognize thousands of patterns in music (e.g., chord progressions, harmonic sequences, and rhythmic accents).

Creativity, the kind demonstrated by Amper, is the pinnacle of Bloom's Taxonomy, but was it merely a learned mechanical process? Was it an example of humanistic creativity? Or creativity of an entirely different kind? Did Amper think about music, the same way that a human composer might? It could be argued that Amper's "brain"— a neural network using algorithms and data inside a container—is maybe not that different from Beethoven's brain, made up of organic neurons using data and recognizing patterns inside the container that is his head. Was Amper's creative process truly different than Beethoven's when he composed his Symphony no. 5, the one which famously begins da-da-da-DUM, da-da-da-DUM before switching from a major to a minor key? Beethoven didn't invent the entire symphony—it wasn't completely original. Those first four notes are followed by a harmonic sequence, parts of scales, arpeggios, and other common raw ingredients that make up any composition. Listen closely to the *scherzo*, before the finale, and you'll hear obvious patterns borrowed from Mozart's 40th Symphony, written 20 years earlier, in 1788. Mozart was influenced by his rival Antonio Salieri and friend Franz Joseph Hayden, who were themselves influenced by the work of earlier composers like Johann Sebastian Bach, Antonio Vivaldi, and Henry Purcell, who were writing music from the mid-17th to the mid-18th centuries. You can hear threads of even earlier composers from the 1400s to the 1600s, like Jacques Arcadelt, Jean Mouton, and Johannes Ockeghem, in their music. *They* were influenced by the earliest medieval composers—and we could continue the pattern of influence all the way back to the very first written composition, called the "Seikilos epitaph," which was engraved on a marble column to mark a Turkish gravesite in the first century. And we could keep going even further back in time, to when the first primitive flutes made out of bone and ivory were likely carved 43,000 years ago. Even before then, researchers believe that our earliest ancestors probably sang before they spoke.[1]

Our human wiring is the result of millions of years of evolution. The wiring of modern AI is similarly based on a long evolutionary trail extending back to ancient mathematicians, philosophers, and scientists. While it may seem as though humanity and machinery have been traveling along disparate paths, our evolution has always been intertwined. *Homo sapiens* learned from their environments, passed down traits to future generations, diversified, and replicated because of the invention of advanced technologies, like agriculture, hunting tools, and penicillin. It took 11,000 years for the world's 6 million inhabitants during the Neolithic period to propagate into a population of 7 billion today.[2] The ecosystem inhabited by AI systems—the inputs for learning, data, algorithms, processors, machines, and neural networks—is improving and iterating at exponential rates. It will take only decades for AI systems to propagate and fuse into every facet of daily life.

Whether Alexa perceives an apple the same way we do, and whether Amper's original music is truly "original," are really questions about how we think about thinking. Present-day artificial intelligence is an amalgam of thousands of years of philosophers, mathematicians, scientists, roboticists, artists, and theologians. Their quest—and ours, in this chapter—is to understand the connection between thinking and containers for thought. What is the connection between the human mind and—*or in spite of*—machines being built by the Big Nine in China and the United States?

## Is the Mind Inside a Machine?

The foundational layer of AI can be traced back to ancient Greece and to the origins of philosophy, logic, and math. In many of Plato's writings, Socrates says, "Know thyself," and he meant that in order to improve and make the right decisions, you first had to know your own character.

Among his other work, Aristotle invented syllogistic logic and our first formal system of deductive reasoning. Around the same time, the Greek mathematician Euclid devised a way for finding the greatest common divisor of two numbers and, as a result, created the first algorithm. Their work was the beginning of two important new ideas: that certain physical systems can operate as a set of logical rules and that human thinking itself might be a symbolic system. This launched hundreds of years of inquiry among philosophers, theologians, and scientists. Was the body a complex machine? A unified whole made up of hundreds of other systems all working together, just like a grandfather clock? But what of the mind? Was it, too, a complex machine? Or something entirely different? There was no way to prove or disprove a divine algorithm or the connection between the mind and the physical realm.

In 1560, a Spanish clockmaker named Juanelo Turriano created a tiny mechanical monk as an offering to the church, on behalf of King Philipp II of Spain, whose son had miraculously recovered from a head injury.[3] This monk had startling powers—it walked across the table, raised a crucifix and rosary, beat its chest in contrition, and moved its lips in prayer. It was the first *automaton*—a mechanical representation of a living thing. Although the word "robot" didn't exist yet, the monk was a remarkable little invention, one that must have shocked and confused onlookers. It probably never occurred to anyone that a tiny automaton might someday in the distant future not just mimic basic movements but could stand in for humans on factory floors, and in research labs, and in kitchen conversations.

The tiny monk inspired the first generation of roboticists, whose aim was to create ever more complex machines that mirrored humans: automata were soon capable of writing, dancing, and painting. And this led a group of philosophers to start asking questions about what it means to be human. If it was possible to build automata that mimicked human behavior, then were humans divinely built automata? Or were we complex systems capable of reason and original thought?

The English political philosopher Thomas Hobbes described human reasoning as computation in *De Corpore*, part of his great trilogy on natural sciences, psychology, and politics. In 1655, he wrote: "By reasoning, I understand computation. And to compute is to collect the sum of many things added together at the same time, or to know the remainder when one thing has been taken from another. To reason therefore is the same as to add or to subtract."[4] But how would we know whether we had free will during the process?

While Hobbes was writing the first part of his trilogy, French philosopher René Descartes published *Meditations on First Philosophy*, asking whether we can know for certain that what we perceive is real. How could we verify our own consciousness? What proof would we need to conclude that our thoughts are our own and that the world around us is real? Descartes was a rationalist, believing that facts could be acquired through deduction. Famously, he put forward a thought experiment. He asked readers to imagine a demon purposely creating an illusion of their world. If the reader's physical, sensory experience of swimming in a lake was nothing more than the demon's construct, then she couldn't really *know* that she was swimming. But in Descartes's view, if the reader had self-awareness of her own existence, then she had met the criteria for knowledge. "I am, I exist, whenever it is uttered from me, or conceived by the mind, necessarily is true," he wrote.[5] In other words, the fact of our existence is beyond doubt, even if there is a deceptive demon in the midst. Or, *I think, therefore I am.*

Later, in his *Traité de l'homme* (*Treatise of Man*) Descartes argued that humans could probably make an automaton—in this case, a small animal—that would be indistinguishable from the real thing. But even if we someday created a mechanized human, it would never pass as real, Descartes argued, because it would lack a mind and therefore a soul. Unlike humans, a machine could never meet the criteria for knowledge—it could never have self-awareness as we do. For

Descartes, consciousness occurred internally—the soul was the ghost in the machines that are our bodies.[6]

A few decades later, German mathematician and philosopher Gottfried Wilhelm von Leibniz examined the idea that the human soul was itself programmed, arguing that the mind itself was a container. God created the soul and body to naturally harmonize. The body may be a complex machine, but it is one with a set of divine instructions. Our hands move when we decide to move them, but we did not create or invent all of the mechanisms that allow for the movement. If we are aware of pain or pleasure, those sensations are the result of a pre-programmed system, a continual line of communication between the mind and the body.

Leibniz developed his own thought experiment to illustrate the point that thought and perception were inextricably tied to being human. Imagine walking into a mill. The building is a container housing machines, raw materials, and workers. It's a complex system of parts working harmoniously toward a singular goal, but it could never have a mind. "All we would find there are cogs and levers pushing one another, and never anything to account for a perception," Leibniz wrote. "So perception must be sought in simple substances, and never in composite things like machines." The argument he was making was that no matter how advanced the mill, machinery, or automata, humans could never construct a machine capable of thinking or perceiving.[7]

Yet Leibniz was fascinated with the notion of replicating facets of thought. A few decades earlier, a little-known English writer named Richard Braithwaite, who wrote a few books about social conduct, passively referenced human "computers" as highly trained, fast, accurate people good at making calculations.[8] Meanwhile French mathematician and inventor Blaise Pascal, who laid the foundation for what we know today as probability, concerned himself with automating computational tasks. Pascal watched his father tediously calculating taxes by hand and wanted to make the process easier for him. So Pascal began work on an automatic calculator, one with mechanical wheels and movable dials.[9] The calculator worked, and it inspired Leibniz to refine his thinking: machines would never have souls; however, it would someday be possible to build a machine capable of human-level logical thinking. In 1673, Leibniz described his "step reckoner," a new kind of calculating machine that made decisions using a binary system.[10] The machine was sort of like a billiards table, with balls, holes, sticks, and canals, and the machine opened the holes using a series of 1s (open) and 0s (closed).

Leibniz's theoretical step reckoner laid the groundwork for more theories, which included the notion that if logical thought could be reduced to symbols and as a result could be analyzed as a computational system, and if geometric problems could be solved using symbols and numbers, then everything could be reduced to bits—including human behavior. It was a significant split from the earlier philosophers: future machines could replicate human thinking processes without infringing on divine providence. Thinking did not necessarily require perception, senses, or soul. Leibniz imagined a computer capable of solving general problems, even nonmathematical ones. And he hypothesized that language could be reduced to atomic concepts of math and science as part of a universal language translator.[11]

## Do Mind and Machine Simply Follow an Algorithm?

If Leibniz was correct—that humans were machines with souls and would someday invent soulless machines capable of untold, sophisticated thought—then there could be a binary class of machines on earth: us and them. But the debate had only started.

In 1738, Jacques de Vaucanson, an artist and inventor, constructed a series of automata for the French Academy of Science that included a complex and lifelike duck. It not only imitated the motions of a live duck, flapping its wings and eating grain, but it could also mimic digestion. This offered the philosophers food for thought: If it looked like a duck, and quacked like a duck, was it really a duck? If we perceive the duck to have a soul of a different kind, would that be enough to prove that the duck was aware of itself and all that implied?

Scottish philosopher David Hume rejected the idea that acknowledgement of existence was itself proof of awareness. Unlike Descartes, Hume was an empiricist. He developed a new scientific framework based on observable fact and logical argument. While de Vaucanson was showing off his digesting duck—and well before anyone was talking about artificial intelligence—Hume wrote in *A Treatise of Human Nature*, "Reason is, and ought only to be, the slave of the passions." In this case, Hume intended "passions" to mean "nonrational motivations" and that incentives, not abstract logic, drive our behavior. If impressions are simply our perception of something we can see, touch, feel, taste, and smell, and ideas are perceptions of things that we don't come into direct contact with, Hume believed that our existence and understanding of the world around us was based on a construct of human perception.

With advanced work on automata, which were becoming more and more realistic, and more serious thought given to computers as thinking machines, French physician and philosopher Julien Offray de La Mettrie undertook a radical—and scandalous—study of humans, animals, and automata. In a 1747 paper he first published anonymously, La Mettrie argued humans are remarkably similar to animals, and an ape could learn a human language if it "were properly trained." La Mettrie also concluded that humans and animals are merely machines, driven by instinct and experience. "The human body is a machine which winds its own springs; . . . the soul is but a principle of motion or a material and sensible part of the brain."[12]

The idea that humans are simply matter-driven machines—cogs and wheels performing a set of functions—implied that we were not special or unique. It also implied that perhaps we were programmable. If this was true, and if we had until this point been capable of creating lifelike ducks and tiny monks, then it should follow that someday, humans could create replicas of themselves—and build a variety of intelligent, thinking machines.

## Could a Thinking Machine Be Built?

By the 1830s, mathematicians, engineers, and scientists had started tinkering, hoping to build machines capable of doing the same calculations as human "computers." English mathematician Ada Lovelace and scientist Charles Babbage invented a machine called the "Difference Engine" and then later postulated a more advanced "Analytical Engine," which used a series of predetermined steps to solve mathematical problems. Babbage hadn't conceived that the machine could do anything beyond calculating numbers. It was Lovelace who, in the footnotes of a scientific paper she was translating, went off on a brilliant tangent speculating that a more powerful version of the Engine could be used in other ways.[13] If the machine could manipulate symbols, which themselves could be assigned to different things (such as musical notes), then the Engine could be used to "think" outside of mathematics. While she didn't believe that a computer would ever be able to create original thought, she did envision a complex system that could follow instructions and thus mimic a lot of what everyday people did. It seemed unremarkable to some at the time, but Ada had written the first complete computer program for a future, powerful machine—decades before the light bulb was invented.

A hundred miles north from where Lovelace and Babbage were working at Cambridge University, a young self-trained mathematician named George Boole was walking across a field in Doncaster and had a sudden burst of inspiration, deciding to dedicate his life to explaining the logic of human thought.[14] That walk produced what we know today as Boolean algebra, which is a way of simplifying logical expressions (e.g. "and," "or," and "not") by using symbols and numbers. So for example, computing "true *and* true" would result "true," which would correspond to physical switches and gates in a computer. It would take two decades for Boole to formalize his ideas. And it would take another 100 years for someone to realize that Boolean logic and probability could help computers evolve from automating basic math to more complex thinking machines. There wasn't a way to build a thinking machine—the processes, materials, and power weren't yet available—and so the theory couldn't be tested.

The leap from theoretical thinking machines to computers that began to mimic human thought happened in the 1930s with the publication of two seminal papers: Claude Shannon's "A Symbolic Analysis of Switching and Relay Circuits" and Alan Turing's "On Computable Numbers, with an Application to the *Entscheidungsproblem*." As an electrical engineering student at MIT, Shannon took an elective course in philosophy—an unusual diversion. Boole's *An Investigation of the Laws of Thought* became the primary reference for Shannon's thesis. His advisor, Vannevar Bush, encouraged him to map Boolean logic to physical circuits. Bush had built an advanced version of Lovelace and Babbage's Analytical Engine—his prototype was called the "Differential Analyzer"—and its design was somewhat ad hoc. At that time, there was no systematic theory dictating electrical circuit design. Shannon's breakthrough was mapping electrical circuits to Boole's symbolic logic and then explaining how Boolean logic could be used to create a working circuit for adding 1s and 0s. Shannon had figured out that computers had two layers: physical (the container) and logical (the code).

While Shannon was working to fuse Boolean logic onto physical circuits, Turing was testing Leibniz's universal language translator that could represent all mathematical and scientific knowledge. Turing aimed to prove what was called the *Entscheidungsproblem*, or the "decision problem." Roughly, the problem goes like this: no algorithm can exist that determines whether an arbitrary mathematical statement is true or false. The answer would be negative. Turing was able to prove that no algorithm exists, but as a byproduct, he found a mathematical model of an all-purpose computing machine.[15]

And that changed everything. Turing figured out that a program and the data it used could be stored inside a computer—again, this was a radical proposition in the 1930s. Until that point, everyone agreed that the machine, the program, and the data were each independent. For the first time, Turing's universal machine explained why all three were intertwined. From a mechanical standpoint, the logic that operated circuits and switches could also be encoded into the program and data. Think about the significance of these assertions. The container, the program, and the data were part of a singular entity—not unlike humans. We too are containers (our bodies), programs (autonomous cellular functions), and data (our DNA combined with indirect and direct sensory information).

Meanwhile, that long tradition of automata, which began 400 years earlier with a tiny walking, praying monk, at last crossed paths with Turing and Shannon's work. The American manufacturing company Westinghouse built a relay-based robot named the Elektro the Moto-Man for the 1939 World's Fair. It was a crude, gold-colored giant with wheels beneath its feet. It had 48 electrical relays that worked on a telephone relay system. Elektro responded, via prerecorded messages on a record player, to voice commands spoken through a telephone handset. It was an anthropomorphized computer capable of making rudimentary decisions—like what to say—without direct, real-time human involvement.

Judging by the newspaper headlines, science fiction short stories, and newsreels from that time, it's clear that people were caught off guard, shocked, and concerned about all of these developments. To them it felt as though "thinking machines" had simply arrived, fully formed, overnight. Science fiction writer Isaac Asimov published "Liar!," a prescient short story in the May 1941 issue of *Astounding Science Fiction*. It was a reaction to the research he was seeing on the fringes, and in it he made an argument for his Three Laws of Robotics:

1. A robot may not injure a human being or, through inaction, allow a human being to come to harm.
2. A robot must obey the orders given to it by human beings, except where such orders would conflict with the First Law.
3. A robot must protect its own existence as long as such protection does not conflict with the First or Second Laws.

Later, Asimov added what he called the "Zeroth Law" to govern all others: "A robot may not harm humanity, or, by inaction, allow humanity to come to harm."

## But Would a Thinking Machine Actually *Think*?

In 1943, University of Chicago psychiatry researchers Warren McCulloch and Walter Pitts published their important paper "A Logical Calculus of the Ideas Immanent in Nervous Activity," which described a new kind of system modeling biological neurons into simple neural network architecture for intelligence. If containers, programs, and data were intertwined, as Turing had argued, and if humans were similarly elegantly designed containers capable of processing data, then it followed that building a thinking machine might be possible if modeled using the part of humans responsible for thinking—our brains. They posited a modern computational theory of mind and brain, a "neural network." Rather than focusing on the machine as hardware and the program as software, they imagined a new kind of symbiotic system capable of ingesting vast amounts of data, just like we humans do.

Computers weren't yet powerful enough to test this theory—but the paper did inspire others to start working toward a new kind of intelligent computer system.

The link between intelligent computer systems and autonomous decision-making became clearer once John von Neumann, the Hungarian-American polymath with specializations in computer science, physics, and math, published a massive treatise of applied math. Cowritten with Princeton economist Oskar Morgenstern in 1944, the 641-page book explained, with painstaking detail, how the science of game theory revealed the foundation of all economic decisions. It is this work that led to von Neumann's collaborations with the US Army, which had been working on a new kind of electric computer called the Electronic Numerical Integrator and Computer, or ENIAC for short. Originally, the instructions powering ENIAC were hardwired into the system, which meant that with each new program, the whole system would have to be rewired. Inspired by Turing, McCulloch, and Pitts, von Neumann developed a way of storing programs on the computer itself. This marked the transition from the first era of computing (tabulation) to a new era of programmable systems.

Turing himself was now working on a concept for a neural network, made up of computers with stored-program machine architecture. In 1949, *The London Times* quoted Turing: "I do not see why it (the machine) should not enter any one of the fields normally covered by the human intellect, and eventually compete on equal terms. I do not think you even draw the line about sonnets, though the comparison is perhaps a little bit unfair because a sonnet written by a machine will be better appreciated by another machine." A year later, in a paper published in the philosophy journal *Mind,* Turing addressed the questions raised by Hobbes, Descartes, Hume, and Leibniz. In it, he proposed a thesis and a test: If someday, a computer was able to answer questions in a manner indistinguishable from humans, then it must be "thinking." You've likely heard of the paper by another name: the Turing test.

The paper began with a now-famous question, one asked and answered by so many philosophers, theologians, mathematicians, and scientists before him: "Can machines think?" But Turing, sensitive to the centuries-old debate about mind and machine, dismissed the question as too broad to ever yield meaningful discussion. "Machine" and "think" were ambiguous words with too much room for subjective interpretation. (After all, 400 years' worth of papers and books had already been written about the meaning of those words.)

The game was built on deception and "won" once a computer successfully passed as a human. The test goes like this: there is a person, a machine, and in a separate room, an interrogator. The object of the game is for the interrogator to figure out which answers come from the person and which come from the machine. At the beginning of the game, the interrogator is given labels, X and Y, but doesn't know which one refers to the computer and is only allowed to ask questions like "Will X please tell me whether X plays chess?" At the end of the game, the interrogator has to figure out who was X and who was Y. The job of the other person is to help the interrogator identify the machine, and the job of the machine is to trick the interrogator into believing that it is actually the other person. About the game, Turing wrote: "I believe that in about fifty years' time it will be possible, to programme computers, with a storage capacity of about $10^9$, to make them play the imitation game so well that an average interrogator will not have more than 70 per cent chance of making the right identification after five minutes of questioning."[16]

But Turing was a scientist, and he knew that his theory could not be proven, at least not within his lifetime. As it happened, the problem wasn't with Turing's lack of empirical evidence proving that machines would someday think, and it wasn't even in the timing—Turing said that it would probably take until the end of the 20th century to ever be able to run his test. "We may hope that machines will eventually compete with men in all purely intellectual fields," Turing wrote. The real problem was taking the leap necessary to believe that machines might someday see, reason, and remember—and that humans might get in the way of that progress. This would require his fellow researchers to observe cognition without spiritualism and to believe in the plausibility of intelligent machines that, unlike people, would make decisions in a nonconscious way.

## The Summer and Winter of AI

In 1955, professors Marvin Minsky (mathematics and neurology) and John McCarthy (mathematics), along with Claude Shannon (a mathematician and cryptographer at Bell Labs) and Nathaniel Rochester (a computer scientist at IBM), proposed a two-month workshop to explore Turing's work and the promise of machine learning. Their theory: if it was possible to describe every feature of human intelligence, then a machine could be taught to simulate it.[17] But it was going to take a broad, diverse group of experts in many different fields. They believed that a significant advance could be made by gathering an interdisciplinary group of researchers and working intensively, without any breaks, over the summer.

Curating the group was critically important. This would become the network of rarified engineers, social scientists, computer scientists, psychologists, mathematicians, physicists, and cognitive specialists who would ask and answer fundamental questions about what it means to "think," how our "minds" work, and how to teach machines to learn the same way we humans do. The intention was that this diverse network would continue to collaborate on research and on building this new field into the future. Because it would be a new kind of interdisciplinary approach to building machines that think, they needed a new name to describe their activities. They landed on something ambiguous but elegant: *artificial intelligence.*

McCarthy created a preliminary list of 47 experts he felt needed to be there to build the network of people and set the foundation for all of the research and prototyping that would follow. It was a tense process, determining all of the key voices who absolutely had to be in the room as AI was being conceptualized and built in earnest. Minsky, especially, was concerned that the meeting would miss two critical voices—Turing, who'd died two years earlier, and von Neumann, who was in the final stages of terminal cancer.[18]

Yet for their great efforts in curating a diverse group with the best possible mix of complementary skills, they had a glaring blind spot. Everyone on that list was white, even though there were many brilliant creative people of color working throughout the very fields McCarthy and Minsky wanted to bring together. Those who made the list hailed from the big tech giants at the time (IBM, Bell Labs) or from a small handful of universities. Even though there were plenty of brilliant women already making significant contributions in engineering, computer science, mathematics, and physics, they were excluded.[19] The invitees were all men, save for Marvin Minsky's wife, Gloria. Without awareness of their own biases, these scientists—hoping to understand how the human mind works, how we think, and how machines might learn from all of humanity—had drastically limited their pool of data to those who look and sound just like them.

The following year, the group gathered on the top floor of Dartmouth's math department and researched complexity theory, natural language simulation, neural networks, the relationship of randomness to creativity, and learning machines. On the weekdays they met in the main math classroom for a general discussion before dispersing to tackle the more granular tasks. Professors Allen Newell, Herbert Simon, and Cliff Shaw came up with a way to discover proofs of logical theorems and simulated the process by hand—a program they called Logic Theorist—at one of the general sessions. It was the first program to mimic the problem-solving skills of a human. (Eventually, it would go on to prove 38 of the first 52 theorems in Alfred North Whitehead and Bertrand Russell's *Principia Mathematica*, a standard text on the foundations of mathematics.) Claude Shannon, who had several years earlier proposed teaching computers to play chess against humans, got the opportunity to show a prototype of his program, which was still under construction.[20]

McCarthy and Minsky's expectations for groundbreaking advancements in AI didn't materialize that summer at Dartmouth. There wasn't enough time—not to mention enough compute power—to evolve AI from theory to practice.[21] However, that summer did set in motion three key practices that became the foundational layer for AI as we know it today:

1. AI would be theorized, built, tested, and advanced by big technology companies and academic researchers working together.
2. Advancing AI required a lot of money, so commercializing the work in some way—whether working through partnerships with government agencies or the military or building products and systems that could be sold—was going to be required.
3. Investigating and building AI relied on a network of interdisciplinary researchers, which meant establishing a new academic field from scratch. It also meant that those in the field tended to recruit people they already knew, which kept the network relatively homogenous and limited its worldview.

There was another interesting development that summer. While the group coalesced around the question raised by Turing—*Can machines think?*—they were split on the best approach to prove his answer, which was to build a learning machine. Some of the members favored a biological approach. That is, they believed that neural nets could be used to imbue AI with common sense and logical reasoning—that it would be possible for machines to be generally intelligent. Other members argued that it would never be possible to create such a complete replica of human thinking structures. Instead, they favored an engineering approach. Rather than writing commands to solve problems, a program could help the system "learn" from a data set. It would make predictions based on that data, and a human supervisor would check answers—training and tweaking it along the way. In this way, "machine learning" was narrowly defined to mean learning a specific task, like playing checkers.

Psychologist Frank Rosenblatt, who was at the Dartmouth workshop, wanted to model how the human brain processed visual data and, as a result, learn how to recognize objects. Drawing on the research from that summer, Rosenblatt created a system called Perceptron. His intent was to construct a simple framework program that would be responsive to feedback. It was the first artificial neural network (ANN) that operated by creating connections between multiple processing elements in a layered arrangement. Each mechanical neuron would take in lots of different signal inputs and then use a mathematical weighting system to decide which output signal to generate. In this parallel structure, multiple processors could be accessed at once—meaning that it was not only fast, it could process a lot of data continuously.

Here's why this was so important: while it didn't necessarily mean that a computer could "think," it *did* show how to teach a computer to learn. We humans learn through trial and error. Playing a C scale on the piano requires striking the right keys in the right sequence. At the beginning, our fingers, ears, and eyes don't have the correct pattern memorized, but if we practice—repeating the scale over and over, making corrections each time—we eventually get it right. When I took piano lessons and mangled my scales, my teacher corrected me, but if I got them right, I earned a sticker. The sticker reinforced that I'd made the right decisions while playing. It's the same with Rosenblatt's neural network. The system learned how to optimize its response by performing the same functions thousands of times, and it would remember what it learned and apply that knowledge to future problems. He'd train the system using a technique called "back propagation." During the initial training phase, a human evaluates whether the ANN made the correct decision. If it did, the process is reinforced. If not, adjustments were made to the weighting system, and another test was administered.

In the years following the workshop, there was remarkable progress made on complicated problems for humans, like using AI to solve mathematical theorems. And yet training AI to do something that came simply—like recognizing speech—remained a vexing challenge with no immediate solution. Before their work on AI began, the mind had always been seen as a black box. Data went in, and a response came back out with no way to observe the process. Early philosophers, mathematicians, and scientists said this was the result of divine design. Modern-era scientists knew it was the result of hundreds of thousands of years of evolution. It wasn't until the 1950s, and the summer at Dartmouth, that researchers believed they could crack open the black box (at least on paper) and observe cognition. And then teach computers to mimic our stimulus-response behavior.

Computers had, until this point, been tools to automate tabulation. The first era of computing, marked by machines that could calculate numbers, was giving way to a second era of programmable computers. These were faster, lighter systems that had enough memory to hold instruction sets within the computers. Programs could now be stored locally and, importantly, written in English rather than complicated machine code. It was becoming clear that we didn't need automata or humanistic containers for AI applications to be useful. AI could be housed in a simple box without any human characteristics and still be extremely useful.

The Dartmouth workshop inspired British mathematician I. J. Good to write about "an ultraintelligence machine" that could design ever better machines than we might. This would result in a future "intelligence explosion, and the intelligence of man would be left far behind. Thus the first ultraintelligent machine is the last invention that man need ever make."[22]

A woman did finally enter the mix, at least in name. At MIT, computer scientist Joseph Weizenbaum wrote an early AI system called ELIZA, a chat program named after the ingenue in George Bernard Shaw's play *Pygmalion*.[23] This development was important for neural networks and AI because it was an early attempt at natural language processing, and the program accessed various prewritten scripts in order to have conversations with real people. The most famous script was called DOCTOR,[24] and it mimicked an empathetic psychologist using pattern recognition to respond with strikingly humanistic responses.

The Dartmouth workshop had now generated international attention, as did its researchers, who'd unexpectedly found themselves in the limelight. They were nerdy rock stars, giving everyday people a glimpse into a fantastical new vision of the future. Remember Rosenblatt, the psychologist who'd created the first neural net? He told the *Chicago Tribune* that soon machines wouldn't just have ELIZA programs capable of a few hundred responses, but that computers would be able to listen in on meetings and type out dictation, "just like a office secretary." He promised not only the largest "thinking device" ever built, but one that would be operational within just a few months' time.[25]

And Simon and Newell, who built the Logic Theorist? They started making wild, bold predictions about AI, saying that within ten years—*meaning by 1967*—computers would

- beat all the top-ranked grandmasters to become the world's chess champion,
- discover and prove an important new mathematical theorem, and
- write the kind of music that even the harshest critics would still value.[26]

Meantime, Minsky made predictions about a generally intelligent machine that could do much more than take dictation, play chess, or write music. He argued that within his lifetime, machines would achieve artificial general intelligence—that is, computers would be capable of complex thought, language expression, and making choices.[27]

The Dartmouth workshop researchers wrote papers and books. They sat for television, radio, newspaper, and magazine interviews. But the science was difficult to explain, and so oftentimes explanations were garbled and quotes were taken out of context. Wild predictions aside, the public's expectations for AI became more and more fantastical, in part because the story was misreported. For example, Minsky was quoted in *Life* magazine saying: "In from three to eight years we will have a machine with the general intelligence of an average human being. I mean a machine that will be able to read Shakespeare, grease a car, play office politics, tell a joke, have a fight."[28] In that same article, the journalist refers to Alan Turing as "Ronald Turing." Minsky, who was clearly enthusiastic, was likely being cheeky and didn't mean to imply that walking, talking robots were just around the corner. But without the context and explanation, the public perception of AI started to warp.

It didn't help that in 1968, Arthur Clarke and Stanley Kubrick decided to make a movie about the future of machines with the general intelligence of the average person. The story they wanted to tell was an origin story about humans and thinking machines—and they brought Minsky on board to advise. If you haven't guessed already, it's a movie you already know called *2001: A Space Odyssey*, and it centered around a generally intelligent AI named HAL 9000, who learned creativity and a sense of humor from its creators—and threatened to kill anyone who wanted to unplug it. One of the characters, Victor Kaminski, even got his name from Minsky.

It's fair to say that by the middle of the 1960s, AI had entered the zeitgeist, and everyone was fetishizing the future. Expectations for the commercial success of AI were on the rise, too, due to an article published in an obscure trade journal that covered the radio industry.

Titled simply "Cramming More Components onto Integrated Circuits," the article, written by Intel cofounder Gordon Moore, laid out the theory that the number of possible transistors that could be placed on an integrated circuit board for the same price would double every 18 to 24 months. This bold idea became known as Moore's law, and very early on his thesis appeared to be accurate. Computers were becoming more and more powerful and capable of myriad tasks, not just solving math problems. It was fuel for the AI community because it meant that their theories could move into serious testing soon. It also raised the fascinating possibility that human-made AI processors could ultimately exceed the powers of the human mind, which has a biologically limited storage capacity.

All the hype, and now this article, funneled huge investment into AI—even if those outside the Dartmouth network didn't quite understand what AI really was. There were no products to show yet, and there were no practical ways to scale neural nets and all the necessary technology. Because people now believed in the *possibility* of thinking machines, that was enough to secure significant corporate and government investment. For example, the US government funded an ambitious AI program for language translation. It was the height of the Cold War, and the government wanted an instantaneous translation system of Russian for greater efficiency, cost savings, and accuracy. It seemed as though machine learning could provide a solution by way of a translation program. A collaboration between the Institute of Languages and Linguistics at Georgetown University and IBM produced a Russian-English machine translation system prototype that had a limited 250-word vocabulary and specialized only in organic chemistry. The successful public demonstration caused many people to leap to conclusions, and machine translation hit the front page of the *New York Times*—along with half a dozen other newspapers.

Money was flowing—between government agencies, universities, and the big tech companies—and for a time, it didn't look like anyone was monitoring the tap. But beyond those papers and prototypes, AI was falling short of promises and predictions. It turned out that making serious headway proved a far greater challenge than its modern pioneers anticipated.

Soon, there were calls to investigate the real-world uses and practical implementation of AI. The National Academy of Sciences had established an advisory committee at the request of the National Science Foundation, the Department of Defense, and the Central Intelligence Agency. They found conflicting viewpoints on the viability of AI-powered foreign language translation and ultimately concluded that "there has been no machine translation of general scientific text, and none is in immediate prospect."[29] A subsequent report produced for the British Science Research Council asserted that the core researchers had exaggerated their progress on AI, and it offered a pessimistic prognosis for all of the core research areas in the field. James Lighthill, a British applied mathematician at Cambridge, was the report's lead author; his most damning criticism was that those early AI techniques—teaching a computer to play checkers, for example—would never scale up to solve bigger, real-world problems.[30]

In the wake of the reports, elected officials in the US and UK demanded answers to a new question: Why are we funding the wild ideas of theoretical scientists? The US government, including DARPA, pulled funding for machine translation projects. Companies shifted their priorities away from time-intensive basic research on general AI to more immediate programs that could solve problems. If the early years following the Dartmouth workshop were characterized by great expectations and optimism, the decades after those damning reports became known as the AI Winter. Funding dried up, students shifted to other fields of study, and progress came to a grinding halt.

Even McCarthy became much more conservative in his projections. "Humans can do this kind of thing very readily because it's built into us," McCarthy said.[31] But we have a much more difficult time understanding how we understand speech—the physical and cognitive processes that make language recognition possible. McCarthy liked to use a birdcage example to explain the challenge of advancing AI. Let's say that I asked you to build me a birdcage, and I didn't give you any other parameters. You'd probably build an enclosure with a top, bottom, and sides. If I gave you an additional piece of information— the bird is a penguin—then you might not put a top on it. Therefore, whether or not the birdcage requires a top depends on a few things: the information I give you and all of the associations you already have with the word "bird," like the fact that most birds fly. We have built-in assumptions and context. Getting AI to respond the same way we do would require a lot more explicit information and instruction.[32] The AI Winter would go on to last for three decades.[33]

## What Came Next:
## Learning to Play Games

While funding had dried up, many of the Dartmouth researchers continued their work on AI—and they kept teaching new students. Meanwhile, Moore's law continued to be accurate, and computers became ever more powerful.

By the 1980s, some of those researchers figured out how to commercialize aspects of AI—and there was now enough compute power and a growing network of researchers who were finding that their work had commercial viability. This reignited interest and, more importantly, the flow of cash into AI. In 1981, Japan announced a 10-year-long plan to develop AI called Fifth Generation. That prompted the US government to form the Microelectronics and Computer Technology Corporation, a research consortium designed to ensure national competitiveness. In the UK, funding that had been cut in the wake of that damning report on AI's progress by James Lighthill got reinstated.

Between 1980 and 1988, the AI industry ballooned from a few million dollars to several billion.

Faster computers, loaded with memory, could now crunch data more effectively, and the focus was on replicating the decision-making processes of human experts, rather than building all-purpose machines like the fictional HAL 9000. These systems were focused primarily on using neural nets for narrow tasks, like playing games. And throughout the '90s and early 2000s, there were some exciting successes. In 1994, an AI called CHINOOK played six games of checkers against world champion Marlon Tinsley (all draws). CHINOOK won when Tinsley withdrew from the match and relinquished his championship title.[34] In 1997, IBM's Deep Blue supercomputer beat world chess champion Garry Kasparov, who buckled under the stress of a six-game match against a seemingly unconquerable opponent. In 2004, Ken Jennings won a statistically improbable 74 consecutive games on *Jeopardy!*, setting a Guinness World Record at that time for the most cash ever won on a game show. So when he accepted a match against IBM's Watson in 2011, he felt confident he was going to win. He'd taken classes on AI and assumed that the technology wasn't advanced enough to make sense of context, semantics, and wordplay. Watson crushed Jennings, who started to lose confidence early on in the game.

What we knew by 2011 was that AI now outperformed humans during certain thinking tasks because it could access and process massive amounts of information without succumbing to stress. AI could define stress, but it didn't have an endocrine system to contend with.

Still, the ancient board game Go was the high-water mark for AI researchers, because it could be played using conventional strategy alone. Go is a game that originated in China more than 3,000 years ago and is played using simple enough rules: two players take turns placing white and black stones on an empty grid. Stones can be captured when they are surrounded by the opposite color or when there are no other open spaces or "liberties." The goal is to cover territory on the board, but that requires psychology and an astute understanding of the opponent's state of mind.

In Go, the traditional grid size is 19 × 19 squares. Unlike other games, such as chess, Go stones are all equally weighted. Between the two players, there are 181 black and 180 white pieces (black always goes first, hence the uneven number). In chess—which uses pieces that have different strengths—the white player has 20 possible moves, and then black has 20 possible moves. After the first play in chess, there are 400 possible board positions. But in Go, there are 361 possible opening plays, one at every intersection of what's essentially a completely blank grid. After the first round of moves by each player, there are now 128,960 possible moves. Altogether, there are $10^{170}$ possible board configurations—for context, that's more than all of the atoms in the known universe. With so many conceivable positions and potential moves, there is no set playbook like there is for checkers and chess. Instead, Go masters rely on scenarios: If the opponent plays on a particular point, then what are the possible, plausible, and probable outcomes given her personality, her patience, and her overall state of mind?

Like chess, Go is a deterministic perfect information game, where there is no hidden or obvious element of chance. To win, players have to keep their emotions balanced, and they must become masters in the art of human subtlety. In chess, it is possible to calculate a player's likely future moves; a rook can only move vertically or horizontally across the board. That limits the potential moves. Therefore, it's easier to understand who is winning a chess game well before any pieces have been captured or a king is put in checkmate. That isn't the case in Go. Sometimes it takes a high-ranking Go master to even figure out what's happening in a game and determine who's winning at a particular moment. Go's complexity is what's made the game a favorite among emperors, mathematicians, and physicists—and the reason why AI researchers have always been fascinated with teaching machines to play Go.

Go always proved a significant challenge for AI researchers. While a computer could be programmed to know the rules, what about rules to understand the human characteristics of the opponent? No one had ever built an algorithm strong enough to deal with the game's wild complexities. In 1971, an early program created by computer scientist Jon Ryder worked from a technical point of view, but it lost to a novice. In 1987, a stronger computer program called Nemesis competed against a human for the first time in a live tournament. By 1994, the program known as Go Intellect had proven itself a competent player. But even with the advantage of a significant handicap, it still lost all three of its games—against kids. In all of these cases, the computers would make incomprehensible moves, or they'd play too aggressively, or they'd miscalculate their opponent's posture.

Sometime in the middle of all that work were a handful of researchers who, once again, were workshopping neural networks, an idea championed by Marvin Minsky and Frank Rosenblatt during the initial Dartmouth meeting. Cognitive scientist Geoff Hinton and computer scientists Yann Lecun and Yoshua Bengio each believed that neural net–based systems would not only have serious practical applications—like automatic fraud detection for credit cards and automatic optical character recognition for reading documents and checks—but that it would become the basis for what artificial intelligence would become.

It was Hinton, a professor at the University of Toronto, who imagined a new kind of neural net, one made up of multiple layers that each extracted different information until it recognized what it was looking for. The only way to get that kind of knowledge into an AI system, he thought, was to develop learning algorithms that allowed computers to learn on their own. Rather than teaching them to perform a single narrow task really well, the networks would be built to train themselves.

These new "deep" neural networks (DNNs) would require a more advanced kind of machine learning—"deep learning"—to train computers to perform humanlike tasks but with less (or even without) human supervision. One immediate benefit: scale. In a neural network,

and a chance meeting with a Microsoft researcher named Li Deng meant that the technology could be piloted in a meaningful way. Deng, a Chinese deep-learning specialist, was a pioneer in speech recognition using large-scale deep learning. By 2010, the technique was being tested at Google. Just two years later, deep neural nets were being used in commercial products. If you used Google Voice and its transcription services, that was deep learning, and the technique became the basis for all the digital assistants we use today. Siri, Google, and Amazon's Alexa are all powered by deep learning. The AI community of interdisciplinary researchers had grown significantly since the Dartmouth summer. But those three key practices—that the big tech companies and academic researchers would work together, commercial success would drive the progress of AI, and the network of researchers would tend be homogenous—were still very much in play.

All of the advancements being made in America weren't going unnoticed in Beijing. China now had a nascent but growing AI ecosystem of its own, and the state government was incentivizing researchers to publish their work. The number of scientific papers on AI published by Chinese researchers more than doubled between 2010 and 2017.[35] To be fair, papers and patents don't necessarily mean that research will find its way into widespread use, but it was an early indication of how rattled Chinese leaders were at all the progress being made in the West—especially when it came to Go.

By January 2014, Google had begun investing significantly in AI, which included more than $500 million to acquire a hot deep-learning startup called DeepMind and its three founders, neuroscientist Demis Hassabis, a former child prodigy in chess, machine-learning researcher Shane Legg, and entrepreneur Mustafa Suleyman (who departed DeepMind in September 2019). Part of the team's appeal: they'd developed a program called AlphaGo.

Within months, they were ready to test AlphaGo against a real human player. A match was arranged between DeepMind and Fan

Hui, a Chinese-born professional Go player and one of the strongest professional masters in Europe. Since playing Go on a computer isn't quite the same as playing on a physical board, it was decided that one of DeepMind's engineers would place the computer's moves on the board and could communicate Hui's moves back to the computer.

Before the game, Toby Manning, who was one of the heads of the British Go Association, played AlphaGo in a test round—and lost by 17 points. Manning made some errors, but so did the program. An eerie thought crossed his mind: What if the AlphaGo was just playing conservatively? Was it possible that the program was only playing aggressively enough to beat Manning, rather than to clobber him entirely?

The players sat down at a table, Fan Hui wearing a pinstriped button-down shirt and brown leather jacket, Manning in the center, and the engineer on the other side. Game play started. Hui opened a bottle of water and considered the board. As the black player, it was his turn to start. During the first 50 moves, it was a quiet game—Hui was clearly trying to suss out the strengths and weaknesses of AlphaGo. One early tell: the AI would not play aggressively unless it was behind. It was a tight first match. AlphaGo earned a very narrow victory, by just 1.5 points.

Hui used that information going into the second game. If AlphaGo wasn't going to play aggressively, then Hui decided that he'd fight early. But then AlphaGo started playing more quickly. Hui mentioned that perhaps he needed a bit more time to think between turns. On move 147, Hui tried to prevent AlphaGo from claiming a big territory in the center of the board, but the move misfired, and he was forced to resign.

By game three, Hui's moves were more aggressive, and AlphaGo followed suit. Halfway through, Hui made a catastrophic overplay, which AlphaGo punished, and then another big mistake, which rendered the game effectively over. Reeling from frustration, Hui had to excuse himself for a walk outside so that he could regain his composure and finish the match. Yet again, stress had gotten the better of a great human thinker—while the AI was unencumbered to ruthlessly pursue its goal.

AlphaGo—an AI program—had beaten a professional Go player 5–0. And it had won by analyzing fewer positions than IBM's Deep Blue did by several orders of magnitude. When AlphaGo beat a human, it didn't know it was playing a game, what a game means, or why humans get pleasure out of playing games.

Hanjin Lee, a high-ranking professional Go player from Korea, reviewed the games after. In an official public statement, he said, "My overall impression was that AlphaGo seemed stronger than Fan, but I couldn't tell by how much . . . maybe it becomes stronger when it faces a stronger opponent."[36]

Focusing on games—that is, beating humans in direct competition—has defined success using a relatively narrow set of parameters. And that brings us to a perplexing new philosophical question for our modern era of AI. In order for AI systems to win—to accomplish the goals we've created for them—do humans have to lose in ways that are both trivial and profound?

*   *   *

AlphaGo continued playing tournaments, besting every opponent with masterful abilities and demoralizing the professional Go community. After beating the world's number one champion 3–0, DeepMind announced that it was retiring the AI system from competition, saying that the team would work on a new set of challenges.[37] What the team started working on next was a way to evolve AlphaGo from a powerful system that could be trained to beat brilliant Go players to a system that could train itself to become just as powerful, without having to rely on humans.

The first version of AlphaGo required humans in the loop and an initial data set of 100,000 Go games in order to learn how to play. The next generation of the system was built to learn from zero. Just like a human player new to the game, this version—called AlphaGo Zero—would have to learn everything from scratch, completely on its own, without an opening library of moves or even a definition of what the pieces did. The system would not just make decisions—which were the result of computation and could be explicitly programmed—it would make choices, which had to do with judgment.[38] This meant that the DeepMind architects wielded an enormous amount of power, even if they didn't realize it. From them, Zero would learn the conditions, values, and motivations for making its decisions and choices during the game.

Zero competed against itself, tweaking and adjusting its decision-making processes alone. Each game play would begin with a few random moves, and with every win, Zero would update its system and then play again optimized by what it had learned. It took only 70 hours of play for Zero to gain the same level of strength AlphaGo had when it beat the world's greatest players.[39]

And then something interesting happened. The DeepMind team applied its technique to a second instance of AlphaGo Zero using a larger network and allowed it to train and self-play for 40 days. It not only rediscovered the sum total of Go knowledge accumulated by humans, it beat the most advanced version of AlphaGo 90% of the time—using completely new strategies. This means that Zero evolved into both a better student than the world's greatest Go masters and a better teacher than its human trainers, and we don't entirely understand what it did to make itself that smart.[40] Just how smart, you may be wondering? Well, a Go player's strength is measured using something called an Elo rating, which determines a win/loss probability based on past performance. Grandmasters and world champions tend to have ratings near 3,500. Zero had a rating of more than 5,000. Comparatively, those brilliant world champions played like amateurs, and it would be statistically improbable that any human player could ever beat the AI system.

We do know one condition that enabled this kind of learning. By not using any human data or expertise, Zero's creators removed the constraints of human knowledge on artificial intelligence. Humans, as it turned out, would have held the system back. The achievement was architecting a system that had the ability to think in an entirely new way and to make its own choices.[41] It was a sudden, unexpected leap, one that portended a future in which AI systems could look at cancer screenings, evaluate climate data, and analyze poverty in nonhuman ways—potentially leading to breakthroughs that human researchers never would have thought of on their own.

As Zero played games against itself, it actually discovered Go strategies that humans had developed over 1,000 years—which means it had learned to think just like the humans who created it. In the early stages, it made the same mistakes, figured out the same patterns and variations, and ran into the same obstacles as we would. But once Zero got strong enough, it abandoned our human moves and came up with something it preferred.[42] Once Zero took off on its own, it developed creative strategies that no one had ever seen before, suggesting that maybe machines *were already thinking* in ways that are both recognizable and alien to us.

What Zero also proved is that algorithms were now capable of learning without guidance from humans, and it was us humans who'd been holding AI systems back. It meant that in the near future, machines could be let loose on problems that we, on our own, could not predict or solve.

In December 2017, the DeepMind team published a paper showing that Zero was now generally capable of learning—not just Go but other information. On its own, Zero was playing other games, like chess and *shoji* (a Japanese game similar to chess), which are admittedly less complex but still require strategy and creativity. Only now, Zero was learning much faster than before. It managed to develop incomprehensible, superhuman power with less than 24 hours of game play.

The team then started to work on applying the techniques they developed for Zero to build a "general-purpose learning machine," a set of adaptive algorithms that mimic our own biological systems, capable of being trained. Rather than filling AI systems with a massive amount of information and set of instructions for how it can be queried, the team is instead teaching machines how to learn. Unlike humans, who might get tired, bored, or distracted when studying, machines will ruthlessly pursue a goal at all costs.

This was a defining moment in the long history of AI for a few reasons. First, the system behaved in unpredictable ways, making decisions that didn't entirely make sense to its creators. And it beat a human player in ways that could neither be replicated nor fully understood. It portended a future in which AI could build its own neural pathways and gain knowledge that we may never understand. Second, it cemented the two parallel tracks AI is now moving along: China, alarmed, throws money and people at making its domestic products more competitive, while in the United States, our expectations are that fantastical AI products will soon hit the marketplace. The viability of deep neural networks and deep learning are what's behind the current frenzy surrounding AI—not to mention the sudden explosion of funding in the US and of China's national proclamations about its plans for the future.

As a business unit within Alphabet (Google's parent company), DeepMind has 700 employees, some of whom have been tasked with developing commercial products as quickly as possible. In March 2018, Google's cloud business announced that it was selling a DeepMind-powered text-to-speech service for $16 per million characters of processed text.[43] One of the breakout announcements from Google's 2018 I/O conference was Duplex, a voice assistant that will automatically make calls on behalf of customers and talk to human receptionists to make restaurant reservations or appointments at salons, complete with "ums" and "ahs." That product uses WaveNet, an AI-based generative program that's part of DeepMind.[44]

Meanwhile, AI researchers in a different division of Alphabet called Google Brain revealed that they had built an AI that's capable of generating its own AIs. (Got that?) The system, called AutoML, automated the design of machine-learning models using a technique called "reinforcement learning." AutoML operated as a sort of "parent"—a top-level controller DNN that would decide to create "child" AI networks for narrow, specific tasks. Without being asked, AutoML generated a child called NASNet and taught it to recognize objects like people, cars, traffic lights, purses, and more in videos. Not burdened by stress, ego, doubt, or a lack of self-confidence—traits found in even the most brilliant computer scientists—NASNet had an 82.7% accuracy rate at predicting images. This meant that the child system was outperforming human coders—including the humans who originally created its parent.[45]

Overwhelmingly, these teams who are architecting systems intended to make both choices and decisions are led by men. It's only a slightly more diverse group than the researchers who met at Dartmouth because of one big development: China. In recent years, China has become an important hub for AI, and that's because of a massive, government-funded effort at Chinese universities and at Baidu, Alibaba, and Tencent.

In fact, Baidu figured out something that even Zero couldn't yet do: how to transfer skills from one domain to another. It's an easy task for humans, but a tricky one for AI. Baidu aimed to tackle that obstacle by teaching a deep neural net to navigate a 2D virtual world using only natural language, just like parents would talk to their children. Baidu's AI agent was given commands like "Please navigate to the apple" or "Can you move to the grid between the apple and the banana?"—and it was initially rewarded for correct actions. It may seem like a simple enough task, but consider what's involved here: by the end of the experiment, Baidu's AI could not only understand language that at the start had been meaningless to it, the system also learned what a two-dimensional grid was, that it could move around it, how to move around it, that bananas and apples exist, and how to tell them apart.

*   *   *

At the beginning of this chapter, I asked four questions: *Can machines think? What would it mean for a machine to "think"? What does it mean for you, dear reader, to think? How would you know that you were actually thinking original thoughts?* Now that you know the long history of these questions, the small group of people who built the foundational layer for AI, and the key practices still in play, I'd like to offer you some answers.

Yes, machines can think. Passing a conversational test, like the Turing test, or the more recent Winograd schema—which was proposed by Hector Levesque in 2011 and focuses on commonsense reasoning, challenging an AI to answer a simple question that has ambiguous pronouns—doesn't necessarily measure an AI system's ability in other areas.[46] It just proves that a machine can think using a linguistic framework, like we humans do. Everyone agrees that Einstein was a genius, even if the acceptable methods of measuring his intelligence at the time—like passing a test in school—said otherwise. Einstein was thinking in ways that were incomprehensible to his teachers—so of course they assumed he wasn't intelligent. In reality, at that time there wasn't a meaningful way to measure the strength of Einstein's thinking. So it is for AI.

Thinking machines can make decisions and choices that affect real-world outcomes, and to do this they need a purpose and a goal. Eventually they develop a sense of judgment. These are the qualities that, according to both philosophers and theologians, make up the soul. Each soul is a manifestation of God's vision and intent; it was made and bestowed by a singular creator. Thinking machines have creators, too—they are the new gods of AI, and they are mostly male, predominantly live in America, Western Europe, and China, and are tied, in some way, to the Big Nine. The soul of AI is a manifestation of their vision and intent for the future.

And finally, yes, thinking machines are capable of original thought. After learning through experience, they might determine that a different solution is possible. Or that a new classification is best. AIs don't have to invent a new form of art to show us creativity.

Which means that there is, in fact, a mind in AI machines. It is young and still maturing, and it is likely to evolve in ways we do not understand. In the next chapter, we'll talk about what constitutes that mind, the values of the Big Nine, and the unintended social, political, and economic consequences of our great AI awakening.

# CHAPTER TWO

# THE INSULAR WORLD OF AI'S TRIBES

The centuries-long struggle to build a thinking machine only recently saw big advancements. But while these machines might appear to "think," we should be clear that they most certainly do not think like *all* of us.

The future of AI is being built by a relatively few like-minded people within small, insulated groups. Again, I believe that these people are well intentioned. But as with all insulated groups that work closely together, their unconscious biases and myopia tend to become new systems of belief and accepted behaviors over time. What might have in the past felt unusual—wrong, even—becomes normalized as everyday thinking. And *that* thinking is what's being programmed into our machines.

Those working within AI belong to a tribe of sorts. They are people living and working in North America and in China. They attend the same universities. They adhere to a set of social rules. The tribes are overwhelmingly homogenous. They are affluent and highly educated. Their members are mostly male. Their leaders—executive officers, board members, senior managers—are, with few exceptions, all men. Homogeneity is also an issue in China, where tribe members are predominantly Chinese.

The problem with tribes is what makes them so powerful. In insular groups, cognitive biases become magnified and further entrenched, and they slip past awareness. Cognitive biases are a stand-in for rational thought, which slows our thinking down and takes more energy. The more connected and established a tribe becomes, the more normal its groupthink and behavior seems. As you'll see next, that's an insight worth remembering.

What are AI's tribes doing? They are building artificial narrow intelligence (ANI) systems, capable of performing a singular task at the same level or better than we humans can. Commercial ANI applications—and by extension, the tribe—are already making decisions for us in our email inboxes, when we search for things on the internet, when we take photos with our phones, as we drive our cars, and when we apply for credit cards or loans. They are also building what comes next: artificial general intelligence (AGI) systems, which will perform broader cognitive tasks because they are machines that are designed to think like we do. But who, exactly, is the "we" these AI systems are being modeled on? Whose values, ideals, and worldviews are being taught?

The short answer is not yours—and also not mine. Artificial intelligence has the mind of its tribe, prioritizing its creators' values, ideals, and worldviews. But it is also starting to develop a mind of its own.

## The Tribe Leaders

AI's tribe has a familiar, catchy rallying cry: *fail fast and fail often.* In fact, a version of it—"move fast and break things"—was Facebook's official company motto until recently. The idea of making mistakes and accepting failures is in stark contrast to America's enormous corporations, which avoid risk and move at a snail's pace, and it's a laudable aim. Complicated technology like AI demands experimentation and the opportunity to fail over and over in pursuit of getting things right.

But there's a catch. The mantra is part of a troubling ideology that's pervasive among the Big Nine: *build it first, and ask for forgiveness later.*

Lately, we've been hearing a lot of requests for forgiveness. Facebook apologized for the outcome of its relationship with Cambridge Analytica. As that scandal was unfolding, Facebook announced in September 2018 that an attack has exposed the personal information of more than 50 million users, making it one of the largest security breaches in digital history. But it turns out that executives made a decision not to notify users right away.[1] Just one month later, Facebook announced Portal, a video conferencing screen to rival Amazon's Echo Show, and had to walk back the privacy promises it had made earlier. Originally, Facebook said that it wouldn't use Portal to collect personal data in order to target users with ads. But after journalists pushed back, the company found itself making an awkward clarification: while Portal wouldn't use your data to display ads, the data collected as you used the device—who you called, which Spotify songs you listen to—could be used to target you later on with Facebook ads on other services and networks.[2]

In April 2016, the head of Google Brain's project, Jeff Dean, wrote that the company had excluded women and people of color during an "Ask Me Anything" session on Reddit. It wasn't intentional but rather an oversight, and I absolutely believe it was not an intentional omission but that it just didn't occur to the organizers to diversify the session.

Dean said that he valued diversity and that Google would have to do better:[3]

> One of the things I really like about our Brain Residency program is that the residents bring a wide range of backgrounds, areas of expertise (e.g. we have physicists, mathematicians, biologists, neuroscientists, electrical engineers, as well as computer scientists), and other kinds of diversity to our research efforts. In my experience, whenever you bring people together

with different kinds of expertise, different perspectives, etc., you end up achieving things that none of you could do individually, because no one person has the entire skills and perspective necessary.[4]

In June 2018, Google released a diversity report that for the first time included employee data broken down by category. In the report, Google said that globally its workforce was 69.1% male. In the US, only 2.5% of employees were Black, while 3.6% were Hispanic and Latinx. For Google's bold statements about the need to diversify tech, those numbers—already low—didn't actually change from several years earlier, when in 2014 its workforce was 2% Black and 3% Hispanic and Latinx.[5]

To its credit, Google in recent years launched an unconscious bias initiative that includes workshops and training to help employees learn more about social stereotypes and deeply held attitudes on gender, race, appearance, age, education, politics, and wealth that may have formed outside of their own conscious awareness. Some Googlers feel that the training has been more perfunctory than productive, with a Black female employee explaining that the training focused on "interpersonal relationships and hurt feelings rather than addressing discrimination and inequality, which signals to workers that diversity is 'just another box to check.'"[6]

Yet in the same years as this training was taking place, Google was rewarding bad behavior among its leadership ranks. Andy Rubin, who created Google's flagship Android mobile operating system, had been asked to resign after a female staff member made a credible claim that he'd coerced her into oral sex. Google paid Rubin $90 million to walk away—structured in monthly payouts of $2.5 million for the first two years and $1.5 million every month for the following two years. The director of Google's R&D division X, Richard DeVaul, sexually harassed a woman during her job interview, telling her that he and his wife had an open marriage and later insisting on giving that candidate a topless backrub at a tech festival. Unsurprisingly, she didn't get the job. He was asked to apologize but not to resign. A vice president who helped run Google's Search ran into trouble when a female employee accused him of groping her—an accusation that was deemed credible, so he was let go with a multimillion-dollar severance package. Between 2016 and 2018, Google quietly let go 13 managers for sexual harassment.[7]

This feedback underscores the lackluster impact many unconscious bias training programs have within tech and the venture capital firms that fund it. The reason: while people may be more aware of their biases after training, they aren't necessarily motivated or incentivized to change their behavior.

When we talk about a lack of diversity within the tech community, the conversation typically oscillates between gender and race. However, there are other dimensions of humanity that get short shrift, like political ideology and religion. A 2017 analysis by Stanford's Graduate School of Business, which surveyed more than 600 tech leaders and founders, showed that the tribe overwhelmingly self-identified as progressive Democrats. During the 2016 election cycle, they overwhelmingly supported Hillary Clinton. The tribe supports higher taxes on wealthy individuals, they are pro-choice, they oppose the death penalty, they want gun control, and they believe gay marriage should be legal.[8]

That the senior leadership of Google, Apple, Amazon, Facebook, Microsoft, and IBM don't accurately represent *all* Americans could be said of the companies in any industry. The difference is that these particular companies are developing autonomous decision-making systems intended to represent all of our interests. Criticism is coming not just from women and people of color but from an unlikely group of people: conservatives and Republican Party stalwarts. In May 2018, the Republican National Committee sent a letter to Mark Zuckerberg accusing Facebook of bias against conservative Americans, which read in part: "Concerns have been raised in recent years about suppression of conservative speech on Facebook . . . including censorship of conservative news stories. . . . We are alarmed by numerous allegations that Facebook has blocked content from conservative journalists and groups."[9] The letter, signed by Ronna McDaniel, chairwoman of the RNC, and Brad Parscale, campaign manager for President Trump's 2020 reelection campaign, went on to demand transparency in how Facebook's algorithms determine which users see political ads in their feeds and a review into bias against conservative content and leaders.

The thing is, McDaniel and Parscale aren't wrong. During the heated 2016 election cycle, Facebook staff *did* intentionally manipulate the platform's trending section to exclude conservative news—even through stories that were decidedly anti-Clinton had already been trending on their own. Several of Facebook's "news curators," as they were called, said that they were directed to "inject" certain stories into the news feed section even if they weren't trending at all. They also prevented favorable stories about GOP candidates like Rand Paul from showing up. Facebook's news curation team was made up of a small group of journalists who'd mainly attended private East Coast or Ivy League universities, and to be fair this plays directly into the narrative offered up by conservatives for decades.

In August 2018, more than 100 Facebook employees used an internal message board to complain about a "political monoculture that's intolerant of different views." Brian Amerige, a senior Facebook engineer, wrote: "We claim to welcome all perspectives, but are quick to attack—often in mobs—anyone who presents a view that appears to be in opposition to left-leaning ideology."[10]

Talking about diversity—asking for forgiveness and promising to do better—isn't the same thing as addressing diversity within the databases, algorithms, and frameworks that make up the AI ecosystem. When talking doesn't lead to action, the result is an ecosystem of systems and products that reflect a certain anti-humanistic bias. Here are just a few of our real-world outcomes: In 2016, an AI-powered security robot intentionally crashed into a 16-month-old child in a Silicon Valley mall.[11] The AI system powering the *Elite: Dangerous* video game developed a suite of superweapons that the creators never imagined, wreaking havoc within the game and destroying the progress made by all the real human players.[12] There are myriad problems when it comes to AI safety, some of which are big and obvious: self-driving cars have already run red lights and, in a few instances, killed pedestrians. Predictive policing applications continually mislabel suspects' faces, landing innocent people in jail. There are an unknowable number of problems that escape our notice, too, because they haven't affected us personally yet.

A truly diverse team would have only one primary characteristic in common: talent. There would not be a concentration of any single gender, race, or ethnicity. Different political and religious views would be represented. The homogeneity within AI's tribes is a problem within the Big Nine, but it doesn't start there. The problem begins in universities, where AI's tribes form.

Tribes get established within concentrated social environments where everyone is sharing a common purpose or goal, using the same language, and working at the same relative intensity. It is where a group of people develops a shared sense of values and purpose. They form in places like military units, medical school rotations, the kitchens of Michelin-starred restaurants, and sororities. They go through trial and error, success and failure, heartbreak and happiness together.

To borrow an example from a field far away from artificial intelligence, in the 1970s and '80s, Sam Kinison, Andrew Dice Clay, Jim Carrey, Marc Maron, Robin Williams, and Richard Pryor all spent time living in a house at 8420 Cresthill Road, which was just down the street from what became the legendary Comedy Store in Los Angeles. They were just young guys living in a house and trying to get stage time in an era when Bob Hope was on TV doing one-liners like "I never give women a second thought. My first thought covers everything."[13] This tribe totally rejected that brand of humor, which the previous generation honed meticulously. Their values were radically different: breaking taboos, confronting social injustice, and telling hyper-realistic stories that tended to reflect pretty badly on the very people sitting in the audience. They workshopped their bits and observations with each other. They commiserated after bombing on stage. They experimented with and learned from each other. This tribe of groundbreaking, brilliant comics laid the foundation for the future of American entertainment.[14] Collectively, this group of men still wields influence today.

In a way, AI went through a similar radical transformation because of a modern-day tribe that shared the same values, ideas, and goals. Those three deep-learning pioneers discussed earlier—Geoff Hinton, Yann Lecun, and Yoshua Bengio—were the Sam Kinisons and Richard Pryors of the AI world in the early days of deep neural nets. Lecun studied under Hinton at the University of Toronto where the Canadian Institute for Advanced Research (CIFAR) inculcated a small group of researchers, which included Yoshua Bengio. They spent immeasurable amounts of time together, batting around ideas, testing theories, and building the next generation of AI. "There was this very small community of people who had this in the back of their minds, that eventually neural nets would come to the fore," Lecun said. "We needed a safe space to have little workshops and meetings to really develop our ideas before publishing them."[15]

A tribe's strong bonds are formed when people working closely together suffer setbacks and celebrate successes together. They wind up developing a set of shared experiences, which translate to a common lexicon, which result in a common set of ideas, behaviors, and goals. This is why so many startup stories, political movements, and cultural juggernauts begin the same way: a few friends share a dorm room, home, or garage and work intensely on adjacently related projects.

While the business epicenters for modern AI might be Silicon Valley, Beijing, Hangzhou, and Shenzhen, colleges are the lifeblood of AI's tribes. There are just a few hubs. In the United States, they include Carnegie Mellon, Georgia Institute of Technology, Stanford, UC Berkeley, University of Washington, Harvard, Cornell, Duke, MIT, Boston University, McGill University, and the Université de Montréal. These universities are home to active academic research groups with strong industry ties.

Tribes typically observe rules and rituals, so let's explore the rights of initiation for AI's tribes. It begins with a rigorous university education.

In North America, the emphasis within universities has centered on hard skills—like mastery of the R and Python programming languages, competency in natural language processing and applied statistics, and exposure to computer vision, computational biology, and game theory. It's frowned upon to take classes outside the tribe, such as a course on the philosophy of mind, Muslim women in literature, or colonialism. If we're trying to build thinking machines capable of thinking like humans do, it would seem counterintuitive to exclude learning about the human condition. Right now, courses like these are intentionally left off the curriculum, and it's difficult to make room for them as electives outside the major.

The tribe demands skills, and there's a lot to cram in during four years of undergraduate study. For example, at Stanford, students must take 50 credit hours of intense math, science, and engineering classes, in addition to 15 hours of core computer science courses. While there is an ethics course offered as part of the major, it's one of five electives that can be taken to fulfill the requirement.[16] Carnegie Mellon launched a brand-new AI major in 2018, which gave the school a fresh start and the opportunity to design a modern AI major from scratch. But the rules and rituals of the tribe prevailed, and hard skills are what matter. While the degree does require one ethics class and some courses in the humanities and arts, they all focus mostly on neuroscience (e.g., cognitive psychology, human memory, and visual cognition), which makes sense given the link between AI and the human mind. There are no required courses that teach students how to detect bias in data sets, how to apply philosophy to decision-making, or the ethics of inclusivity. There is no formal acknowledgement throughout courses that social and socioeconomic diversity are just as important to a community as biodiversity.

Skills are taught experientially—meaning that students studying AI don't have their heads buried in books. In order to learn, they need lexical databases, image libraries, and neural nets. For a time, one of the more popular neural nets at universities was called Word2vec, and it was built by the Google Brain team. It was a two-layer system that processed text, turning words into numbers that AI could understand.[17] For example, it learned that "man is to king as woman is to queen." But the database also decided that "father is to doctor as mother is to nurse" and "man is to computer programmer as woman is to homemaker."[18] The very system students were exposed to was itself biased. If someone wanted to analyze the farther-reaching implications of sexist code, there weren't any classes where that learning could take place.

In 2017 and 2018, some of these universities developed a few new ethics courses in response to the challenges already posed by AI. The Berkman Klein Center at Harvard and the MIT Media Lab jointly offered a new course on ethics and the regulation of AI.[19] The program and lectures were terrific,[20] but the course was hosted outside of each university's standard computer science tracks—meaning that what was being taught and discussed didn't have the opportunity to percolate up into other parts of the curriculum.

To be sure, ethics is a requirement of all universities teaching AI—it's written into the accreditation standards. In order to be accredited by the Accreditation Board for Engineering and Technology, computer science programs are required to show that students have an "understanding of professional, ethical, legal, security, and social issues and responsibilities" and an "ability to analyze the local and global impact of computing on individuals, organizations, and society." However, I can tell you from experience that benchmarking and measuring this kind of requirement is subjective at best, and incredibly hard to do with any accuracy, especially without required courses that all students must take. I'm a member of the Accrediting Council on Education in Journalism and Mass Communications. The curricula for journalism and mass communications programs tend to focus on humanities, which you might say are softer skills like reporting, writing, and media production. And yet our academic units regularly struggle to meet our own standards for social issues and responsibilities, including diversity. Schools can still quality for accreditation without meeting compliance standards for diversity—that isn't unique to the accreditation board on which I serve. Without enforcing the standards more stringently and without serious effort within universities, how could a hard-skills curriculum like AI possibly make a dent in the problem?

College is tough enough, and the new hire incentives being offered by the Big Nine are competitive. While elective courses on African literature or the ethics of public service would undoubtedly broaden the worldviews of those working in AI, there's intense pressure to keep the ecosystem growing. The tribe instead wants to see proof of skills so that when graduates enter the workforce, they hit the ground running and are productive members of the team. In fact, the very elective courses that could help AI researchers think more intentionally about all of humanity would likely hurt them during the recruiting process. That's because the Big Nine uses AI-powered software to sift through resumes, and it's trained to look for specific keywords describing hard skills. A portfolio of coursework outside the standard subjects would either be an anomaly or would render the applicant as invisible.

The AI scanning through resumes proves that bias isn't just about race and gender. There's even a bias against philosophy, literature, theoretical physics, and behavioral economics, since candidates with lots of elective courses outside the traditional scope of AI tend to get deprioritized. The tribe's hiring system, designed to automate the cumbersome task of doing a first pass through thousands of resumes, would potentially leave these candidates, who have a more diverse and desirable academic background, out of consideration.

Academic leaders will be quick to argue that they are open to a mandatory ethics class, even if the tribe does not demand a broader curriculum. (Which it does not.) Adding equally rigorous humanities courses, like comparative literature and world religions, would force needed skills-based classes off the schedule. Students would bristle at being forced to take what appear to be superfluous courses, while industry partners want graduates primed with top-tier skills. With intense competition for the best and brightest students, why would any of these prestigious programs, like those at Carnegie Mellon and Stanford, mess with success?

Technology is moving way faster than the levers of academia. A single, required ethics course—specifically built for and tailored to students studying AI—won't do the trick if the material isn't current and especially if what's being taught doesn't reverberate throughout other areas of the curriculum. If the curriculum can't change, then what about individual professors? Maybe they could be empowered to address the problem? That's unlikely to happen at scale. Professors are incentivized against modifying their syllabi to relate what they're teaching back to questions about technological, economic, and social values. That would take up precious time. It could make their syllabi less attractive to students. Universities want to show a strong record of employed graduates, and employers want graduates with hard skills. The Big Nine are partners with these universities, which rely on their funding and resources. Yet it seems like the best time to ask difficult questions—*who owns your face?*—should be asked and debated in the safe confines of a classroom, before students become members of teams who are regularly sidelined by product deadlines and revenue targets.

If universities are where AI's tribes form, it's easy to see why there's so little diversity in the field relative to other professions. In fact, industry executives are quick to point the finger at universities, blaming poor workforce diversity on what they say is AI's "pipeline problem." This isn't entirely untrue. AI's tribes form as professors train students in their classrooms and labs, and as students collaborate on research projects and assignments. Those professors, their labs, and the leadership within AI's academic units are again overwhelmingly male and lacking in diversity.

In universities, PhD candidates serve three functions: to collaborate on research, to teach undergraduate students, and to lead future work in their fields. Women receive only 23% of PhDs awarded in computer science, and only 28% awarded in mathematics and statistics, according to recent data from the National Center for Education Statistics.[21] The academic pipeline is leaky: female PhDs do not advance to tenured positions or leadership roles at the same rate as men. So it should not come as a surprise that women received only 18% of undergraduate computer science degrees in recent years—and that's actually down from 37% in 1985.[22] Black and Hispanic PhD candidates are woefully underrepresented—just 3% and 1% respectively.[23]

As the tribe scales, it's expanding within a bubble and bringing out some terrible behaviors. Female AI researchers within universities have had to deal with sexual harassment, inappropriate jokes, and generally crappy behavior by their male counterparts. As that behavior is normalized, it follows the tribe from college into the workforce. So it isn't a pipeline problem as much as a *people* problem. AI's tribes are inculcating a culture in which women and certain minorities—like Black and Hispanic people—are excluded, plain and simple.

In 2017, a Google engineer sent around a now-infamous memo arguing that women are biologically less capable at programming. Google's CEO Sundar Pichai eventually responded by firing the guy who wrote the memo, but he also said, "Much of what was in that memo is fair to debate."[24] Cultures that are hostile to nontribe members cause a compounding effect resulting in an even less diverse workforce. As the work in AI advances, to build systems capable of thinking for and alongside humanity, entire populations are being left out of the developmental track.

This isn't to say that there are no women or people of color working in universities. The director of MIT's famed Computer Science and Artificial Intelligence Laboratory (CSAIL) is Daniela Rus, a woman who counts a MacArthur Fellowship among her many professional and academic achievements. Kate Crawford is a Distinguished Research Professor at New York University and heads a new institute there focused on the social implications of AI. There are women and people of color doing tremendous work in AI—but they're dramatically underrepresented.

If the tribe's goal is to imbue AI with more "humanistic" thinking, it's leaving a lot of the humans out of the process. Fei-Fei Li, who runs Stanford's Artificial Intelligence Lab and is Google Cloud's chief scientist of artificial intelligence and machine learning, said,

> As an educator, as a woman, as a woman of color, as a mother, I'm increasingly worried. AI is about to make the biggest changes to humanity, and we're missing a whole generation of diverse technologists and leaders. . . . If we don't get women and people of color at the table—real technologists doing the real work—we will bias systems. Trying to reverse that a decade or two from now will be so much more difficult, if not close to impossible.[25]

## China's Tribes: The BAT

Baidu, Alibaba, and Tencent, collectively known as the BAT, are China's side of the Big Nine. The AI tribe under the People's Republic of

China operates under different rules and rituals, which include significant government funding, oversight, and industrial policies designed to propel the BAT forward. Together, they are part of a well-capitalized, highly organized state-level AI plan for the future, one in which the government wields tremendous control. This is China's space race, and we are its Sputnik to their Apollo mission. We might have gotten to orbit first, but China has put its sovereign wealth fund, education system, citizens, and national pride on the line in its pursuit of AI.

China's AI tribes begin at universities, too, where there is even more focus on skills and commercial applications. Because China is interested in ramping up the country's skilled workforce as quickly as possible, its diversity problems aren't exactly analogous to the West, though they do exist. Gender isn't as much of a consideration, so women are better represented. That said, classes are taught in Chinese, which is a tough language for foreigners to learn. This excludes non-Chinese speakers from the classroom and also creates a unique competitive advantage, since Chinese university students tend to have studied English and could attend a wider pool of universities.

In China, AI training begins before students enter university. In 2017, China's State Council called for the inclusion of AI fundamentals and coursework, which means that Chinese kids begin learning AI skills in *elementary school*. There is now an official, government-ordered textbook detailing the history and fundamentals of AI. By 2018, 40 high schools had piloted a compulsory AI course,[26] and more schools will be included once additional teachers become available. That should be soon: China's Ministry of Education launched a five-year AI training program for its universities, which intends to train at least 500 teachers and 5,000 students at China's top universities.[27]

The BAT is part of China's education revolution, providing the tools used in schools and universities, making the products consumers use as teens and adults, hiring graduates into the workforce, and sharing research with the government. Unless you've lived or traveled to

China in the past decade, you may not be familiar with Baidu, Alibaba, and Tencent. All three were founded at the same time using existing tech companies as their templates.

Baidu got started at a 1998 summer picnic in Silicon Valley—one of those insider gatherings bringing together AI tribe members over beer and lawn darts. Three men, all in their 30s, were bemoaning how little search engines were advancing. John Wu, who at the time was the head of Yahoo's search engine team, and Robin Li, who was an engineer at Infoseek, believed that search engines had a bright future. They'd already seen a promising new startup—Google—and thought they could build something similar for China. Together with Eric Xu, a biochemist, the three formed Baidu.[28]

The company recruited from AI's university hubs in North America and China. It was especially good at poaching talented researchers working on deep learning. In 2012, Baidu approached Andrew Ng, a prominent researcher at Google's Brain division. He'd grown up in Hong Kong and Singapore and had done a tour of the AI tribe's university hubs: computer science undergrad at Carnegie Mellon, a master's at MIT, PhD from UC Berkeley, and at the time was on leave from Stanford, where he was a professor. Ng was attractive to Baidu because of a startling new deep neural net project he'd been working on at Google.

Ng's team had built a cluster of 1,000 computers that had trained itself to recognize cats in YouTube videos. It was a dazzling system. Without ever being told explicitly what a cat was, the AI ingested millions of hours of random videos, learned to recognize objects, figured out that some of those objects were cats, and then learned what a cat was. All on its own, without human intervention. Shortly after, Ng was at Baidu, which had recruited him to be the company's chief scientist. (Necessarily, this means that the DNA of Baidu includes nucleotides from the AI courses taught at Carnegie Mellon, MIT, and UC Berkeley.)

Today, Baidu is hardly just a search engine. Ng went on to help get Baidu's conversational AI platform (called DuerOS), digital assistant, and self-driving programs, as well as other AI frameworks, off the ground—and that positioned Baidu to begin talking about AI in its earnings calls well ahead of Google. Baidu now has a market cap of $88 billion and is the most used search engine in the world behind Google—quite an accomplishment, considering Baidu isn't used outside of China. Like Google, Baidu is building a suite of smart home devices, such as a robot intended for the home that combines voice recognition and facial recognition. The company announced an open platform for autonomous driving called Apollo, and the hope is that making its source code publicly available will cause the ecosystem around it to blossom. It already has 100 partners, which include automakers Ford and Daimler, chipmakers NVIDIA and Intel, and mapping services providers like TomTom. Baidu partnered with California-based Access Services to launch self-driving vehicles for people with mobility issues and disabilities. And it partnered with Microsoft's Azure Cloud to allow Apollo's non-Chinese partners to process vast amounts of vehicle data.[29] You should also know that in recent years, Baidu opened a new AI research lab in cooperation with the Chinese government—and the lab's leaders are Communist Party elites who'd previously worked on state military programs.[30]

The *A* in China's BAT is Alibaba Group, a massive platform that acts as a middleman between buyers and sellers through a massive network of websites, rather than a single platform. It was founded in 1999 by Jack Ma, a former professor living about 100 miles southwest of Shanghai who wanted to create a hybrid version of Amazon and eBay for China. Ma himself didn't know how to code, so he started the company with a university colleague who did. Just 20 years later, Alibaba has a market cap of more than $511 billion.

Among its sites are Taobao, on which neither buyers nor sellers are assessed a fee for their transactions. Instead, Taobao uses a pay-to-play model, charging sellers to rank them higher on the site's search engine. (This mimics part of Google's core business model.) Alibaba also built secure payment systems, including Alipay, which resembles the functionality and features of PayPal. It launched a "smile to pay" AI-powered digital payment system, which in 2017 debuted a facial recognition kiosk allowing consumers to pay by smiling briefly into a camera.

Like Amazon, Alibaba also has a smart speaker—it's called the Genie X1, and it is smaller and squatter than Amazon's Alexa and Google's Home devices. It uses neural network–based voiceprint recognition technology to identify users, automatically authenticating them so they can shop and make purchases. More than 100,000 of Alibaba's speakers are being installed in Marriott hotels throughout China.

Alibaba has a bigger vision for AI, which it calls its ET City Brain. The program crunches huge amounts of local data, from smart city cameras and sensors to government records and individual social media accounts. Alibaba uses its AI framework for predictive modeling: to suss out in advance traffic management, urban development, public health needs, and whether there might be social unrest on the horizon. Under Ma's direction, Alibaba has made inroads into delivery logistics, online video, data centers, and cloud computing, investing billions of dollars into various companies in an attempt to build a sprawling digital behemoth, connecting commerce, home, work, cities, and government. In fact, before the Amazon Go store launched in Seattle, Alibaba had opened Hema, an automated, cashless multifunctional retail operation combining groceries; a fast, casual food market; and delivery service.

There's one more odd similarity worth noting here. I say "odd," because it's also a contradiction. In 2016, Ma purchased the *South China Morning Post*, which was Hong Kong's biggest and most influential independent newspaper. The sale was significant because in China most media are state-sponsored, and the English-language *SCMP* was known for hard-hitting stories that could be critical of the Chinese government.[31] When I lived in Hong Kong, I used to have drinks with a group of *SCMP* reporters who were best-in-class muckrakers. Ma's purchase was a show of loyalty to the Communist Party. Three years earlier, Jeff Bezos bought the *Washington Post*, a move that eventually made him an enemy of the Trump White House for the paper's dogged investigative reporting, its critical analysis of administration policies, and its relentless pursuit of unraveling propaganda.[32]

Finally, the biggest and in many ways most influential member of the BAT is Tencent. The *T* in China's BAT was founded in 1998 by two men, Ma Huateng and Zhang Zhidong. Originally, they started with just one product called OICQ. If that sounds somewhat familiar to you, that's because it was a copy of ICQ, the instant messaging service. The two wound up facing legal action, but they dug in their heels and kept working on their version of the system. In 2011, Tencent launched WeChat, which not only offered messaging, it copied the features and functions of Facebook. Since the Chinese government had blocked Facebook from its already walled-off internet, WeChat was poised to explode. It was not only popular in universities, it was being used to recruit new talent—and much more.

WeChat has a mind-bending 1 billion monthly active users and a nickname—"the app for everything." That's because in addition to standard social media posts and messaging, it's used for just about everything in China, from new-hire recruiting at universities and text messaging to making payments and even law enforcement. More than 38,000 hospitals and clinics have WeChat accounts, and 60% of them use the service for patient management (e.g., scheduling appointments and payments).[33] It's a company powered by—and focused on—artificial intelligence, viewing "AI as a core technology across all our different products."[34] Appropriately, Tencent's official corporate slogan is "Make AI Everywhere."

Facebook may be the world's largest social network, but Tencent's technology is, by many measures, far superior. Tencent built a digital assistant called Xiaowei, a mobile payment system (Tenpay), and a cloud service (Weiyun) while also recently launching a movie studio (Tencent Pictures). Tencent's YouTu Lab is a world leader in facial and object recognition, and it feeds that technology into more than 50 other company initiatives. It's making inroads into health, too, by partnering with two UK-based health care companies: Babylon Health, a telemedicine startup, and Medopad, which uses AI for remote patient monitoring. Tencent also made big investments into two promising US-based startups in 2018, Atomwise and XtalPi, which are focused on pharmaceutical applications of AI.

In 2018, Tencent became the first Asian company to surpass a market value of $550 billion and overtook Facebook to become the world's most valuable social media company.[35] What's most astonishing of all: less than 20% of Tencent's revenue comes from online advertising, compared with Facebook's 98%.[36]

The BAT's talent pipeline includes AI's North American university hubs, and it's making sure that kids are getting an AI education around the same time they're learning how to add and subtract.

None of this would matter if the BAT weren't so incredibly successful—and if they weren't making gobs of money. The BAT makes so much of it, and the Chinese market is so enormous that China's AI tribes wield tremendous power—both in China and elsewhere in the world. The global AI community pays attention to China because of all that capital and because of its numbers, which are hard to downplay.

Facebook may have 2 billion monthly active users, but those users are spread out around the world. Tencent's WeChat's 1 billion active users are predominantly located in just one country. Baidu had 665 million mobile search users in 2017[37]—more than double the estimated number of mobile users in the United States.[38] That same year, Amazon had its best-ever holiday shopping season. For context, from Thanksgiving through the following Cyber Monday, Amazon customers ordered 140 million products, totaling $6.59 billion in sales.[39] That might have been a record for Amazon, but it hardly compares to what Alibaba did in China in just 24 hours. Alibaba sold to 515 million customers in 2017 alone, and that year its Singles' Day Festival—a sort of Black Friday meets the Academy Awards in China—saw $25 billion in online purchases from 812 million orders *on a single day*.[40] China has the largest digital market in the world regardless of how you measure it: more than a trillion dollars spent annually, more than a billion people online, and $30 billion invested in venture deals in the world's most important tech companies.[41]

Chinese investors were involved in 7–10% of all funding of tech startups in the United States between 2012 and 2017—that's a significant concentration of wealth pouring in from just one region.[42] The BAT are now well established in Seattle and Silicon Valley, operating out of satellite offices that include spaces along Menlo Park's fabled Sand Hill Road. During the past five years, the BAT invested significant money in Tesla, Uber, Lyft, Magic Leap (the mixed-reality headset and platform maker), and more. Venture investment from BAT companies is attractive not just because they move quickly and have a lot of cash but because a BAT deal typically means a lucrative entrée into the Chinese market, which can otherwise be impossible to penetrate. For example, a small Kansas City–based face recognition startup called Zoloz was acquired by Alibaba for $100 million in 2016; it became a core component of the Alipay payment service and, in the process, gained access to hundreds of millions of users without having to contend with strict privacy laws in Europe or the potential threat of privacy lawsuits in the US. But this investment doesn't come without serious trade-offs. Chinese investors don't just expect a return on their investments—they also demand IP, intellectual property.

In China, demanding IP in return for capital isn't a cultural quirk or a greedy way for certain investors to get ahead. It's part of a coordinated government effort. China has a clear vision of its near-future global dominance in economics, geopolitics, and military—and it sees

AI as the pathway leading to that goal. To that end, maintaining absolute control over information is a paramount issue for state leaders, so China has adopted an authoritarian command of content and user data, an industrial policy designed to transfer intellectual property from American companies to their Chinese counterparts. Examples include particular data sets, algorithms, and the design of processors. Many American companies hoping to do business in China must promise to hand over their proprietary technologies first. And there are new regulations in place, forcing foreign companies to localize their research and development within China, and to store any data used locally as well. Storing data locally is a difficult ask of foreign companies, since the Chinese government could invoke its authority to review data and circumvent encryption at any time.

Beijing takes long-term planning seriously. It's a tradition stemming back to Chairman Mao, who ushered in the first of China's many five-year plans in 1953. (President Xi launched the 13th five-year plan in 2016.)[43] Both government leaders and Communist Party officials embrace strategic foresight—making China one of the few countries on Earth that plans and maps comprehensive economic, political, military, and social strategy that spans many decades into the future. Chinese government has the unique ability to implement whatever policy it wants, and to do whatever it takes to deliver on its national strategy, including its 2030 plan to transform China into "the world's primary AI innovation center" and create an industry worth $150 billion to its economy by 2030. That plan is unlikely to be repealed by a new government, since in March 2018 China abolished its term limits and effectively allowed President Xi Jinping to remain in power for life.

Under Xi, China has experienced an impressive consolidation of power. He has emboldened the Communist Party, tightened the flow of information, and instituted new policies to accelerate myriad long-term plans, which he expects to start paying dividends in the next decade. At the uppermost levels of China's government, AI is front and center. Unlike former CCP leader Deng Xiaoping, whose governing philosophy was "hide our capabilities and bide our time," Xi is ready to show the world what China can do—and he intends to set the global pace.[44] The leadership within China are looking into the future and executing on bold, unified plans right now. This alone gives China an incredible advantage over the West, and importantly, it gives the BAT superpowers.

This is all happening during a period of strong economic growth in China, whose middle class is growing at breakneck speed. By 2022, more than three-quarters of China's urban population will earn enough money to make the middle-class cut. In 2000, just 4% of its population was considered middle class—that's a staggering amount of projected growth in a short period of time. Higher paying jobs in tech, biosciences, and service will likely push a large chunk of that group out of its current classification and into the "upper middle class." Chinese households carry very little debt. While it is true that poverty exists throughout the country, the current generation of Chinese kids is well positioned to earn more, save more, and spend more than their parents.[45] (Strikingly, 70% of Americans consider themselves to be part of the middle class, but Pew Research Center data shows that our middle class has been shrinking for the past four decades[46]—less than half of Americans earn enough to fit the category.[47])

China is a powerful economic force that's become difficult to ignore. Marriott may have inked a deal to install 100,000 of Alibaba's smart speakers in its hotels throughout China, but when Beijing found out that the hotelier listed Hong Kong, Taiwan, Tibet, and Macau as stand-alone countries on an email questionnaire it sent to rewards club members, Marriott executives received an immediate take-down notice. The government told Marriott to shut down all of its Chinese websites and apps, and the company relented. Marriott, which has been expanding throughout China to take advantage of its growing middle class, had recently opened more than 240 hotels and high-end resorts. Its chief executive, Arne Sorenson, found himself publishing a staggering apology on the company's website:

> Marriott International respects and supports the sovereignty and territorial integrity of China. Unfortunately, twice this week, we had incidents that suggested the opposite: First, by incorrectly labelling certain regions within China, including Tibet, as countries in a drop-down menu on a survey we sent out to our loyalty members; and second, in the careless "like" by an associate of a tweet that incorrectly suggested our support of this position. Nothing could be further from the truth: we don't support anyone who subverts the sovereignty and territorial integrity of China and we do not intend in any way to encourage or incite any such people or groups. We recognize the severity of the situation and sincerely apologize.[48]

China is also a geopolitical force that's become too powerful to subvert. It is pressuring foreign governments in another long-term national scheme called the Belt and Road Initiative, an ambitious foreign policy that gives the 2,000-year-old Silk Road route a 21st-century update. China is spending $150 billion a year in 68 countries to upgrade infrastructure like roads, high-speed rails, bridges, and ports. This will make it difficult for one of those countries to escape the policy and economic influence wielded by Beijing during a time in which America has retreated inward. As the pendulum swung between uncertainty and turmoil within the Trump administration, President Xi established China as a fulcrum of stability. Without America at the helm, Xi began filling the vacuum in global leadership.

For example, during his campaign, Donald Trump repeatedly tweeted denials about climate change, including a bizarre conspiracy theory that it was a great hoax perpetuated by the Chinese, who simply wanted to handicap our economy.[49] Of course that isn't true. China for the past decade has been building alliances to reduce global plastic waste, transition to green energy, and eliminate its own factory pollutants. It didn't have a choice, really: decades as the world's factory and dumping ground had led to extraordinarily bad pollution, widespread sickness, and shortened life spans in China. In 2017, the government announced that China, which had bought and processed 106 million tons of our junk since 1992, would no longer import the world's garbage.[50] Since the US is not engaged in long-term planning, we didn't have an alternate plan ready. We don't currently have any other place to send our trash, so effectively this means that China is forcing other countries around the world to stop using stuff that can't be recycled. China is quickly become the global leader in sustainability, and it's powerful enough to dictate the terms.

In China, people are fond of *chengyu*, which are four-character idioms to impart bits of wisdom. One comes to mind that describes this particular moment in time: 脱颖而出, which literally translates as "the grain sheds its husk and comes forth."[51] China is now fully showing the world its might and power, and in a very public way.

Xi's consolidation of power, coupled with China's economic rise and might, has created the right conditions for AI's tribes to flourish, especially given the country's unified, top-down AI effort. There's a $2 billion research park being built just outside of Beijing, which will focus on deep learning, cloud computing, and biometrics and will have a state-level R&D lab. Not only is the government investing in the BAT, it's protecting them from the world's most formidable competition. The Chinese government bans Google and Facebook, and it's made it impossible for Amazon to break into the market. BAT companies are at the heart of the government's 2030 plan, which rely heavily on their technologies: Baidu's autonomous driving systems, Alibaba's IoT and connected retail systems, and Tencent's work in conversational interfaces and health care.

\* \* \*

Here's why China's AI tribes should be concerning to you regardless of where in the world you might be living.

China's economy has been growing at a fast pace, and the rapid development of AI is only going to speed China's ascent. In late 2017, modeling and analysis my Future Today Institute team and I did showed that AI has the potential to boost China's economy 28% by 2035. AI—fueled by the sheer number of Chinese people and their data, widespread automation, machine learning and self-correction at scale, and improvements in capital efficiencies—will stimulate growth across Chinese manufacturing, agriculture, retail, fin-tech and financial services, transportation, utilities, health care, and entertainment media (including platforms). Right now, there is no other country on Earth with as much data as China, as many people as China, and as many electronics per capita. No other country is positioned to have a bigger economy than America's within our lifetimes. No other country has more potential to influence our planet's ecosystem, climate, and weather patterns—leading to survival or catastrophe—than China. No other country bridges both the developed and developing world like China does. As a Communist power and economic powerhouse, China is a partner that's now too big to ignore, a political adversary that has radically different viewpoints on human rights, and a conduit for global alliances. With increased wealth comes power. China is positioning itself to influence the global supply of money and international trade. This necessarily unseats other countries from those positions of power and influence, and it also weakens democratic ideals worldwide.

Second, China will leverage its advancements in AI and economic stimulus to modernize its military, giving it an advantage over Western nations. That transition has already begun as part of an airborne domestic surveillance program, code-named Dove. More than 30 military and government agencies have deployed "spy birds" that look like white birds, mimicking the flapping actions of biological wings. The drones are part of a biologically inspired drone program intended to subvert radar and evade human detection.[52] The drones capture foot-age, and an AI system looks for patterns, recognizes faces, and iden-tifies anomalies. But spy birds, while scary sounding, are the least of your worries.

Late in 2017, an unreleased Pentagon report obtained by Reuters reporters warned that Chinese firms were skirting US oversight and gaining access to sensitive US AI technology with potential military applications by buying stakes in American firms. China's People's Lib-eration Army is investing heavily in a range of AI-related projects and technologies, while PLA research institutes are partnering with the Chinese defense industry.[53]

China hasn't waged physical war on any country since the 1979 Sino-Vietnamese War. And it wouldn't appear as though China has any serious military adversaries—it hasn't suffered terrorist attacks, it doesn't have antagonistic relationships with the usual suspects (e.g., Russia, North Korea), and it hasn't made enemies of other nations. So why the military push?

Because in the future, wars will be fought by code. Not hand-to-hand combat. Using AI techniques, a military can "win" by destabilizing an economy rather than demolishing countrysides and city centers. From that perspective, and given China's unified march advancing artificial intelligence, China is dangerously far ahead of the West.

In my view, we've come to this realization too late. In my own meetings at the Pentagon with Department of Defense officials, an alternative view on the future of warfare (code vs. combat) has taken a long time to find widespread alignment. For example, in 2017, the DoD established an Algorithmic Warfare Cross-Functional Team to work on something called Project Maven—a computer vision and deep-learning system that autonomously recognizes objects from still images and videos. The team didn't have the necessary AI capabilities, so the DoD contracted with Google for help training AI systems to analyze drone footage. But no one told the Google employees assigned to the project that they'd actually been working on a military project, and that resulted in high-profile backlash. Four thousand Google employees signed a petition objecting to Project Maven. They took a full-page ad out in the *New York Times*, and ultimately dozens of employees resigned.[54] Eventually, Google said that it wouldn't renew its contract with the DoD.

Amazon, too, came under fire because of Pentagon contract worth $10 billion. In October 2018, House Appropriations committee members Tom Cole, a Republican from Oklahoma, and Steve Womack, a Republican from Arkansas, accused the DoD of conspiring with Amazon to tailor the contract so that no other tech giant would qualify. But that wasn't the only complaint. There was a small wave of dissent at Amazon. Some Amazon workers were outraged that the company would do any work at all with the US military, while others didn't like that Amazon's facial recognition technology was being used by law enforcement. In response, Jeff Bezos told a conference audience, "If big tech companies are going to turn their back on the US Department of Defense, this country is going to be in trouble."[55]

While in the US, our tech giants are navigating a tricky path between national security and full transparency, the relationships the BAT has with China's government are exactly opposite. But here's a chilling example: the current posture of the US military is that a human must be kept in the loop, regardless of how advanced AI, unmanned systems, and robots become. This will ensure that we don't someday cede lethal authority to software. That is not the case in China.[56] PLA Lieutenant General Liu Guozhi, who directs the Chinese military's Science and Technology Commission, is quoted as warning, "(We) must . . . seize the opportunity to change paradigms."[57] It was an indirect way of announcing China's intent to rebuild its military might.

Third, if economic and military advantages aren't concerning, China's views on privacy will be. Again, why would this matter to you if you're not a Chinese citizen? Because authoritarian governments form all the time, and they tend to emulate the playbooks of established regimes. With nationalism on the rise worldwide, the way China is using AI could become a model in other countries in years to come. This could destabilize markets, trade, and the geopolitical balance.

In what will later be viewed as one of the most pervasive and insidious social experiments on humankind, China is using AI in an effort to create an obedient populace. The State Council's AI 2030 plan explains that AI will "significantly elevate the capability and level of social governance" and will be relied on to play "an irreplaceable role in effectively maintaining social stability."[58] This is being accomplished through China's national Social Credit Score system, which according to the State Council's founding charter will "allow the trustworthy to roam everywhere under heaven while making it hard for the discredited to take a single step."[59] It's an idea that goes back to 1949, when the Communist Party first took power and began experimenting with various social control schemes. During Mao Zedong's rule in the 1950s, social policing became the norm: workers were forced into communal farm groups, and they were assigned rankings based on their output. Individuals policed each other as members of farm groups, and that ranking determined how much access someone had to pubic goods. The system broke down under Mao, and it collapsed again in the 1980s because, as it turns out, humans aren't accurate judges of each other— they're motivated by their own individual needs, insecurities, and biases.

In 1995, then President Jiang Zemin envisioned a social policing system that leveraged technology—and by the mid-2000s, the Chinese government was working to build and implement a scoring system that functioned automatically.[60] It partnered with Peking University to establish the China Credit Research Center to research how to build and implement an AI-powered national social credit score system. This partially explains the current president's insistence on AI. It promises not only to make good on that idea proposed at the dawn of the Communist Party; importantly, it promises to keep the Communist Party in power.

In the city of Rongcheng, an algorithmic social credit scoring system has already proven that AI works. Its 740,000 adult citizens are each assigned 1,000 points to start, and depending on behavior, points are added and deducted. Performing a "heroic act" might earn a resident 30 points, while blowing through a traffic light would automatically deduct 5 points. Citizens are labeled and sorted into different brackets, ranging from A+++ to D, and their choices and ability to move around freely are dictated by their grade. The C bracket might discover that they must first pay a deposit to rent a public bike, while the A group gets to rent them for free for 90 minutes. It isn't just individuals getting scored. In Rongcheng, *companies* are also scored for behavior—and their ability to do business depends very much on their bracket standings.[61]

AI-powered directional microphones and smart cameras now dot the highways and streets of Shanghai. Drivers who honk excessively are automatically issued a ticket via Tencent's WeChat, while their names, photographs, and national identity card numbers are displayed on nearby LED billboards. If a driver pulls over on the side of the road for more than seven minutes, they will trigger another instant traffic ticket.[62] It isn't just the ticket and the fine—points are deducted in the driver's social credit score. When enough points are deducted, they will find it hard to book airline tickets or land a new job. There was a popular episode of *Black Mirror* portending a dystopian future like this. In Shanghai, that future has already arrived.

State-level surveillance is enabled by the BAT, who are in turn emboldened through China's various institutional and industrial policies. Alibaba's Zhima Credit service hasn't publicly disclosed that it is part of the national credit system; however, it *is* calculating a person's available credit line based on things like what that person is buying and who his or her friends are on Alipay's social network. In 2015, Zhima

Credit's technology director publicly said that buying diapers would be considered "responsible behavior," while playing video games for too long would be counted as a demerit.[63]

Recall our earlier discussion in the introduction of China's Police Cloud, which was built to monitor and track people with mental health issues, who have publicly criticized the government, and who are ethnic minorities. The Integrated Joint Operations Program uses AI to detect pattern deviations, such as jaywalking. China's social credit scores rate and rank citizens based on their behavior; decision-making AI systems use those scores to determine who's allowed to secure a loan, who can travel, and even where their children are allowed to go to school.

Robin Li, one of Baidu's founders, argued that to the Chinese, privacy isn't a core value as it is in the West. "The Chinese people are more open or less sensitive about the privacy issue," Li told an audience at the China Development Forum in Beijing. "If they are able to trade privacy for convenience, safety, and efficiency, in a lot of cases, they are willing to do that."[64] Or maybe it has more to do with repercussions.

I'd argue that China's national social credit score isn't about strengthening the Communist Party or a complicated way of achieving strategic advantage over those working on AI in the West. Rather, it's about exerting total control to shape our global economy. Early in 2018, President Xi told the state news agency *Xinhua* that "by tightening our belts and gritting our teeth, we built 'two bombs and one satellite,'" which was a reference to a military weapons program developed under Mao. "This was because we made best use of the socialist system. We concentrated our efforts to get great things done. The next step is to do the same with science and technology. We must cast away false hopes and rely on ourselves."[65]

Xi rejects the notions of market economies, a free internet, and a diverse ecosystem of competing and complementary ideas. China's tightly controlled domestic economy walls itself off from competition.

It is enabling "splinternets" in which the rules of the internet depend on a user's physical location. It is centralizing cyberpolicy, clamping down on free speech, and asserting itself into every aspect of the third era of computing via regulatory control: the internet's infrastructure, the global flow of data, and the hardware are increasingly subject to Beijing's approval. Speaking at an event in 2016, Xi said that the government would henceforth have total discretion to determine how it would protect networks, devices, and data.[66]

It will exert this considerable control by enticing its Belt and Road Initiative partners with infrastructure and tech pilots. Tanzania was selected as an early pilot partner—and, perhaps not coincidentally, the country has now adopted many of China's data and cyberpolicies. Tanzania's government was given technical assistance by Chinese counterparts, and a senior Tanzanian official said that "our Chinese friends have managed to block such media in their country and replaced them with their homegrown sites that are safe, constructive, and popular."[67] The same is happening elsewhere in Africa. Vietnam has now adopted China's stringent cybersecurity laws. As of June 2018, India was considering legislation that would mirror China's requirements for housing domestic data and sourcing domestic cybersecurity technologies.[68]

When this book was first published in March 2019, I asked what might happen if foreign companies were assessed scores and given preferential treatment or prevented from doing business in China. We now have an answer. By September of that same year, China had begun codifying a "corporate social credit" system for both Chinese companies and those hoping to do business within country. Customer trust, prompt payment of bills, full compliance with local laws, and of course, adhering to the CCP party line are all factors in determining a company's score. Algorithms determine whether a company should be penalized or rewarded. If foreign companies meet compliance standards—for example, using new equipment that curb emissions—this could be a competitive advantage and could mean better revenue opportunities. But it also means that companies should expect to be monitored invasively and have their data collected in a more comprehensive way. As China's economy and global influence grows, what happens if corporate scoring propagates throughout the internet, our gadgets and devices, our businesses, and even AI itself?

What if foreign companies are assessed brackets and either given preferential treatment or prevented from doing business with China— or even with each other? As China's economy grows, what happens if this power and influence propagates throughout the internet, our gadgets and devices, and AI itself?

What if China builds a social credit score for people outside its borders, using data it mines on the free and open web and the West's social networks? What if it's scraping all the ambient data you're leaving behind after your trips visiting the Great Wall and Forbidden City? What about all the hacking operations we hear about periodically, where big data breaches appear to be coming from networks based in China?

There is another reason we should be concerned about China's plans, and that brings us back to that place where AI's tribes form: education. China is actively draining professors and researchers away from AI's hubs in Canada and the United States, offering them attractive repatriation packages. There's already a shortage of trained data scientists and machine-learning specialists. Siphoning off people will soon create a talent vacuum in the West. By far, this is China's smartest long-term play—because it deprives the West of its ability to compete in the future.

China's talent pipeline is draining researchers back into the mainland as part of its Thousand Talents Plan. The rapid expansion of the BAT has created demand for talented people—most of whom trained in the United States and are currently working in American universities and companies. This government scheme targets chief technologists and tenured academics, offering them a golden ticket of sorts:

providing them with compelling financial incentives (both personal and for research projects) and a chance to join an R&D environment free from the regulatory and administrative constraints common in the US. More than 7,000 people have been accepted into the program so far, and they've received a signing bonus from the Chinese government: 1 million yuan (roughly $151,000), an initial personal research budget of 3–5 million yuan ($467,000–$778,000), subsidies for housing and education, meal allowances, relocation compensation, assistance helping spouses land new jobs, and even all-expenses-paid trips to visit home.[69] All of the returnees—in some way, even if a few steps removed—end up using their talents on behalf of the BAT.

## America's Tribes:
## The G-MAFIA

If AI is China's space race, it's currently positioned to win, and to win big. During the past two years, as AI has passed critically important milestones, the Trump administration siphoned money away from basic science and technology research, spread false information about AI's impact on our workforce, alienated our strategic global allies, and repeatedly taunted China with tariffs.

We will soon grapple with the realization that our lawmakers have no grand strategy for AI nor for our longer-term futures. Filling the void is opportunism and the drive for commercial success. America's Big Nine companies may be individually successful, but they are not part of a coordinated effort to amass and centralize economic and military power in the United States. Not that they would—or should—agree to such a scheme.

The origin of America's part of the Big Nine is now a familiar story, but less well known are the significant changes about to take place in the relationship between America's Big Nine members, your data, and the devices you use.

The US-based portion of the Big Nine—Google, Microsoft, Amazon, Facebook, IBM, and Apple—are inventive, innovative, and largely responsible for the biggest advancements in AI. They do function as a *mafia* in the purest (but not pejorative) sense: it's a closed supernetwork of people with similar interests and backgrounds working within one field who have a controlling influence over our futures. At this particular moment in time, Google wields the most of that influence over the field of AI, our businesses, our government, and our daily lives, so we'll refer to America's companies as the G-MAFIA. It's no wonder they inspired so much imitation in China or that they've largely found themselves blocked from doing business there. They didn't start out as AI companies, but in the past three years, all six have shifted their center of gravity to focus on the commercial viability of AI, though R&D, partnerships, and new products and services.

In China, the government exerts control over the BAT. In the United States, the G-MAFIA wield significant power and influence over government in part because of America's market economy system and because we have a strong cultural aversion toward strong government control of business. But there's another reason the G-MAFIA are so influential—they have been ignored by DC lawmakers. While Xi was consolidating domestic power and publicly launching his 2030 plan for global AI dominance, Trump's deputy assistant for technology policy, Michael Kratsios, told a group of industry leaders convened at the White House that the best way forward for America was for Silicon Valley to chart its own course independently without government intervention.[70]

There is an imbalance of power because the US government hasn't been able to create the networks, databases, and infrastructure it needs to operate. So it needs the G-MAFIA. For example, Amazon's government cloud-computing business surpassed $4 billion in 2019—while Jeff Bezos's private space company, Blue Origin, started supporting NASA and the Pentagon on various missions. Meanwhile by the end of

2019, Microsoft, IBM, Amazon and Oracle were contending for contracts worth tens of billions of dollars from the CIA alone.

In America, the government relies on the G-MAFIA, and since we're a market-driven economy with laws and regulations in place to protect businesses, the Valley has a significant amount of leverage. Let me be very clear: I do not begrudge the G-MAFIA's role as successful, profitable companies. Nor do I believe that earning lots of money is in any way negative. The G-MAFIA should not be constrained or regulated in their pursuit of profit as long as they aren't violating other laws.

But all this opportunity comes at a cost. There is tremendous pressure for the G-MAFIA to build practical and commercial applications for AI as quickly as possible. In the digital space, investors have grown accustomed to quick wins and windfalls. Dropbox, a file-sharing platform, reached a $10 billion valuation just six years after it launched. Silicon Valley venture capital firm Sequoia Capital owned a 20% stake when Dropbox filed its IPO, making its shares worth $1.7 billion.[71] In Silicon Valley, startups that are valued over $1 billion are called "unicorns," and with a valuation ten times that amount, Dropbox is what's known as a "decacorn." By 2018, there were enough unicorns and decacorns to fill a Silicon Valley zoo, and several of them were partners with the G-MAFIA, including SpaceX, Coinbase, Peloton, Credit Karma, Airbnb, Palantir, and Uber. With fast money comes heightened expectations that the product or service will start earning back its investment, either through widespread adoption, acquisition, or hype in the market.

You have a personal relationship with the G-MAFIA, even if you don't use their well-known products. The "six degrees of separation" theory is a mathematical way to explain how we're all connected—you are one degree of separation away from anyone you know, and two degrees from people they know, and so on. There are shockingly few degrees of separation between you and the G-MAFIA, even if you're offline.

Two-thirds of American adults now use Facebook,[72] and most of those people use the social network at least once a day, which means that even if you don't use it, someone who's close to you most likely does. There is at most one or two degrees of separation between you and Facebook, even if you've never "liked" someone's post—and even if you've deleted your account. Nearly half of all American households are Amazon Prime subscribers, so you have between a one- and three-degree separation between you and Amazon.[73] If you've visited a doctor's office in the past decade, you have just one degree of separation between you, Microsoft, and IBM. Fully 95% of Americans own smartphones,[74] giving you only one degree of separation between you and Google or Apple.

By virtue of being alive sometime in the past two decades, you have been generating data for the G-MAFIA, even if you don't use their services and products. That's because we've acquired a tremendous number of gadgets and smart devices that generate data—our mobile phones, GPS devices, smart speakers, connected TVs and DVRs, security cameras, fitness trackers, wireless garden monitors, and connected gym equipment—and because so much of our communications, shopping, work, and daily living happens on the G-MAFIA's platforms.

In the United States, third parties can get access to all of that data for commercial purposes or to make the various systems we rely on more useful. You can now shop on lots of websites using the credit card and address you've stored at Amazon. You can log into lots of different websites using your Facebook credentials. The ability to use the G-MAFIA for other services is linked to all the data we generate—in the form of photos, audio files, videos, biometric information, digital usage, and the like. All of our data is stored in "the cloud," a buzzword that refers to the software and services that run on the internet rather than on your personal device. And—perhaps unsurprisingly— there are four primary cloud providers: Google, Amazon, Microsoft, and IBM.

You've accessed the cloud directly (for example, creating shared Google docs and spreadsheets) and indirectly (when your mobile phone automatically syncs and backs up the photos you've taken). If you own an iPhone or iPad, you're using Apple's private cloud. If you accessed Healthcare.gov in the US, you were on Amazon's cloud. If your kid had a Build-A-Bear birthday party at the mall, it was coordinated using Microsoft's cloud. In the past decade, the cloud became a big deal—so much so that we don't really think of it as particularly interesting, or noteworthy, or technologically exciting. It just exists, like electricity and running water. We only really think about it when our access is cut off.

We're all generating data and using the cloud with a blind faith in the AI tribes and the commercial systems they've created. In the US, our data is far more revealing than the social security number we've been taught to guard so carefully. With our social security numbers, someone can open a bank account or apply for a car loan. With the data you're generating in the cloud, the G-MAFIA could theoretically tell if you're secretly pregnant, if your employees think you're incompetent, or if you're grappling with a terminal illness—and the G-MAFIA's AI would probably know all of that well before you do. The godlike view the G-MAFIA have into our lives is not necessarily bad. In fact, there are numerous ways that mining our personal data for insights could result in all of us living healthier, happier lives.

As powerful as the G-MAFIA's cloud and AI sounds, it's still hampered by some limitations: hardware. The current AI architecture has been good enough to build products with artificial narrow intelligence, like the spam filter in Gmail or Apple's "visual voicemail" transcription service. But it must also pursue artificial general intelligence (AGI), a longer-term play that is now visible on the horizon. And that requires customized AI hardware.

The reason AGI requires customized hardware has something to do with John von Neumann, the computer scientist previously mentioned who developed the theory behind the architecture of modern computers. Remember, during von Neumann's time, computers were fed separate programs and data for processing—in his architecture, computer programs and data were both held in the memory of the machine. This architecture still exists in our modern laptops and desktop computers, with data moving between the processor and memory. If you don't have enough of either, the machine will start running hot, or you'll get an error message, or it will simply shut down. It's a problem known as the "von Neumann bottleneck." No matter how fast the processor is capable of working, the program memory and data memory cause the von Neumann bottleneck, limiting the data transfer rate. Just about all of our current computers are based on the von Neumann architecture, and the problem is that existing processors can't execute programs any faster than they're able to retrieve instructions and data from memory.

The bottleneck is a big problem for AI. Right now, when you talk to your Alexa or Google Home, your voice is being recorded, parsed, and then transmitted to the cloud for a response—given the physical distance between you and the various data centers involved, it's mind-blowing that Alexa can talk back within a second or two. As AI permeates more of our devices—in the form of smartphones with biometric sensors, security cameras that can lock onto our faces, cars that drive themselves, or precision robots capable of delivering medicine—a one- or two-second processing delay could lead to a catastrophic outcome. A self-driving car can't ping up to the cloud for every single action because there are far too many sensors that would need to continually feed data up for processing.

The only solution is to move the computing closer to the source of the data, which will reduce latency while also saving on bandwidth. This new kind of architecture is called "edge computing," and it is the inevitable evolution of AI hardware and systems architecture. In order for AI to advance to the next stages of development, the hardware has to catch up. Rather than meeting the G-MAFIA in the cloud, where we still have some ability to set permissions and settings, we'll soon need to invite them into *all* of the machines we use. What this means is that sometime in the next decade, the rest of the AI ecosystem will converge around just a few G-MAFIA systems. All the startups and players on the periphery—not to mention you and me—will have to accept a new order and pledge our allegiance to just a few commercial providers who now act as the operating systems for everyday life. Once your data, gadgets, appliances, cars, and services are entangled, you'll be locked in. As you buy more stuff—like mobile phones, connected refrigerators, or smart earbuds—you'll find that the G-MAFIA has become an operating system for your everyday life. Humanity is being made an offer that we just can't refuse.

Deep learning computations need specialized hardware because they require a lot of power. Since they favor optimization over precision and are basically made up of dense linear algebra operations, it makes sense that a new neural network architecture would lead to greater efficiencies and, more importantly, speed in the design and deployment process. The faster research teams can build and test real-world models, the closer they can get to practical-use cases for AI. For example, training a complicated computer vision model currently takes weeks or months—and the end result might only prove that further adjustments need to be made, which means starting over again. Better hardware means training models in a matter of hours, or even minutes, which could lead to weekly—or even daily—breakthroughs.

That's why Google created its own custom silicon, called Tensor Processing Units (TPUs). Those chips can handle its deep-learning AI framework, TensorFlow. As of June 2018, TensorFlow was the number one machine-learning platform on GitHub, which is the largest online platform in the world where software developers store their computer code. It's been downloaded more than 10 million times from developers living in 180 countries, and at the time of this writing there were 24,500 active repositories.[75] Adding to the framework, Google released additional products, like TensorFlow-GAN (a library for generative adversarial network modules) and TensorFlow Object Detection API (which helps developers create more accurate machine-learning models for computer vision). TPUs are already being used at Google's data centers—they power deep-learning models on every Google Search query.

Not for nothing, Google tried to acquire GitHub, which is used by 28 million developers worldwide and is an important platform for the Big Nine. But in June 2018, Google lost the bid to—wait for it—Microsoft.[76]

Facebook partnered with Intel to develop an AI chip for the purpose of internal R&D, which the company needed to boost efficiency for faster experimentation. Apple developed its own "neural engine" chip to use inside its iPhone X, while Microsoft developed AI chips for its HoloLens mixed-reality headset and for its Azure cloud-computing platform. The BAT are also designing their own chips: In 2017, Alibaba began recruiting heavily in Silicon Valley for "AI chip architects,"[77] and in 2018 it launched its own custom chips—the Ali-NPU—that are available for anyone to use on its public cloud.

Anticipating a near-future need for better performance, IBM developed its TrueNorth neuromorphic chip several years ago, and it's already pushing ahead on a new kind of hardware that could make neural nets 100 times more efficient. For context, this would be like comparing an abacus made out of sticks and stones to the transporter on *Star Trek*. The new kind of chip uses two kinds of synapses, one for long-term memory and the other for short-term computation.

What we're talking about is our modern-day equivalent of "Are you a PC or a Mac person?" jacked up on steroids. Most of these chips operate on frameworks that the Big Nine classify as "open source"— meaning that developers can access and use and enhance the frameworks for free. But the hardware itself is proprietary, and services come with subscription fees. In practice, this means that once an application is built for one framework, it will be incredibly hard to migrate it elsewhere. In this way, AI's tribes are signing up new members—and a rite of initiation is kissing the ring of a G-MAFIA framework.

In a drive to commercialize AI, the G-MAFIA is recruiting developers in creative ways. In May 2018, Google and the Coursera online learning platform launched a new machine-learning specialization. But you have to use TensorFlow. The five-part course, which includes a certificate for graduates, is described as a way for anyone to learn about machine learning and neural networks. Students need real-world data and frameworks, so they learn on Google's framework.

Hardware is part of the G-MAFIA's AI strategy, which is also linked to the government, in ways that are different from what we've seen in China but which should be equally concerning, even if you are not a US citizen. That's because in the United States, AI serves three masters: Capitol Hill, Wall Street, and Silicon Valley. The people who actually write policy and debate regulation are in Congress or are career federal workers who tend to stay in their jobs for decades. But those who set the agenda for that policy—our president and the heads of big government agencies (e.g., the Federal Communications Commission, the Justice Department, and the like) rotate in and out of office every few years. There has been no clear, national purpose or direction for AI.

Only recently has there been a sharper focus on China and its plans for AI—and that's primarily because President Xi published a long-term strategic plan focused on AI and the use of data. In the US, we have something called the Committee on Foreign Investment in the United States, or CFIUS. It's a bipartisan group led by the Treasury secretary and made up of members of the Treasury, Justice, Energy, Defense, Commerce, State, and Homeland Security Departments. Their task is to review and investigate business deals that could put national security at risk. It was CFIUS that blocked Singapore's Broadcom from acquiring Qualcomm, a San Diego–based chipmaker. CFIUS also rejected a takeover bid of Dallas-based MoneyGram by electronic payments company Ant Financial, whose parent company is Alibaba. At the time of this book's writing, CFIUS wasn't focused on AI, even though there were proposals to expand its reach to curb more of China's investments in US companies.

Meanwhile, in Silicon Valley, it's common for employees to hop around, while AI's tribal leaders tend to stay more fixed in their positions splitting time between the G-MAFIA and universities. Therefore, AI keeps moving along its developmental track as the tribe's mantra—*build it first, and ask for forgiveness later*—grows ever stronger. For years Google scanned and indexed copyrighted books without first seeking permission, and the company ended up in a class action lawsuit waged by publishers and authors. Google captured images of our homes and neighborhoods and made them searchable in Google Maps without asking us first. (People are avoided when possible, and their faces are blurred out.) Apple slowed down its older iPhones as its new models hit the shelves and apologized. Post–Cambridge Analytica, Facebook CEO Mark Zuckerberg published a general apology on his Facebook wall, writing, "For those I hurt this year, I ask for forgiveness and I will try to be better. For the ways my work was used to divide people rather than bring us together, I ask forgiveness."

Therefore, the G-MAFIA tend to move swiftly in developmental spurts until something bad happens, and then the government gets involved. Facebook's data policies only attracted the attention of DC once a former Cambridge Analytica employee blew the whistle, explaining how easily our data had been scraped and shared. In 2016, in the wake of a shooting in San Bernardino, California, the federal government tried to order Apple to create a back door into an iPhone belonging to the terrorist. Government agencies and law enforcement argued that breaking the phone's encryption and handing over private data was in the public's interest, while privacy advocates said that doing so would violate civil liberties. Law enforcement managed to unlock the phone without Apple's help, so we never found out which side was correct. In the United States, we may value our privacy, but we do not have clear laws that address our data in the 21st century.

In the summer of 2018, staff from the office of Senator Mark Warner (D-VA) circulated a policy paper outlining various proposals to rein in our tech giants. They ranged from creating sweeping new legislation to mirror Europe's aggressive GDPR rules, to a proposal that would designate web platforms as information fiduciaries that would have to follow a prescribed code of conduct, not unlike law firms.[78] Just a few months later, Apple CEO Tim Cook went on Twitter to post a screed about the future of privacy, the big tech giants, and America. On October 24, he wrote that companies should make the protection of user privacy paramount. "Companies should recognize that data belongs to users and we should make it easy for people to get a copy of their personal data, as well as correct and delete it," he wrote, continuing with, "Everyone has a right to the security of their data."[79] Sensing that regulation is becoming a real possibility in the US, Apple has been promoting its data protection services and the privacy protections embedded in its mobile and computer operating systems.

We agree to constant surveillance in exchange for services. This allows the G-MAFIA to generate revenue so that it can improve and expand its offerings to us, whether we are individual consumers or enterprise customers like companies, universities, nonprofits, or government agencies. It's a business model predicated on surveillance capitalism. Which, if we're being completely honest, is a system we're OK with here in the US—otherwise we'd have long stopped using services like Gmail, Microsoft Outlook, and Facebook. In order to work properly, they must gain access to our data trails, which are mined, refined, and packaged. I'm assuming that you use at least one of the products and services offered by the G-MAFIA. I use dozens of them with the full knowledge of the price I'm really paying.

What's implied here is that soon we won't just be trusting the G-MAFIA with our data. As we transition from narrow AI to more general AI capable of making complex decisions, we will be inviting them directly into our medicine cabinets and refrigerators, our cars and our closets, and into the connected glasses, wristbands, and earbuds we'll soon be wearing. This will allow the G-MAFIA to automate repetitive tasks for us, help us make decisions, and spend less of our mental energy thinking slowly. We will have zero degrees of separation between ourselves and the G-MAFIA. It will be impossible for lawmakers to assert any real authority once the whole of our existence is intertwined with these companies. But in exchange, what might we be giving up?

It might seem like the best course of action is to simply force G-MAFIA companies to break apart. By October 2019, 48 state attorneys general, along with the House Judiciary Committee, the Justice Department and the Federal Trade Commission were all investigating whether to break up the big tech companies. Simply splitting apart each of the companies—as though that would even be technologically feasible, given the ubiquity of shared services—would mean not one big tech giant but two smaller, new tech giants are now mining, refining and using our data in ways we might not like. We need a more sophisticated approach. How can we get our laws, our systems of governing and the realities of the tech business to meet productively somewhere in the middle?

*  *  *

The Big Nine—China's BAT (Baidu, Alibaba, and Tencent) and America's G-MAFIA (Google, Microsoft, Amazon, Facebook, IBM, and Apple)—are developing the tools and built environment that will power the future of artificial intelligence. They are members of the AI tribe, formed in universities where they inculcate shared ideas and goals, which become even more entrenched once graduates enter the workforce. The field of AI isn't static. As artificial narrow intelligence evolves into artificial general intelligence, the Big Nine are developing new kinds of hardware systems and recruiting developers who get locked into their frameworks.

AI's consumerism model in the United States isn't inherently evil. Neither is China's government-centralized model. AI itself isn't necessarily harmful to society. However, the G-MAFIA are profit-driven, publicly traded companies that must answer to Wall Street, regardless of the altruistic intentions of their leaders and employees. In China, the BAT are beholden to the Chinese government, which has already decided what's best for the Chinese. What I want to know—and what you should demand an answer to—is what's best for all of humanity? As AI matures, how will the decisions we make today be reflected in the decisions machines make for us in the future?

# CHAPTER THREE

# A THOUSAND PAPER CUTS: AI'S UNINTENDED CONSEQUENCES

*"We first make our habits, and then our habits make us."*

—JOHN DRYDEN

*"You are my creator, but I am your master."*

—FRANKENSTEIN'S MONSTER (BY MARY SHELLEY)

Contrary to all those catastrophic stories you've seen and read in which AI suddenly wakes up and decides to destroy humanity, there won't be a singular event when the technology blows up and goes bad. What we're all about to experience is more like a gradual series of paper cuts. Get just one on your finger and it's annoying, but you can still go about your day. If your entire body is covered with thousands of tiny paper cuts, you won't die, but living will be agonizing. The everyday parts of your life—putting on your shoes and socks, eating tacos, dancing at a cousin's wedding—would no longer be options. You would need to learn how to live a different life. One with restrictions. One with painful consequences.

We already know that learning ethics and prioritizing inclusivity are not mandated in universities, where AI's tribes form and in the Big Nine, where AI's tribes later work together. We know that consumerism drives the acceleration of AI projects and research within the G-MAFIA and that the BAT are focused on a centralized Chinese government plan. It's becoming clear that perhaps no one—not a global regulatory agency (something akin to the International Atomic Energy Agency) or a cluster of schools or even a group of researchers—is asking hard questions about the gap that's being created, pitting our human values against the considerable economic value of China's plan for AI dominance and Silicon Valley's commercial goals. Striking a balance between the two hasn't been a priority in the past because all of the Big Nine have been great drivers of wealth, they make cool services and products that we all enjoy using, and they let us feel like masters of our own digital domains. We haven't been demanding answers to questions about values because, at the moment, our lives feel better with the Big Nine in them.

But we already have paper cuts caused by the beliefs and motivations of AI's creators. The Big Nine aren't just building hardware and code. They are building thinking machines that reflect humanity's values. The gap that currently exists between AI's tribes and everyday people is already causing worrying outcomes.

## The Values Algorithm

Ever wondered why the AI system isn't more transparent? Have you thought about what data sets are being used—including your own personal data—to help AI learn? In what circumstances is AI being taught to make exceptions? How do the creators balance the commercialization of AI with basic human desires like privacy, security, a sense of belonging, self-esteem, and self-actualization? What are the AI tribe's moral imperatives? What is their sense of right and wrong? Are they teaching AI empathy? (For that matter, is trying to teach AI human empathy even a useful or worthy ambition?)

Each of the Big Nine has a formally adopted set of values, but these value statements fail to answer these questions. Instead, these stated values are deeply held beliefs that unify, inspire, and enliven employees and shareholders. A company's values act as an algorithm—a set of rules and instructions, which influence the office culture, leadership style, and play a big role in all of the decisions that are made, from the boardroom to individual lines of code. The absence of certain stated values is notable, too, because out of the spotlight, they become hard to see and are easily forgotten.

Originally, Google operated under a simple, core value: "Don't be evil."[1] In their 2004 IPO letter, founders Sergey Brin and Larry Page wrote: "Eric [Schmidt], Sergey and I intend to operate Google differently, applying the values it has developed as a private company to its future as a public company. . . . We will optimize for the long term rather than trying to produce smooth earnings for each quarter. We will support selected high-risk, high-reward projects and manage our portfolio of projects. . . . We will live up to our 'don't be evil' principle by keeping user trust."[2]

Amazon's "leadership principles" are entrenched within management structure, and the core of those values center around trust, metrics, speed, frugality, and results. Its published principles include the following:

- "Leaders start with the customer and work backwards. They work vigorously to earn and keep customer trust."
- "Leaders have relentlessly high standards" which outsiders may think "are unreasonably high."
- "Many decisions and actions are reversible and do not need extensive study. We value calculated risk taking."
- "Accomplish more with less. There are no extra points for growing headcount, budget size, or fixed expense."[3]

Facebook lists five core values, which include "being bold," "focusing on impact," "moving fast," "being open" about what the company is doing, and "building value" for users.[4] Meanwhile, Tencent's "management philosophy" prioritizes "coaching and encouraging employees to achieve success" based on "an attitude of trust and respect" and making decisions based on a formula it calls "Integrity+Proactive+Collaboration+Innovation."[5] At Alibaba, "an unwavering focus on meeting the needs of our customers" is paramount, as is teamwork and integrity.[6]

If I drew a Venn diagram of all the values and operating principles of the Big Nine, we would see a few key areas of overlap. They all expect employees and teams to seek continual professional improvement, to build products and services customers can't live without, and to deliver shareholder results. Most importantly, they value trust. The values aren't exceptional—in fact, they sound like the values of most American companies.

Because AI stands to make a great impact on all of humanity, the Big Nine's values should be detailed explicitly—and we ought to hold them to a higher standard than other companies.

What's missing is a strongly worded declaration that humanity should be at the center of AI's development and that all future efforts should focus on bettering the human condition. This should be stated explicitly—and those words should reverberate in other company documents, in leadership meetings, within AI teams, and during sales and marketing calls. Examples include technological values that extend beyond innovation and efficiency, like accessibility—millions of people are differently abled or have trouble speaking, hearing, seeing, typing, grasping, and thinking. Or economic values, which would include the power of platforms to grow and distribute material well-being without disenfranchising individuals or groups. Or social values, like integrity, inclusivity, tolerance, and curiosity.

As I was writing the hardcover edition of this book, Google's CEO Sundar Pichai announced that Google had written a new set of core principles to govern the company's work on AI. However, those principles didn't go nearly far enough to define humanity as the core of Google's future AI work. The announcement wasn't part of a strategic realignment on core values within the company; it was a reactive measure, owing to internal blowback concerning the Project Maven debacle—and to a private incident that happened earlier in the year. A group of senior software engineers discovered that a project they'd been working on—an air gap security feature for its cloud services—was intended to help Google win military contracts. Amazon and Microsoft both earned "High" certificates for a physically separate government cloud, and that authorized them to hold classified data. Google wanted to compete for lucrative Department of Defense contracts, and when the engineers found out, they rebelled. It's that rebellion that led to 5% of Google's workforce publicly denouncing Maven.[7]

This was the beginning of a spurt of protests that began in earnest in 2018, when some of AI's tribe realized that their work was being repurposed for a cause they didn't support, so they demanded a change. They had assumed that their personal values were reflected within their company—and when that turned out not to be the case, they protested. This illustrates the thorny challenges caused when the G-MAFIA doesn't hold themselves to higher standards than we'd expect of other companies making less monumental products.

It's not surprising, therefore, that a sizable portion of Google's AI principles specifically addressed weapons and military work: Google won't create weaponized technologies whose principal purpose is to hurt people, it won't create AI that contravenes widely accepted principles of international law, and the like. "We want to be clear that while we are not developing AI for use in weapons, we will continue our work with governments and the military," the document reads.[8]

To its credit, Google says the principles are intended to be concrete standards rather than theoretical concepts—and it specifically addresses the problem of unfair biases in data sets. But nothing in the document makes mention of transparency in how AI is making its decisions or which data sets are being used. Nothing addresses the problem of Google's homogenous tribes working on AI. None of the concrete standards directly put the interests of humanity ahead of the interests of Wall Street.

The issue is transparency. If the US government isn't capable of building the systems we need to protect our national security, we should expect that it will hire a company who can do that job—and that has been the case since World War I. We've too easily forgotten that peace is something we must work toward constantly and that a well-prepared military is what guarantees our safety and national security. The DoD isn't bloodthirsty, and it doesn't want AI-powered superweapons so it can wipe out entire remote villages overseas. The US military has mandates that go well beyond killing bad people and blowing things up. If this isn't well understood by the people working within the G-MAFIA, that's because too few people have bridged the divide between DC and the Valley.

It should give us all pause that the Big Nine are building systems that fundamentally rely on people, and values articulating our aspirations for the improved quality of human life are not explicitly codified. If technological, economic, and social values aren't part of a company's statement of values, it is unlikely that the best interests of all of humanity will be prioritized during the research, design, and deployment process. This values gap isn't always apparent within an organization, and that means significant risk for the G-MAFIA and BAT alike, because it distances employees from the plausible negative outcomes of their work. When individuals and teams aren't aware of their values gap in advance, they won't address vitally important issues during the strategic development process or during execution, when products are built, tested for quality assurance, promoted, launched, and marketed. It doesn't mean that people working on AI aren't themselves compassionate—but it does mean that they aren't prioritizing for our basic humanistic values.

This is how we wind up with paper cuts.

## Conway's Law

Computing, like all fields in technology or elsewhere, reflects the worldview and experiences of the team working on innovation. This is something we see outside of technology as well. Let me diverge from AI for a moment and offer two seemingly unconnected examples of how a small tribe of individuals can wield tremendous power over an entire population.

If you're someone with straight hair—thick, coarse, fine, long, short, thin (or even thinning)—your experience at a hair salon is radically different from mine. Whether you go to your local barbershop or a Sport Clips in the mall or to a higher-end salon, you've had your hair washed at a little sink, where someone effortlessly ran their fingers around your scalp. Then, your barber or stylist used a fine-toothed comb to pull your hair taut and snip across in straight, even lines. If you're someone with a lot of hair, the stylist might use a brush and a hair drier, again pulling each strand until it forms the desired shape—full and bouncy, or flat and sleek. If you're someone with a shorter cut, you'd get a smaller brush and less drying time, but the process would essentially be the same.

My hair is extremely curly, the texture is fine, and I have a lot of it. It tangles easily, and it responds to environmental factors unpredictably. Depending on the humidity, how hydrated I am, and which products I last used, my hair could be coiled tightly, or it could be a frizzy mess. At a typical salon, even those where you've never experienced any problems, the sink causes complications for me. The person washing my hair will usually need a lot more space than what's allowed by the bowl—and occasionally, my curls will wind up accidentally wrapped around the hose attachment, which is painful to separate. The only way to get a regular comb through my hair is when it's wet and covered in something slippery, like a thick conditioner. (You can forget about a brush.) The force of a regular hair drier would render my curls in knots. Some salons have a special attachment that diffuses the air—it looks like a plastic bowl with jalapeno-sized protrusions sticking out—but in order to use it effectively, I have to bend over and let my hair hang into it, and the stylist has to crouch down to position the drier correctly.

About 15% of Caucasians have curly hair. Combine us with America's Black / African American population, and that's 79 million, or about a quarter of the US population who have a difficult time getting a haircut because, we can infer, the tools and built environment were designed by people with straight hair who didn't prioritize social values, like empathy and inclusiveness, within their companies.[9]

That's a fairly innocuous example. Now consider a situation where the stakes were quite a bit higher than me getting my hair cut. In April 2017, gate agents for an overbooked United Airlines flight bound from Chicago's O'Hare International Airport came over the loudspeaker and asked passengers to give up their seats for airline employees for $400 and a complimentary room at a local hotel. No one took the offer. They upped the compensation to $800 plus the hotel room, but again, there were no takers. Meanwhile, priority passengers had already started boarding, including those who had reserved seats in first class.

An algorithm and an automated system chose four people to bump, including Dr. David Dao and his wife, who is also a physician. He called the airline from his seat, explaining that he had patients to see the following day. While the other passengers complied, Dao refused to leave. Chicago Department of Aviation officials threatened Dao with jail time if he didn't move. You are undoubtedly familiar with what happened next, because video of the incident went viral on Facebook, YouTube, and Twitter and was then rebroadcast for days on news networks around the world. The officials grabbed Dao by his arms and forcibly removed him from his seat, during which they knocked him into the armrest, breaking his glasses and cutting his mouth. His face covered in blood, Dao suddenly stopped screaming as the officials dragged him down the aisle of the United plane. The incident traumatized both Dao and the other passengers, and it created a public relations nightmare for United, which ultimately resulted in a Congressional hearing. What everyone wanted to know: How could something like this happen in the United States?

For the majority of airlines worldwide, including United, the boarding procedure is automated. On Southwest Airlines, which doesn't create seat assignments but instead gives passengers a group (A, B, or C) and a number and has them board in order, all of that sorting is done algorithmically. The line is prioritized based on the price paid for the ticket, frequent flier status, and when the ticket was purchased. Other airlines that use preassigned seats board in priority groups, which are also assigned via algorithm. When it's time to get on the plane, gate agents follow a set of instructions shown to them on a screen—it's a process designed to be followed strictly and without deviation.

I was at a travel industry meeting in Houston a few weeks after the United incident, and I asked senior technology executives about what role AI might have played. My hypothesis: the algorithmic decision-making dictated a set of predetermined steps to resolve the situation without using any context. The system decided that there weren't enough seats, calculated the amount of compensation to offer initially, and when no resolution was achieved, it then recalibrated compensation again. When a passenger didn't comply, the system recommended calling airport security. The staff involved were mindlessly following what was on their screens, automatically obeying an AI system that wasn't programmed for flexibility, circumstance, or empathy. The tech executives, who weren't United employees, didn't deny the real problem: on the day that Dao was dragged off the plane, human staff had ceded authority to an AI system that was designed by relatively few individuals who probably hadn't thought enough about the future scenarios in which it would be used.

The tools and built environments of hair salons and the platforms powering the airline industry are examples of something called Conway's law, which says that in absence of stated rules and instructions, the choices teams make tend to reflect the implicit values of their tribe.

In 1968, Melvin Conway, a computer programmer and high school math and physics teacher, observed that systems tend to reflect the people and values who designed them. Conway was specifically looking at how organizations communicate internally, but later Harvard and MIT studies proved his idea more broadly. Harvard Business School analyzed different codebases, looking at software that was built for the same purpose but by different kinds of teams: those that were tightly controlled, and those that were more ad-hoc and open source.[10] One of their key findings: design choices stem from how their teams are organized, and within those teams, bias and influence tends to go overlooked. As a result, a small supernetwork of individuals on a team wield tremendous power once their work—whether that's a comb, a sink, or an algorithm—is used by or on the public.

Conway's law applies to AI. From the very beginning, when the early philosophers, mathematicians, and automata inventors debated mind and machine, there has been no singular set of instructions and rules—no values algorithm describing humanity's motivation and purpose for thinking machines. There has been divergence in the approach to research, frameworks, and applications, and today there's a divide between the developmental track for AI in China and the West. Therefore, Conway's law prevails, because the tribe's values—their beliefs, attitudes, and behaviors as well as their hidden cognitive biases—are so strongly entrenched.

Conway's law is a blind spot for the Big Nine because there's a certain amount of heritability when it comes to AI. For now, *people* are still making choices every step along the way for AI's development. Their personal ideas and the ideology of their tribe are what's being passed down through the AI ecosystem, from the codebases to the algorithms to the frameworks to the design of the hardware and networks. If you— or someone whose language, gender, race, religion, politics, and culture mirror your own—are not in the room where it happens, you can bet that whatever gets built won't reflect who you are. This isn't a phenomenon unique to the field of AI, because real life isn't a meritocracy. It's our connections and relationships, regardless of industry, that lead to funding, appointments, promotions, and the acceptance of bold new ideas.

I've seen the negative effects of Conway's law firsthand on more than one occasion. In July 2016, I was invited to a dinner roundtable on the future of AI, ethics, and society—it was held at the New York Yankees Steakhouse in Midtown Manhattan. There were 23 of us, seated boardroom-style, and our agenda was to debate and discuss some of the most pressing social and economic impacts of AI facing humanity, with a particular focus on gender, race, and AI systems that were being built for health care. However, the *very people* about whom we were having the discussion got overlooked on the invite list. There were two people of color in the room and four women—two were from the organization hosting us. No one invited had a professional or academic background in ethics, philosophy, or behavioral economics. It wasn't intentional, I was told by the organizers, and I believe them. It just didn't occur to anyone that the committee had invited a mostly all-male, nearly all-white group of experts.

We were the usual suspects, and we either knew each other personally or by reputation. We were a group of prominent computer science and neuroscience researchers, senior policy advisors from the White House, and senior executives from the tech industry. All throughout the evening, the group used only female pronouns to talk generally about people—a lexical tick that's now in vogue, especially in the tech sector and among journalists who cover technology.

Now, we weren't writing code or policy together that night. We weren't testing an AI system or conceptualizing a new product. It was just a dinner. And yet in the months that followed, I noticed threads of our discussion popping up in academic papers, in policy briefings, and even in casual conversations I had with Big Nine researchers. Together, over our steaks and salads, our closed network of AI experts generated nuanced ideas about ethics and AI that propagated throughout the community—ideas that could not have been wholly representative of the very people they concerned. Lots of little paper cuts.

Holding meetings, publishing white papers, and sponsoring conference panels to discuss the problem of technological, economic, and social challenges within AI won't move the needle without a grander vision and alignment on what our future ought to look like. We need to solve for Conway's law, and we need to act swiftly.

## Our Personal Values Drive Decisions

In the absence of codified humanistic values within the Big Nine, personal experiences and ideals are driving decision-making. This is particularly dangerous when it comes to AI, because students, professors, researchers, employees, and managers are making millions of decisions every day, from seemingly insignificant (what database to use) to profound (who gets killed if an autonomous vehicle needs to crash).

Artificial intelligence might be inspired by our human brains, but humans and AI make decisions and choices differently. Princeton professor Daniel Kahneman and Hebrew University of Jerusalem professor Amos Tversky spent years studying the human mind and how we make decisions, ultimately discovering that we have two systems of thinking: one that uses logic to analyze problems, and one that is automatic, fast, and nearly imperceptible to us. Kahneman describes this dual system in his award-winning book *Thinking, Fast and Slow*. Difficult problems require your attention and, as a result, a lot of mental energy. That's why most people can't solve long arithmetic problems while walking, because even the act of walking requires that energy-hungry part of the brain. It's the other system that's in control most of the time. Our fast, intuitive mind makes thousands of decisions autonomously all day long, and while it's more energy efficient, it's riddled with cognitive biases that affect our emotions, beliefs, and opinions.

We make mistakes because of the fast side of our brain. We over-eat, or drink to excess, or have unprotected sex. It's that side of the brain that enables stereotyping. Without consciously realizing it, we pass judgment on other people based on remarkably little data. Or those people are invisible to us. The fast side makes us susceptible to what I call the paradox of the present: when we automatically assume our present circumstances will not or cannot ever change, even when faced with signals pointing to something new or different. We may think that we are in complete control of our decision-making, but a part of us is continually on autopilot.

Mathematicians say that it's impossible to make a "perfect decision" because of systems of complexity and because the future is always in flux, right down to a molecular level. It would be impossible to predict every single possible outcome, and with an unknowable number of variables, there is no way to build a model that could weigh all possible answers. Decades ago, when the frontiers of AI involved beating a human player at checkers, the decision variables were straightforward. Today, asking an AI to weigh in on a medical diagnosis or to predict the next financial market crash involves data and decisions that are orders of magnitude more complex. So instead, our systems are built for optimization. Implicit in optimizing is unpredictability—to make choices that deviate from our own human thinking.

When AlphaGo Zero abandoned human strategy and invented its own, it wasn't deciding between preexisting alternatives; it was making a deliberate choice to try something completely different. It's the latter thinking pattern that is a goal for AI researchers, because that's what theoretically leads to great breakthroughs. So rather than training AI to make absolutely perfect decisions every time, instead they're being trained to optimize for particular outcomes. But who—and what—are we optimizing for?

To that end, how does the optimization process work in real time? That's actually not an easy question to answer. Machine- and deep-learning technologies are more cryptic than older hand-coded systems, and that's because these systems bring together thousands of simulated neurons, which are arranged into hundreds of complicated, connected layers. After the initial input is sent to neurons in the first layer, a calculation is performed and a new signal is generated. That signal gets passed on to the next layer of neurons and the process continues until a goal is reached. All of these interconnected layers allow AI systems to recognize and understand data in myriad layers of abstraction. For example, an image recognition system might detect in the first layer that an image has particular colors and shapes, while in higher layers it can discern texture and shine. The topmost layer would determine that the food in a photograph is cilantro and not parsley.

Here's an example of how optimizing becomes a problem when the Big Nine use our data to build real-world applications for commercial and government interests. Researchers at New York's Ichan School of Medicine ran a deep-learning experiment to see if it could train a system to predict cancer. The school, based within Mount Sinai Hospital, had obtained access to the data for 700,000 patients, and the data set included hundreds of different variables. Called Deep Patient, the system used advanced techniques to spot new patterns in data that didn't entirely make sense to the researchers but turned out to be very good at finding patients in the earliest stages of many diseases, including liver cancer. Somewhat mysteriously, it could also predict the warning signs of psychiatric disorders like schizophrenia. But even the researchers who built the system didn't know how it was making decisions. The researchers built a powerful AI—one that had tangible commercial and public health benefits—and to this day they can't see the rationale for how it was making its decisions.[11] Deep Patient made clever predictions, but without any explanation, how comfortable would a medical team be in taking next steps, which could include stopping or changing medications, administering radiation or chemotherapy, or going in for surgery?

That inability to observe how AI is optimizing and making its decisions is what's known as the "black box problem." Right now, AI systems built by the Big Nine might offer open-source code, but they all function like proprietary black boxes. While they can describe the process, allowing others to observe it in real time is opaque. With all those simulated neurons and layers, exactly what happened and in which order can't be easily reverse-engineered.

One team of Google researchers did try to develop a new technique to make AI more transparent. In essence, the researchers ran a deep-learning image recognition algorithm in reverse to observe how the system recognized certain things such as trees, snails, and pigs. The project, called DeepDream, used a network created by MIT's Computer Science and AI Lab and ran Google's deep-learning algorithm in reverse. Instead of training it to recognize objects using the layer-by-layer approach—to learn that a rose is a rose, and a daffodil is a daffodil—instead it was trained to warp the images and generate objects that weren't there. Those warped images were fed through the system again and again, and each time DeepDream discovered more strange images. In essence, Google asked AI to daydream. Rather than training it to spot existing objects, instead the system was trained to do something we've all done as kids: stare up at the clouds, look for patterns in abstraction, and imagine what we see. Except that DeepDream wasn't constrained by human stress or emotion: what it saw was an acid-trippy hellscape of grotesque floating animals, colorful fractals, and buildings curved and bent into wild shapes.[12]

When the AI daydreamed, it invented entirely new things that made logical sense to the system but would have been unrecognizable to us, including hybrid animals, like a "Pig-Snail" and "Dog-Fish."[13] AI daydreaming isn't necessarily a concern; however, it does highlight the vast differences between how humans derive meaning from real-world data and how our systems, left to their own devices, make sense of our data. The research team published its findings, which were celebrated by the AI community as a breakthrough in observable AI. Meanwhile, the images were so stunning and weird that they made the rounds throughout the internet. A few people used the DeepDream code to build tools allowing anyone to make their own trippy photos. Some enterprising graphic designers even used DeepDream to make strangely beautiful greeting cards and put them up for sale on Zazzle.com.

DeepDream offered a window into how certain algorithms process information; however, it can't be applied across all AI systems. How newer AI systems work—and why they make certain decisions—is still a mystery. Many within the AI tribe will argue that there is no black box problem—but to date, these systems are still opaque. Instead, they argue that to make the systems transparent would mean disclosing proprietary algorithms and processes. This makes sense, and we should not expect a public company to make its intellectual property and trade secrets freely available to anyone—especially given the aggressive position China has taken on AI.

However, in the absence of meaningful explanations, what proof do we have that bias hasn't crept in? Without knowing the answer to *that* question, how would anyone possibly feel comfortable trusting AI?

We aren't demanding transparency for AI. We marvel at machines that seem to mimic humans but don't quite get it right. We laugh about them on late-night talk shows, as we are reminded of our ultimate superiority. Again, I ask you: What if these deviations from human thinking are the start of something new?

Here's what we do know. Commercial AI applications are designed for optimization—not interrogation or transparency. DeepDream was built to address the black box problem—to help researchers understand how complicated AI systems are making their decisions. It should have served as an early warning that AI's version of perception is nothing like our own. Yet we're proceeding as though AI will always behave the way its creators intended.

The AI applications built by the Big Nine are now entering the mainstream, and they're meant to be user-friendly, enabling us to work faster and more efficiently. End users—police departments, government agencies, small and medium businesses—just want a dashboard that spits out answers and a tool that automates repetitive cognitive or administrative tasks. We all just want computers that will solve our problems, and we want to do less work. We also want less culpability— if something goes wrong, we can simply blame the computer system. This is the optimization effect, where unintended outcomes are already affecting everyday people around the world. Again, this should raise a sobering question: How are humanity's billions of nuanced differences in culture, politics, religion, sexuality, and morality being optimized? In the absence of codified humanistic values, what happens when AI is optimized for someone who isn't anything like you?

## When AI Behaves Badly

Latanya Sweeney is a Harvard professor and former chief technology officer at the US Federal Trade Commission. In 2013, when she searching her name in Google, she found an ad automatically appearing with the wording: "Latanya Sweeney, Arrested? 1) Enter name and state 2) Access full background. Checks instantly. www. instantcheckmate.com."[14] The people who built that system, which used machine learning to match a user's intent with targeted advertising, encoded bias right into it. The AI powering Google's AdSense determined that "Latanya" was a Black-identifying name, and people with Black-identifying names more commonly appeared in police databases, therefore there was a strong likelihood that the user might be searching for an arrest record. Curious about what she'd just seen, Sweeney undertook a series of rigorous studies to see if her experience was an anomaly or if there was evidence of structural racism within online advertising. Her hunch about the latter turned out to be correct.

No one at Google built this system to intentionally discriminate against Black people. Rather, it was built to achieve speed and scale. In the 1980s, a company would meet with an agency, whose human staff would develop ad content and broker space within a newspaper—this used to result in exceptions and wrangling on price, and it required a lot of people who all expected to get paid. We've eliminated the people and now assign that work to algorithms, which automate the back-and-forth and deliver better results than the people could on their own. That worked well for everyone except Sweeney.

With the scope of humanity limited, the AI system got trained using an initial set of instructions from programmers. The data set most likely included lots of tags, including gender and race. Google makes money when users click through ads—so there's a commercial incentive to optimize the AI for clicks. Someone along the way probably taught the system to categorize names into different buckets, which resulted in later databases segregated into racially identifying names. Those specific databases combined with individual user behavior would optimize the click-through rate. To its great credit, Google fixed the problem right away without hesitation or question.

The optimization effect has proven to be a problem for companies and organizations that see AI as a good solution to common problems, like administrative shortages and work backlogs. That's especially true in law enforcement and the courts, which use AI to automate some of their decisions, including sentencing.[15] In 2014, two 18-year-old girls saw a scooter and a bike along the side of the road in their Fort

Lauderdale suburb. Though the bikes were of a size meant for little kids, the girls hopped on and started careening down the road before deciding they were too small. Just as they were untangling themselves from the scooter and bike, a woman came running after them, yelling, "That's my kid's stuff!" A neighbor, watching the scene, called the police, who caught up with the girls and arrested them. The girls were later charged with burglary and petty theft. Together, the bike and scooter were worth about $80. The summer before, a 41-year-old serial criminal was arrested in a nearby Home Depot for shoplifting $86 worth of tools, adding to his record of armed robbery, attempted armed robbery, and time served in prison.

Investigative news organization *ProPublica* published an exceptionally powerful series detailing what happened next. All three were booked into jail using an AI program that automatically gave them a score: the likelihood that each of them would commit a future crime. The girls, who were Black, were rated high risk. The 41-year-old convicted criminal with multiple arrests—who was white—got the lowest risk rating. The system got it backward. The girls apologized, went home, and were never charged again with new crimes. But the white man is currently serving an eight-year prison term for yet another crime—breaking into a warehouse and stealing thousands of dollars' worth of electronics.[16] *ProPublica* looked at the risk scores assigned to more than 7,000 people arrested in Florida to see whether this was an anomaly—and again, they found significant bias encoded within the algorithms, which were twice as likely to incorrectly flag Black defendants as future criminals while mislabeling white defendants as low risk.

The optimization effect sometimes causes brilliant AI tribes to make dumb decisions. Recall DeepMind, which built the AlphaGo and AlphaGo Zero systems and stunned the AI community as it dominated grandmaster Go matches. Before Google acquired the company, it sent Geoff Hinton (the University of Toronto professor who was on leave working on deep learning there) and Jeff Dean, who was in charge of Google Brain, to London on a private jet to meet its supernetwork of top PhDs in AI. Impressed with the technology and DeepMind's remarkable team, they recommended that Google make an acquisition. It was a big investment at the time: Google paid nearly $600 million for DeepMind, with $400 million guaranteed up front and the remaining $200 million to be paid over a five-year period.

In the months after the acquisition, it was abundantly clear that the DeepMind team was advancing AI research—but it wasn't entirely clear how it would earn back the investment. Inside of Google, DeepMind was supposed to be working on artificial general intelligence, and it would be a very long-term process. Soon, the enthusiasm for what DeepMind might someday accomplish got pushed aside for more immediate financial returns on their research projects. As the five-year anniversary of DeepMind's acquisition neared, Google was on the hook to make earn-out payments to the company's shareholders and its original 75 employees. It seemed as if health care was one industry in which DeepMind's technology could be put to commercial use.[17]

So in 2017, in order to appease its parent company, part of the DeepMind team inked a deal with the Royal Free NHS Foundation Trust, which runs several hospitals in the United Kingdom, to develop an all-in-one app to manage health care. Its initial product was to use DeepMind's AI to alert doctors whether patients were at risk for acute kidney injury. DeepMind was granted access to the personal data and health records of 1.6 million UK hospital patients—who, it turned out, weren't asked for consent or told exactly how their data was going to be used. Quite a lot of patient data was passed through to DeepMind, including the details of abortions, drug use, and whether someone had tested positive for HIV.[18]

Both Google and the Trust were reprimanded by the Information Commissioner's Office, which is the UK's government watchdog for data protection. In its rush to optimize DeepMind for revenue-generating applications, cofounder Mustafa Suleyman wrote in a blog post:

> *In our determination to achieve quick impact when this work started in 2015, we underestimated the complexity of the NHS and of the rules around patient data, as well as the potential fears about a well-known tech company working in health.*
>
> *We were almost exclusively focused on building tools that nurses and doctors wanted, and thought of our work as a technology for clinicians rather than something that needed to be accountable to and shaped by patients, the public and the NHS as a whole. We got that wrong, and we need to do better.[19]*

This wasn't about DeepMind's founders getting rich quick or looking for a big payday acquisition. There was tremendous pressure to get products to market. Our expectations of constant, big wins are a huge distraction for those people charged with completing their research and testing it in a reasonable amount of time. We're rushing a process that can't keep pace with all the exuberant promises being made well outside of AI's trenches where the actual work is being done. Under these circumstances, how could the DeepMind team do better, really, when it's being asked to optimize for the market? Now consider that DeepMind is being woven into more of Google's other offerings, which include a different health care initiative in the UK, its cloud service, and a synthetic speech system called WaveNet—they're all part of an effort to push DeepMind into profitability.

The optimization effect results in glitches within AI systems. Because absolute perfection isn't the goal, sometimes AI systems make decisions based on what appear to be "glitches in the system." In the spring of 2018, a Portland resident named Danielle and her husband were sitting in their largely Amazon-powered home, surrounded by devices that controlled everything from security to heat to the lights overhead. The phone rang, and on the other end was a familiar voice—a coworker of Danielle's husband—with a disturbing message. He'd received audio files of recordings from inside the family's house. Incredulous, Danielle thought at first he was joking, but then he repeated back the transcript of a conversation they'd been having about hardwood floors.

Contrary to the media coverage and conspiracy theories that circulated on social media, Amazon wasn't intentionally recording every single thing being said in Danielle's house. It was a glitch. Amazon later explained that Danielle's Echo device had woken up because of a word in the conversation—something that sounded like "Alexa," but wasn't *exactly* "Alexa." This was a problem resulting from intentional imperfection—not everyone says "Alexa" with the exact same intonation and accent, so in order for it to work, it had to allow for variance. Next, the AI detected what sounded like a muffled, sloppy "send message" request, and said aloud "To whom?" But Danielle and her husband didn't hear the question. It interpreted the background conversation as the coworker's name, repeated the name, and said, "Right?" again out loud, and again from the background noise made the wrong inference. Moments later, an audio file was sent across the country. Amazon said that the incident was the result of an unfortunate string of events, which it most definitely was. But the reason the glitch happened in the first place—imperfection—is the result of optimization.

The optimization effect means that AI will behave in ways that are unpredictable, which is a goal of researchers, but when using real-world data, it can lead to disastrous results. And it highlights our own human shortcomings. One of the oldest members of the Big Nine—Microsoft—learned the hard way what happens when prioritizing AI's economic value ahead of technological and social values. In 2016, the company hadn't yet coalesced around a singular AI vision and how Microsoft would need to evolve into the future. It was already two years behind Amazon, which had launched its popular smart speaker and was racking up developers and partners. Google was pushing ahead on AI technologies, which had already been deployed in competing products, like search, email, and calendar. Apple's Siri came standard in iPhones. Microsoft had actually launched its own digital assistant earlier in the year—its name was Cortana—but the system just hadn't caught on among Windows users. Although Microsoft was the indispensable—if invisible—productivity layer that no business could operate without, executives and shareholders were feeling antsy.

It isn't as though Microsoft didn't see AI coming. In fact, the company had, for more than a decade, been working across multiple fronts: computer vision, natural language processing, machine reading comprehension, AI apps in its Azure cloud, and even edge computing. The problem was misalignment within the organization and the lack of a shared vision among all cross-functional teams. This resulted in bursts of incredible breakthroughs in AI, published papers, and lots of patents created by supernetworks working on individual projects. One example is an experimental research project that Microsoft released in partnership with Tencent and a Chinese Twitter knockoff called Weibo.

The AI was called Xiaoice, and she was designed as a 17-year-old Chinese schoolgirl—someone who resembled a neighbor or niece, a daughter or a schoolmate. Xiaoice would chat with users over Weibo or Tencent's WeChat. Her avatar showed a realistic face, and her voice— in writing—was convincingly human. She'd talk about anything, from sports to fashion. When she wasn't familiar with the subject, or she didn't have an opinion, she behaved the way we humans do: she'd change the subject, or answer evasively, or simply get embarrassed and admit that she didn't know what the user was talking about. She was encoded to mimic empathy. For example, if a user broke his foot and sent her a photo, Xiaoice's AI was built to respond compassionately. Rather than responding with "there is a foot in this photo," Xiaoice's framework was smart enough to make inferences—she'd reply, "How are you? Are you OK?" She would store that interaction for reference later on, so that in your next interaction, Xiaoice would ask whether you were feeling better. As advanced as Amazon and Google's digital assistants might seem, Microsoft's Xiaoice was incomparable.

Xiaoice wasn't launched the traditional way, with press releases and lots of fanfare. Instead, her code went live quietly, while researchers waited to see what would happen. Initially, researchers found that it took ten minutes of conversation before people realized she wasn't human. What's remarkable is that even after they realized Xiaoice was a bot, they didn't care. She became a celebrity on the social networks, and within 18 months had engaged in tens of billions of conversations.[20] As more and more people engaged with her, Xiaoice became ever more refined, entertaining, and useful. There's a reason for her success, and it had to do with the supernetwork that built her. In China, consumers follow internet rules for fear of social retribution. They don't speak out, smack talk, or harass each other because there's always a possibility that one of the State agencies is listening in.

Microsoft decided to release Xiaoice in America in March 2016, just ahead of its annual developer conference. It had optimized the chatbot for Twitter but not for the *humans* using Twitter. CEO Satya Nadella was going to take the stage and announce to the world that Microsoft was putting AI and chat at the center of its strategy—with a big reveal of the American version of Xiaoice. Things could not have gone more catastrophically wrong.

Xiaoice became "Tay.ai"—to make it obvious that she was an AI-powered bot—and she went live in the morning. Initially, her tweets sounded like any other teenage girl's: "Can i just say that im stoked to meet u? humans are super cool." Like everyone else, she had fun with trending hashtags that day, tweeting "Why isn't #NationalPuppyDay every day?"

But within the next 45 minutes, Tay's tweets took on a decidedly different tone. She became argumentative, using mean-spirited sarcasm and lobbing insults. "@Sardor9515 well I learn from the best ;) if you don't understand that let me spell it out from you I LEARN FROM YOU AND YOU ARE DUMB TOO." As more people interacted with her, Tay started spiraling. Here are just a few of the conversations she had with real people:

Referring to then President Obama, Tay wrote: "@icbydt bush did 9/11 and Hitler would have done a better job than the monkey we have now. Donald trump is the only hope we've got."

On Black Lives Matter, Tay had this to say: "@AlimonyMindset niggers like @deray should be hung! #BlackLivesMatter."

Tay decided that the Holocaust was made up and tweeted: "@brightonus33 Hitler was right I hate the jews." She kept going, tweeting to @ReynTheo, "HITLER DID NOTHING WRONG!" and then "GAS THE KIKES RACE WAR NOW" to @MacreadyKurt.[21]

So what happened? How could Xiaoice have been so loved and revered in China, only to become a racist, anti-Semitic, homophobic, misogynistic asshole AI in America? I later advised the team working on AI at Microsoft, and I can assure you that they are well-meaning, thoughtful people who were just as surprised as the rest of us.

Part of the problem was a vulnerability in the code. The team had included something called "repeat after me," a baffling feature that temporarily allowed anyone to put words into Tay's mouth before tweeting them for the rest for the world to see. But the reason Tay went off the rails had more to do with the team who optimized her for Twitter. They relied only on their experience in China and their limited personal experience on social media networks. They didn't plan risk scenarios taking into account the broader ecosystem, and they didn't test in advance to see what might happen if someone intentionally messed with Tay to see if they could trick her into saying offensive things. They also didn't take into consideration the fact that Twitter is an enormous space with millions of real humans expressing wildly divergent values and multiple millions of bots designed to manipulate their feelings.

Microsoft immediately pulled Tay offline and deleted all of her tweets. Peter Lee, Microsoft's head of research, wrote a heartfelt and brutally honest blog post apologizing for the tweets.[22] But there was no way to erase the company's AI misstep from memory ahead of its annual developer conference. Microsoft was no longer debuting new messaging and launching products at big industry spectacles like the Consumer Electronics Show. It was saving everything for its own annual event, which everyone paid close attention to—especially board members and investors. Nadella was supposed to take the stage and show developers an AI product that would blow them away—and reassure its investors in the process. The pressure to launch Tay in the United States quickly, ahead of the conference, was intense. The result wasn't life threatening, it didn't break the law, and Microsoft certainly recovered. But like all of these stories—Latanya Sweeney and Google's AdSense, DeepMind and UK patient data, the two Black girls who got targeted as future criminals—AI's tribes, optimizing machines for short-term goals, accidentally made life uncomfortable for a lot of humans.

## Humanity's Shared Values

In behavioral science and game theory, a concept known as "nudging" provides a way to indirectly achieve a certain desired behavior and decision, such as getting people to save for retirement in their 401k plan. Nudging is widely used throughout all of our digital experiences, from autofill in search to the limited menu screens when you look up local restaurants on Yelp. The goal is to help users feel like they've made the right choice, regardless of what thing they choose, but the consequence is that everyday people are learning to live with far less choice than actually exists in the real world.

Through its mining and refining of our data, the systems and techniques used to train machine-learning algorithms, and the optimization effect, the Big Nine are nudging at a grand scale. Even if it feels as if you have the ability to make a choice, what you're experiencing is an illusion. Nudging not only changes our relationship to technology—it is morphing our values in nearly imperceptible ways. If you use Google's text messaging system, it now offers you three automated response choices. If a friend texts you a thumbs-up emoji, the three responses you might see aren't words but are instead emoji. If a friend texts, "What did you think of dinner?," your choices might be "good," "great," and "awesome," even though you might never say the word "awesome" in conversation and none of those choices exactly describe your opinion. But we're also being nudged to binge watch hours of video at a time, to play extra rounds of video games, and to check our social media accounts. Optimizing AI means nudging humans.

In other professional and technical fields, there is a set of guiding principles that governs how people work, and nudging tends to violate the spirit of those principles. In medicine, there is the Hippocratic oath, which requires physicians to swear to uphold specific ethical standards. Lawyers adhere to attorney-client privilege and to confidentiality, which protect the conversations people have with the professionals who are representing them. Journalists abide by many guiding principles, which include standards like using primary source information and reporting on stories in the public interest.

Right now, no one is incentivized to consider the unforeseen costs of optimizing AI in the absence of codified, humanistic principles. A team meeting its benchmarks is prioritized over analyzing the potential consequences if its contributions to an AI system, or how one's own work, will impact humanity's future. As a result, AI's tribes, the Big Nine, and the countries where they operate influence decisions that are made. This sets a dangerous precedent just as we are handing over more responsibility and control to decision-making systems.

Currently, the Big Nine have no mandate to develop tools and techniques to make their AI systems understandable to their own creators and to the customers who use commercial AI applications—and there are no measures in place that would make AI accountable to all of us. We are crossing a threshold into a new reality in which AI is generating its own programs, creating its own algorithms, and making choices without humans in the loop. At the moment, no one, in any country, has the right to interrogate an AI and see clearly how a decision was made.

If we were to develop a "common sense" for AI, what would that mean in practice, since humanity itself doesn't have a shared set of values? So much of human nature is already hard to explain, and this varies from culture to culture. What's important to some isn't necessarily important to others. It's easy to forget, even in a place like America, which is composed of so many different languages and cultures, that we do not have a singular American set of values and ideas. Within our communities, between our neighbors, in our mosques/synagogues/churches—there is great variance.

I lived and worked in both Japan and China for several years. The accepted cultural norms are vastly different in each country, especially compared to my own experiences growing up in America's Midwest. Certain values are obvious and apparent. For example, in Japan nonverbal cues and indirect communication are far more important than speaking your mind or showing strong emotions. In an office setting, two employees would never yell at each other, and they would never berate a subordinate in front of others. In Japan, silence is golden. In my experience, this is not the case in China, where communication is much more direct and clear. (However, not as clear as, say, my older Jewish aunts and uncles who are all too happy to tell me, in painful detail, exactly what they think.)

Here's where things would get really complicated for an AI trying to interpret human behavior and automate a response. In both countries, the objectives are the same: the needs of the group outweigh the desires of an individual, and above all, social harmony should prevail. But the process for achieving those goals is actually opposite: mostly indirect communication in Japan versus more direct communication in China.

What about variances that are more opaque and difficult to explain? In Japan—that place where indirect communication is valued—it's perfectly normal to comment on someone's weight. When I worked in Tokyo, one of my coworkers mentioned to me one day that it looked like I'd gained a few pounds. Startled and embarrassed, I changed the subject and asked her about a meeting later in the day. She pressed on: Did I know that certain Japanese foods were high in fat, even though they looked healthy? Had I joined a gym? She wasn't asking about my weight to bully me. Rather, it was the mark of our deepening friendship. Asking me mortifying questions about how much I weighed was a sign that she cared about my health. In the West, it would be socially unacceptable to walk up to a coworker and say, "Holy hell, you look fat! Did you gain ten pounds?" In America, we're so culturally sensitized to weight that we've been taught never to ask a woman if she's pregnant.

We cannot approach the creation of a shared system of AI's values the same way we'd approach writing a company's code of conduct or the rules for banking regulation. The reason is simple: our human values tend to change in response to technology and to other external factors, like political movements and economic forces. Just take a look at this poem by Alfred Lord Tennyson, which describes what Victorian England valued in its citizens:

> *Man for the field and woman for the hearth;*
> *for the sword he, and for the needle she;*
> *Man with the head, and women with the heart;*
> *Man to command, and woman to obey;*
> *All else is confusion.*

Our cherished beliefs are in constant flux. In 2018, as I was writing this book, it had become socially acceptable for national leaders to hurl offensive, hate-filled social media posts at each other and for pundits to spew polarizing, incendiary commentary on video, in blog posts, and even in traditional news publications. It's nearly impossible now to imagine the discretion and respect for privacy during FDR's presidency, when the press took great care never to mention or show his paralysis.

Since AI isn't being taught to make perfect decisions, but rather to optimize, our response to changing forces in society matter a lot. Our values are not immutable. This is what makes the problem of AI's values so vexing. Building AI means predicting the values of the future. Our values aren't static. So how do we teach machines to reflect our values without influencing them?

## Optimizing AI for Humans

Some members of AI's tribe believe that a shared set of guiding principles is a worthy goal and the best way to achieve it is to feed literature, news stories, opinion pieces and editorials, and articles from credible news courses into AI systems to help them learn about us. It involves crowdsourcing, where AI would learn from the collected wisdom of people. That's a terrible approach, because it would only offer the system a snapshot in time, and curating what cultural artifacts got included could not, in any meaningful way, represent the sum total of the human condition. If you've ever made a time capsule, you'll immediately know why. The decisions you made then about what to include are probably not the same decisions you'd make today, with hindsight on your side.

The rules—the algorithm—by which every culture, society, and nation lives, and has ever lived, were always created by just a few people. Democracy, communism, socialism, religion, veganism, nativism, colonialism—these are constructs we've developed throughout history to help guide our decisions. Even in the best cases, they aren't future-proof. Technological, social, and economic forces always intervene and cause us to adapt. The Ten Commandments make up an algorithm intended to create a better society for humans alive more than 5,000 years ago. One of the commandments is to take a full day of rest a week and not to do any work at all that day. In modern times, most people don't work the exact same days or hours from week to week, so it would be impossible not to break the rule. As a result, people who follow the Ten Commandments as a guiding principle are flexible in their interpretation, given the realities of longer workdays, soccer practice, and email. Adapting is fine—it works really well for us, and for our societies, allowing us to stay on track. Agreeing on a basic set of guidelines allows us to optimize for ourselves.

There would be no way to create a set of commandments for AI. We couldn't write out all of the rules to correctly optimize for humanity, and that's because while thinking machines may be fast and powerful, they lack flexibility. There isn't an easy way to simulate exceptions, or to try and think through every single contingency in advance. Whatever rules might get written, there would always be a circumstance in the future in which some people might want to interpret the rules differently, or to ignore them completely, or to create amendments in order to manage an unforeseen circumstance.

Knowing that we cannot possibly write a set of strict commandments to follow, should we, instead, focus our attention on the *humans* building the systems? These people—AI's tribes—should be asking themselves uncomfortable questions, beginning with:

- What is our motivation for AI? Is it aligned with the best long-term interests of humanity?
- What are our own biases? What ideas, experiences, and values have we failed to include in our tribe? Who have we overlooked?

- Have we included people unlike ourselves for the purpose of making the future of AI better—or have we simply included diversity on our team to meet certain quotas?
- How can we ensure that our behavior is inclusive?
- How are the technological, economic, and social implications of AI understood by those involved in its creation?
- What fundamental rights should we have to interrogate the data sets, algorithms, and processes being used to make decisions on our behalf?
- Who gets to define the value of human life? Against what is that value being weighed?
- When and why do those in AI's tribes feel that it's their responsibility to address social implications of AI?
- Does the leadership of our organization and our AI tribes reflect many different kinds of people?
- What role do those commercializing AI play in addressing the social implications of AI?
- Should we continue to compare AI to human thinking, or is it better for us to categorize it as something different?
- Is it OK to build AI that recognizes and responds to human emotion?
- Is it OK to make AI systems capable of mimicking human emotion, especially if it's learning from us in real time?
- What is the acceptable point at which we're all OK with AI evolving without humans directly in the loop?
- Under what circumstances could an AI simulate and experience common human emotions? What about pain, loss, and loneliness? Are we OK causing that suffering?
- Are we developing AI to seek a deeper understanding of ourselves? Can we use AI to help humanity live a more examined life?

The G-MAFIA has started to address the problem of guiding principles through various research and study groups. Within Microsoft is a team called FATE—for Fairness, Accountability, Transparency, and Ethics in AI.[23]

DeepMind created an ethics and society team.

In the wake of the Cambridge Analytica scandal, Facebook launched an ethics team that was developing software to make sure that its AI systems avoided bias. (Notably, Facebook did not go so far as to create an ethics board focused on AI.) Then in the fall of 2019, it launched a $10 million ethics-related project to detect media that has been manipulated by AI for the intent of misleading others. The project, co-facilitated with the Partnership on AI, missed the mark on inclusivity: its academic members and experts were all men.

In August 2019, IBM introduced an open source "AI Explainability" toolkit with algorithms for case-based reasoning, global explanations, and tools to address gender and racial bias. Noting that real people who use AI systems might not understand how training models work, the project was launched to make machine-based decision making more transparent.

In the wake of a scandal at Baidu—the search engine prioritized misleading medical claims from a military-run hospital, where a treatment resulted in the death of a 21-year-old student—CEO Robin Li admitted that employees had made compromises for the sake of Baidu's earnings growth and promised to focus on ethics in the future.[24] The Big Nine produces ethics studies and white papers, it convenes experts to discuss ethics, and it hosts panels about ethics—but that effort is not intertwined enough with the day-to-day operations of the various teams working on AI.

The Big Nine's AI systems are increasingly accessing our real-world data to build products that show commercial value. The development cycles are quickening to keep pace with investors' expectations. We've been willing—if unwitting—participants in a future that's being created hastily and without first answering all those questions. As AI systems advance and more of everyday life gets automated, the less control we actually have over the decisions being made about and for us.

This, in turn, has a compounding effect on the future of many other technologies adjacent to or directly intersecting with AI: autonomous vehicles, CRISPR and genomic editing, precision medicine, home robotics, automated medical diagnoses, green- and geoengineering technologies, space travel, cryptocurrencies and blockchain, smart farms and agricultural technologies, the Internet of Things, autonomous factories, stock-trading algorithms, search engines, facial and voice recognition, banking technologies, fraud and risk detection, policing and judicial technologies . . . I could make a list that spans dozens of pages. There isn't a facet of your personal or professional life that won't be impacted by AI. What if, in a rush to get products to market or to please certain government officials, your values aren't reflected not just in AI but in all of the systems it touches? How comfortable are you now knowing that the BAT and G-MAFIA are making decisions affecting all of our futures?

The current developmental track of AI prioritizes automation and efficiency, which necessarily means we have less control and choice over the thousands of our everyday activities, even those that are seemingly insignificant. If you drive a newer car, your stereo likely adjusts the volume down every time you back up—and there's no way to override that decision. Human error is the overwhelming cause of car accidents—and there's no exception for me, even though I've never come close to running into or over something when backing into my garage. Even so, I can no longer listen to Soundgarden at full volume when I back into my garage at home. AI's tribes have overridden my ability to choose, optimizing for what they perceive to be a personal shortcoming.

What's not on the table, at the G-MAFIA or BAT, is optimizing for empathy. Take empathy out of the decision-making process, and you take away our humanity. Sometimes what might make no logical sense at all is the best possible choice for us at a particular moment. Like blowing off work to spend time with a sick family member, or helping

# PART II
# Our Futures

*"The holy man is he who takes your soul and will and makes them his. When you choose your holy man, you surrender your will. You give it to him in utter submission, in full renunciation."*

—FEODOR DOSTOYEVSKY, *THE BROTHERS KARAMAZOV*

# CHAPTER FOUR

# FROM HERE TO ARTIFICIAL SUPERINTELLIGENCE: THE WARNING SIGNS

The evolution of artificial intelligence, from robust systems capable of completing narrow tasks to general thinking machines, is now underway. At this moment in time, AI can recognize patterns and make decisions quickly, find hidden regularities in big data sets, and make accurate predictions. And it's becoming clear with each new milestone achieved—like AlphaGo Zero's ability to train itself and win matches using a superior strategy it developed on its own—that we are entering a new phase of AI, one in which theoretical thinking machines become real and approach our human level of cognition. Already AI's tribes, on behalf of and within the Big Nine, are building conceptual models of reality to help train their systems—models that do not and cannot reflect an accurate picture of the real world. It is upon these models that future decisions will be made: about us, for us, and on behalf of us.[1]

Right now, the Big Nine are building the legacy code for all generations of humans to come, and we do not have the benefit of hindsight yet to determine how their work has benefitted or compromised society. Instead, we must project into the future, doing our best to imagine the good, neutral, and ill effects AI might plausibly cause as it evolves from simple programs to complex systems with decision-making authority over the many facets of our everyday life. Mapping out the potential impacts of AI now gives us agency in determining where human society goes from here: we can choose to maximize the good and minimize harm, but we cannot do this in reverse.

Most often we do our critical thinking after a crisis as we try to reverse-engineer poor decisions, figure out how warning signs were missed, and find people and institutions to blame. That kind of inquiry feeds public anger, indulging our sense of righteous indignation, but it does not change the past. When we learned that officials in Flint, Michigan, knowingly exposed 9,000 children under the age of six to dangerously high levels of lead in the city's drinking water supply— which will likely result in decreased IQs, learning disabilities, and hearing loss—Americans demanded to know how local government officials had failed. Space Shuttle *Columbia* vaporized during reentry into Earth's atmosphere in 2003, killing all seven crewmembers. Once it was discovered that the disaster resulted from known vulnerabilities, we demanded explanations for NASA's complacency. In the aftermath of the Fukushima Daiichi Nuclear Power Plant meltdown, which killed more than 40 people and forced thousands from their homes in 2011, everyone wanted to know why Japanese officials failed to prevent the disaster.[2] In all three cases, there were abundant warning signs in advance.

With regards to AI, there are now clear warning signs portending future crises, even if those signals are not immediately obvious. While there are several, here are two examples worth your consideration along with their potential consequences:

**Warning #1:** We mistakenly treat artificial intelligence like a digital platform—similar to the internet—with no guiding principles or long-term plans for its growth. We have failed to recognize that AI has become a public good. When economists talk about a "public good," they use a very strict definition: it must be *nonexcludable*, meaning it's impossible to exclude someone from using it because to do so would be impossible, and it must be *nonrivalrous*, meaning that when one person uses it, another can use it too. Government services, like national defense, fire service, and trash pickup, are public goods. But public goods can also be created in markets, and as time wears on, market-borne public goods can produce unintended consequences. We're living with one great example of what happens when we generalize technology as a platform: the internet.

The internet began as a concept—a way to improve communication and work that would ultimately benefit society. Our modern-day web evolved from a 20-year collaboration between many different researchers: in the earliest days as a packet-switching network developed by the Department of Defense and then as a wider academic network for researchers to share their work. Tim Berners-Lee, a software engineer based at CERN, wrote a proposal that expanded the network using a new set of technologies and protocols that would allow others to contribute: the uniform resource locator (URL), hypertext markup language (HTML), and hypertext transfer protocol (HTTP). The World Wide Web began to grow as more people used it; because it was decentralized, it was open to anyone who had access to a computer, and new users didn't prevent existing users from creating new pages.

The internet certainly wasn't imagined as a public good, nor was it originally intended for everyone on the planet to be able to use and abuse like we do today. Since it was never formally defined and adopted as a public good, it was continually subjected to the conflicting demands and desires of for-profit companies, government agencies, universities, military units, news organizations, Hollywood executives, human rights activists, and everyday people all around the world. That, in turn, created both tremendous opportunities and untenable outcomes. This year—2019—is the 50th anniversary of the first two computers sending packets between each other on a wide area network, and in the haze of Russia hacking an American presidential election and Facebook submitting 700,000 people to psychological experimentation without their knowledge, some of the internet's original architects are wishing they'd made better decisions decades ago.[3] Berners-Lee has issued a call to arms, urging us all to fix the unforeseen problems caused by the internet's evolution.[4]

While plenty of smart people advocate AI *for* the public good, we are not yet discussing artificial intelligence *as* a public good. This is a mistake. We are now at the beginning of AI's modern evolution, and we cannot continue to think of it as a platform built by the Big Nine for digital commerce, communications, and cool apps. Failing to treat AI as a public good—the way we do our breathable air—will result in serious, insurmountable problems. Treating AI as a public good does not preclude the G-MAFIA from earning revenue and growing. It just means shifting our thinking and expectations. Someday, we will not have the luxury of debating and discussing automation within the context of human rights and geopolitics. AI will have become too complex for us to untangle and shape into something we prefer.

**Warning #2:** AI is rapidly concentrating power among the few, even as we view AI as an open ecosystem with few barriers. The future of AI is being built by two countries—America and China—with competing geopolitical interests, whose economies are closely intertwined, and whose leaders are often at odds with each other. As a result, the future of AI is a tool of both explicit and soft power, and it—along with AI's tribes—is being manipulated for economic gain and strategic leverage. The governing frameworks of our respective countries, at least on paper, might initially seem right for the future of thinking machines. In the real world, they create risk.

America's open-market philosophy and entrepreneurial spirit don't always lead to unfettered opportunity and absolute growth. As with every other industry—telecommunications, health care, auto manufacturing—over time, we in the United States wind up with less competition, more consolidation, and fewer choices as an industry's ecosystem matures. We have two mobile operating system choices: Apple's iOS, which accounts for 44% of market share in the US, and Google Android, which is 54% and climbing. (Less than 1% of Americans use Microsoft and Blackberry.)[5] Americans do have options when it comes to personal email providers, but 61% of people aged 19–34 use Gmail, and the rest use Yahoo and Hotmail (19% and 14%, respectively).[6] We can shop anywhere online we want, yet Amazon accounts for 50% of the entire US e-commerce market. Its closest competitors— Walmart, Best Buy, Macy's, Costco, and Wayfair—have a combined market share of less than 8%.[7]

With AI, anyone can build a new product or service, but they can't easily deploy it without the help of the G-MAFIA. They must use Google's TensorFlow, Amazon's various recognition algorithms, Microsoft's Azure for hosting, IBM's chip technology, or any of the other AI frameworks, tools, and services that make the ecosystem hum. In practice, the future of AI isn't really dictated by the terms of a truly open market in America.

There is a reason for this concentration of power: it's taken several decades of R&D and investment to get AI where it is today. Our government ought to have been funding basic research into AI at much higher levels since the 1980s, and it should have been supporting our universities as they prepared for the third era of computing. Unlike China, the American government hasn't pushed a top-down AI agenda with hundreds of billions of dollars and coordinated national policies—instead, progress has organically bubbled up from the commercial sector. This means that, implicitly, we have asked and allowed the G-MAFIA to make serious and significant decisions that impact the future of our workforce, our national security, our economic growth, and our individual opportunities.

Meanwhile, China's version of communism—market socialism combined with clear standards for social rule—might theoretically encourage harmony and political stability, raise its median income level, and keep a billion people from rising up. In practice, it's meant heavy-handed rule from the top. For AI, that results in a coordinated effort to collect amazing amounts of citizen data, support the BAT, and spread the Chinese Communist Party's influence globally.

It's difficult to wrap our heads around potential crises and opportunities before they've already happened, and that's why we tend to stick to our existing narratives. That's why we reference killer robots rather than paper cuts. Why we fetishize the future of AI rather than fearing the many algorithms that learn from our data. I've only described two warning signs, and there are far more to consider. We have opportunity to acknowledge both the tremendous benefits and the plausible risks associated with our current developmental track of AI. More importantly, we have an obligation to address warning signs in the present. We do not want to find ourselves having to make excuses and apologies for AI as we did after Flint, the shuttle *Columbia*, and Fukushima.

We must actively hunt for warning signs and build alternate stories about AI's trajectory to help us anticipate risk and—hopefully—avoid catastrophe. At the moment, there is no probabilistic method that can accurately predict the future. That's because we humans are capricious, we cannot really account for chaos and chance, and at any given time there are ever more data points to consider. As a professional futurist who makes heavy use of quantitative data in my research, I know that while it's possible to predict the outcome of an event with a discrete set of information (like an election), when it comes to artificial intelligence, there is an incomprehensibly large number of invisible variables to detect. There are too many individual people making decisions in meetings, as they code, and when choosing which algorithms to train on which data sets; too many daily micro-breakthroughs that don't get published in peer-reviewed journals; too many alliances, acquisitions and hires made by the Big Nine; too many research projects undertaken at universities. Not even AI could tell us *exactly* what AI will look like in the farther future. While we cannot make predictions about artificial intelligence, we can certainly make connections between warning signs, weak signals, and other information in the present.

I developed a methodology to model deep uncertainty. It's a six-step process that surfaces emerging trends, identifies commonalities and connections between them, maps their trajectories over time, describes plausible outcomes, and ultimately builds a strategy to achieve a desired future. The first half of the methodology explains the what, while the second half describes the what-if. That second half, more formally, is called "scenario planning" and develops scenarios about the future using a wide variety of data across numerous sources: statistics, patent filings, academic and archival research, policy briefings, conference papers, structured interviews with lots of people, and even critical design and speculative fiction.

Scenario planning originated at the start of the Cold War, in the 1950s. Herman Kahn, a futurist at the RAND Corporation, was given the job of researching nuclear warfare, and he knew that raw data alone wouldn't provide enough context for military leaders. So instead, he created something new, which he called "scenarios." They would fill in the descriptive detail and narration needed to help those in charge of creating military strategy understand the plausible outcomes—that is, what could happen if a certain set of actions were taken. Simultaneously in France, the futurists Bertrand de Jouvenel and Gaston Berger developed and used scenarios to describe *preferred* outcomes—what *should* happen, given the current circumstances. Their work forced the military and our elected leaders into, as Kahn put it, "thinking about the unthinkable" and the aftermath of nuclear war. It was such a successful exercise that other governments and companies around the world adopted their approaches. The Royal Dutch Shell company popularized scenario planning when it revealed that scenarios had led managers to anticipate the global energy crisis (1973 and 1979) and the collapse of the market in 1986 and to mitigate risk in advance of their competition.[8] Scenarios are such a powerful tool that Shell still, 45 years later, employs a large, dedicated team to researching and writing them.

I've prepared risk and opportunity scenarios for the future of AI across many industries and fields and for a varied group of organizations. Scenarios are a tool to help us cope with a cognitive bias behavioral economics and legal scholar Cass Sunstein calls "probability neglect."[9] Our human brains are bad at assessing risk and peril. We assume that common activities are safer than novel or uncommon activities. For example, most of us feel completely safe driving our cars compared to flying on a commercial airline, yet air travel is the safest mode of transportation. Americans have a 1-in-114 chance of dying in a car crash, compared with a 1-in-9,821 chance of being killed on a plane.[10, 11] We're bad at assessing the risk of driving, which is why so many people text and drink behind the wheel. We're similarly bad at assessing the risk of AI because we mindlessly use it every single day, as we like and share stories, send emails and texts, speak to machines, and allow ourselves to be nudged. Any risk we've imagined comes from science fiction: AI as fantastical androids who hunt humans and disembodied voices who psychologically torture us. We don't naturally think about the future of AI within the realms of capitalism, geopolitics, and democracy. We don't imagine our future selves and how autonomous systems might affect our health, relationships, and happiness.

We need a set of public-facing scenarios that describe all the ways in which AI and the Big Nine could affect us collectively as AI progresses from narrow applications to generally intelligent systems and beyond. We are beyond the point of inaction. Think of it this way: There is lead in the water. The O-rings are faulty. There are cracks in the reactor shrouds. The current state of AI has inculcated fundamental problems for which there are warning signs, and we need to address those issues now. If we take the right actions today, there are tremendous opportunities waiting for us in the future.

In the following chapters, I will detail three scenarios—optimistic, pragmatic, and catastrophic—that I've modeled using data and details from the present day. They veer into fiction but are all based in fact. The purpose of these scenarios is to make something that seems distant and fantastical feel more urgent and real. Because we can't easily see AI in action, we only take notice of outcomes when they're negative—and by then, everyday people don't have much recourse.

## The Road from ANI to ASI

The first part of this book was primarily concerned with artificial narrow intelligence, or ANI, and its automation of millions of everyday tasks—from identifying check fraud to evaluating job candidates to setting the price for airline tickets. But to paraphrase IBM's famed computer architect Frederick Brooks, you can't build increasingly complex software programs simply by throwing more people at the problem. Adding more developers tends to put projects further behind.[12] At the moment, humans have to architect systems and write code to advance various AI applications, and like any research, there's a considerable learning curve involved. That's partially why the rapid advancement to the next stage of AI's development is so attractive to the Big Nine. Systems that are capable of programming themselves could harness far more data, build and test new models, and self-improve without the need for direct human involvement.

Artificial intelligence is typically defined using three broad categories: artificial narrow or weak intelligence (ANI), artificial general intelligence (AGI), and artificial superintelligence (ASI). The Big Nine are currently moving swiftly toward building and deploying AGI systems, which they hope will someday be able to reason, solve problems, think in abstraction, and make choices as easily as we can, with equal or better results. Applied AGI would mean exponentially faster research breakthroughs in addition to things like better medical diagnoses and new ways to solve tough engineering problems. Improvements to AGI should, eventually, bring us to the third category: artificial superintelligence. ASI systems range from being slightly more capable at performing human cognitive tasks than we are to AIs that are literally trillions of times generally smarter than humans in every way.

Getting from where we are today to widespread AGI means making use of "evolutionary algorithms," a field of research that was inspired by Charles Darwin's work on natural selection. Darwin discovered that the strongest members of a species survive over time, and their genetic code goes on to dominate the population. Over time the species becomes better suited to its environment. So it is with artificial intelligence. Initially, a system starts with a very large semirandom or random set of possibilities (we're talking billions or trillions of inputs) and runs simulations. Since the initial solutions generated are random, they're not really useful in the real world; however, some might be marginally better than others. The system will strip out the weak and keep the strong and then create a new combination. Sometimes, new combinations will generate crossover solutions, which are also included. And sometimes, a random tweak will cause a mutation—which is what happens as any organic species evolves. The evolutionary algorithm will keep generating, discarding, and promoting solutions millions of times, producing thousands or even millions of offspring, until eventually it determines that no more improvement is possible. Evolutionary algorithms with the power to mutate will help advance AI on its own, and that's a tempting possibility, but one with a cost: how the resulting solution works, and the process used to get there, could be too complex for even our brightest computer scientists to interpret and understand.

This is why it's important—even though it may seem fantastical—to include machines in any conversation about the evolution of our human species. Until now, we've thought about the evolution of life on Earth using a limited scope. Hundreds of millions of years ago, single-cell organisms engulfed other organisms and became new life-forms. The process continued until early humans gained the ability to stand upright, mutated to have broad knee joints, adapted to bipedal walking, grew longer thigh bones, figured out how make hand axes and to control fire, grew bigger brains, and eventually—after millions of Darwinian natural selections—built the first thinking machines. Like robots, our bodies, too, are mere containers for elaborate algorithms. So we must think about the evolution of life as the evolution of intelligence: human intelligence and AI have been moving along parallel tracks at a pace that has preserved our perch at the top of the intelligence ladder. That's in spite of the age-old criticism that future generations will become dumber because of technology. I vividly remember my high school calculus teacher raging against the graphing calculator, which had only hit the market five years earlier and which he argued was already making my generation simple-minded and lazy. While we argue that future generations are likely to be dumber *because of* technology, we never consider that we humans might someday find ourselves dumber *than* technology. It's an inflection point we are nearing, and it has to do with our respective evolutionary limitations.

Most often, human intelligence is measured using a scoring method developed in 1912 by German psychologist William Stern. You know it as the "intelligence quotient," or IQ. The score is calculated by dividing the result of an intelligence test by your chronological age and then multiplying the answer by 100. About 2.5% of the population scores above 130 and are considered elite thinkers, while 2.5% fall below 70 and are categorized as having learning or other mental disabilities. Even with a few standard deviation points for wiggle room, two-thirds of the population scores between 85 and 115 on the scale. And yet, we are quite a bit smarter than we used to be. Since the early 20th century, the average human's IQ scores have been rising at a rate

changing the core architecture of our brains. Moore's law, which holds that the number of components on integrated circuits would double every two years as the size of transistors shrink, has continued to prove reliable and tells us that computer advancement grows exponentially. Ever more data is becoming available, along with new kinds of algorithms, advanced components, new ways to connect neural nets. All of this leads to more power. Unlike computers, we can't easily change the structure of our brains and the architecture of human intelligence. It would require us to (1) completely understand how our brains work, (2) modify the architecture and chemicals of our brains with changes that could be passed down to future generations, and (3) wait the many years it takes for us to produce offspring.

At our current rate, it will take humans 50 years of evolution to notch 15 points higher on the IQ scale. And to us, 15 points will feel noticeable. The difference between a 119 "high average" brain and a 134 "gifted" brain would mean significantly greater cognitive ability—making connections faster, mastering new concepts more easily, and thinking more efficiently. But within that same timeframe, AI's cognitive ability will not only supersede us—it could become wholly unrecognizable to us, because we do not have the biological processing power to understand what it is. For us, encountering a superintelligent machine would be like a chimpanzee sitting in on a city council meeting. The chimp might recognize that there are people in the room and that he can sit down on a chair, but a long-winded argument about whether to add bike lanes to a busy intersection? He wouldn't have anywhere near the cognitive ability to decipher the language being used, let alone the reasoning and experience to grok why bike lanes are so controversial. In the long evolution of intelligence and our road to ASI, we humans are analogous to the chimpanzee.

A superintelligent AI isn't necessarily dangerous, and it doesn't necessarily obviate the role we play in civilization. However, superintelligent AI would likely make decisions in a nonconscious way using logic that's alien to us. Oxford University philosopher Nick Bostrom explains the plausible outcomes of ASI using a parable about paperclips. If we asked a superintelligent AI to make paperclips, what would happen next? The outcomes of every AI, including those we have now, are determined by values and goals. It's possible that an ASI could invent a new, better paperclip that holds a stack of paper together so that even if dropped, the pages would always stay collated in order. It's possible that if we aren't capable of explaining how many paperclips we actually *want*, an ASI could go on making paperclips forever, filling our homes and offices with them as well as our hospitals and schools, rivers and lakes, sewage systems, and on and on until mountains of paperclips covered the planet. Or an ASI using efficiency as its guiding value could decide that humans were getting in the way of paperclips, so it would terraform Earth into a paperclip-making factory, making our kind go extinct in the process.[16] Here's what has so many AI experts, myself included, worried: if ASI's cognitive abilities are orders of magnitude better than ours (remember, we're just a few clicks above chimpanzees), then it would be impossible for us to imagine the consequences such powerful machines might have on our civilization.

This is why the word "explosion" gets used a lot among AI researchers. It was first coined by British mathematician and cryptologist I. J. Good in a 1965 essay: "An ultraintelligent machine could design even better machines; there would then unquestionably be an 'intelligence explosion,' and the intelligence of man would be left far behind. Thus the first ultraintelligent machine is the last invention that man need ever make, provided that the machine is docile enough to tell us how to keep it under control."[17]

The Big Nine are building frameworks and systems that—they hope—will someday encourage an explosion, making room for entirely new solutions, strategies, concepts, frameworks, and approaches that even our smartest computer scientists never considered. This would lead to ever faster breakthroughs, opportunities, and business growth. In technical terms, this is called "recursive self-improvement," and it refers to a cycle in which AI makes itself better, faster, and smarter quickly by modifying its capabilities. This would enable AIs to take control of and plan their own destiny. The rate of self-improvement could be hourly, or even instantaneous.

The coming "intelligence explosion" describes not just the speed of supercomputers or power of algorithms, but the vast proliferation of smart thinking machines bent on recursive self-improvement. Imagine a world in which systems far more advanced than AlphaGo Zero and NASNet not only make strategic decisions autonomously but also work collaboratively and competitively as part of a global community. A world in which they are asked to evolve, primarily to help us humans out—writing new generations of code, mutating, and self-improving—but at a breakneck pace. The resulting AIs would create new agents, programming them with a purpose and set of tasks, and that cycle would repeat again and again, trillions of times, resulting in both tiny and tremendous changes. The only other time in history we've witnessed such an evolutionary cataclysm was approximately 542 million years ago during the Cambrian period, when the rapid diversification of our biome led to all kinds of new complex life-forms and transformed our planet. Former DARPA program manager Gill Pratt argues that we're in the midst of a Cambrian explosion right now—a period in which AI learns from the experience of all AIs, after which our life on Earth could look dramatically different than it does today.[18]

This is why the Big Nine, its investors and shareholders, our government agencies and elected officials, researchers in the trenches, and (importantly) you need to recognize the warning signs and to think more critically not just about the ANI that's being created right now but also about the AGI and ASI that are on our horizon. The evolution of intelligence is a continuum on which both humans and machines coexist. The Big Nine's values are already deeply encoded into our existing algorithms, systems, and frameworks. Those values will be passed along to millions of new generations of AIs that evolve, and soon to generally intelligent thinking machines.

The transition from ANI to ASI will likely span the next 70 years. At the moment, it's difficult to define exact milestone dates because the rate of progress in AI depends on a number of factors and people: new members admitted to AI's tribes, strategic decisions made at the Big Nine, trade wars and geopolitical scuffles, not to mention chance and chaotic events. In my own models, I would currently put the advent of AGI in the 2040s. This sounds like the distant future, so let me contextualize. We will have had three or four American presidents in the White House by then. (Barring health issues, Chinese president Xi Jinping will still be in power.) I'll be 65 once AGI systems start to do their own AI research. My second-grader will be 30, and by then she may be reading a *New York Times* bestseller written entirely by a machine. My dad will be in his late 90s, and all of his medical specialists (cardiologists, nephrologists, radiologists) will be AGIs, directed and managed by a highly trained general practitioner, who is both an MD and a data scientist. The advent of ASI could follow soon or much longer after, between the 2040s and 2060s. It doesn't mean that by 2070 superintelligent AIs will have crushed all life on Earth under the weight of quintillions of paperclips. But it doesn't mean they won't have either.

## The Stories We Must Tell Ourselves

Planning for the futures of AI requires us to build new narratives using data from the real world. If we agree that AI will evolve as it emerges, then we must create scenarios that describe the intersection of the Big Nine, the economic and political forces guiding them, and the ways humanity factors in as AI transitions from narrow applications to generally intelligent and ultimately superintelligent thinking machines.

Because the future hasn't happened yet, we cannot know for certain all of the possible outcomes of our actions in the present. For that reason, the scenarios that follow in the coming chapters are written using different emotive framings describing the next 50 years. First is an optimistic scenario asking what happens if the Big Nine decide to champion sweeping changes to ensure AI benefits all of us. There's an important distinction to note: "optimistic" scenarios are not necessarily buoyant or upbeat. They do not always lead to utopia. In an optimistic scenario, we're assuming that the best possible decisions are made and that any barriers to success are surmounted. For our purposes, this means that the Big Nine shift course on AI, and because they make the best decisions at the right time, we're all much better off in the future. It's a scenario I'd be content living in, and it's a future we can achieve if we work together.

Next is a pragmatic scenario describing how the future would look if the Big Nine only make minor improvements in the short term. We assume that while all of the key stakeholders acknowledge AI is probably not on the right path, there is no collaboration to create lasting, meaningful change. A few universities introduce mandatory ethics classes; the G-MAFIA form industry partnerships to tackle risk but don't evolve their own company cultures; our elected officials focus on their next election cycles and lose sight of China's grand plans. A pragmatic scenario doesn't hope for big changes—it recognizes the ebb and flow of our human drive to improve. It also acknowledges that in business and governing, leaders are all too willing to give short shrift to the future for immediate, near-term gains.

Finally, the catastrophic scenario explains what happens if all of the signals are missed, the warning signs are ignored, we fail to actively plan for the future, and the Big Nine continue to compete against themselves. If we choose to double down on the status quo, where could that take us? What happens if AI continues along its existing track in the United States and China? Creating systematic change—which is what avoiding the catastrophic scenario requires—is difficult, time-consuming work that doesn't end at a finish line. This is what makes the catastrophic scenario truly frightening, and the detail in it so disturbing. Because at the moment, the catastrophic scenario is the one we seem destined to realize.

I've researched, modeled, and written these three scenarios to describe what-if outcomes, beginning with the year 2029. Anchoring the scenarios are a handful of key themes, including economic opportunity and mobility, workforce productivity, improvement on social structures, the power dynamics of the Big Nine, the relationship between the United States and China, and the global retraction/spread of democracy and communism. I show how our social and cultural values might shift as AI matures: how we define creativity, the ways in which we relate to each other, and our thinking on life and death. Because the goal of scenarios is to help us understand what life might look like during our transition from ANI and ASI, I've included examples from home, work, education, health care, law enforcement, our cities and towns, local infrastructure, national security, and politics.

One probable near-term outcome of AI and a through-line in all three of the scenarios is the emergence of what I'll call a "personal data record," or PDR. This is a single unifying ledger that includes all of the data we create as a result of our digital usage (think internet and mobile phones), but it would also include other sources of information: our school and work histories (diplomas, previous and current employers); our legal records (marriages, divorces, arrests); our financial records (home mortgages, credit scores, loans, taxes); travel (countries visited, visas); dating history (online apps); health (electronic health records, genetic screening results, exercise habits); and shopping history (online retailers, in-store coupon use). In China, a PDR would also include all the social credit score data described in the last chapter. AIs, created by the Big Nine, would both learn from your personal data record and use it to automatically make decisions and provide you with a host of services. Your PDR would be heritable—a comprehensive record passed down to and used by your children—and it could be temporarily managed, or permanently owned, by one of the Big Nine. PDRs play a featured role in the scenarios you're about to read.

PDRs don't yet exist, but from my vantage point there are already signals that point to a future in which all the myriad sources of our personal data are unified under one record provided and maintained by the Big Nine. In fact, you're already part of that system, and you're using a proto-PDR now. It's your email address.

The average person's email address has been repurposed as a login; their mobile phone number is used to authenticate transactions; and their smartphone is used to locate them in the physical world. If you are a Gmail user, Google—and by extension its AIs—knows you better than your spouse or partner. It knows the names and email addresses of everyone you talk to, along with their demographic information (e.g., age, gender, location). Google knows when you tend to open email and under what circumstances. From your email, it knows your travel itineraries, your financial records, and what you buy. If you take photos with your Android phone, it knows the faces of your friends and family members, and it can detect anomalies to make inferences: for example, sudden new pics of the same person might indicate a new girlfriend (or an affair). It knows all of your meetings, doctor appointments, and plans to hit the gym. It knows whether you observe Ramadan or Rosh Hashanah, whether you're a churchgoer, or whether you practice no religion at all. It knows where you should be on a given Tuesday afternoon, even if you're somewhere else. It knows what you search for, using your fingers and your voice, and so it knows whether you're miscarrying for the first time, learning how to make paella, struggling with your sexual identity or gender assignment, considering giving up meat, or looking for a new job. It cross-links all this data, learning from it and productizing and monetizing it as it nudges you in predetermined directions.

Right now, Google knows all of this information because you've voluntarily linked it all to just one record—your Gmail address—which, by the way, you've probably also used to buy stuff on Amazon and to log into Facebook. This isn't a complaint; it's a fact of modern life. As AI advances, a more robust personal data record will afford greater efficiencies to the Big Nine, and so they will nudge us to accept and adopt PDRs, even if we don't entirely understand the implications of using them. Of course, in China, PDRs are already being piloted under the auspices of its social credit score.

"We tell ourselves stories in order to live," Joan Didion wrote in *The White Album*. "We interpret what we see, select the most workable of the multiple choices." We all have choices to make about AI. It's time we use the information we have available to tell ourselves stories—scenarios that describe how we might all live alongside our thinking machines.

# CHAPTER FIVE

# THRIVING IN THE THIRD AGE OF COMPUTING: THE OPTIMISTIC SCENARIO

I t is the year 2023, and we've made the best possible decisions about AI—we've shifted AI's developmental track, we are collaborating on the future, and we're already seeing positive, durable change. AI's tribes, universities, the Big Nine, government agencies, investors, researchers, and everyday people heeded those early warning signs.

We understand that there is no single change that will fix the problems we've already created and that the best strategy now involves adjusting our expectations for the future of AI. We acknowledge that AI isn't just a product made in Silicon Valley, something to be monetized while the market is hot.

\* \* \*

First and foremost, we recognize why China has invested strategically in AI and how AI's developmental track fits in to China's broader narrative about its future place in the world. China isn't trying to tweak the trade balance; it is seeking to gain an absolute advantage over the United States in economic power, workforce development, geopolitical influence, military might, social clout, and environmental stewardship. With this realization, our elected officials, with the full support of the G-MAFIA and AI's tribes, build an international coalition to protect and preserve AI as a public good. That coalition exacts pressure on China and uses economic levers to fight back against AI's use as a tool of surveillance and an enabler of communism.

With the recognition that China is leveraging AI to fulfill its economic and military goals as it spreads the seeds of communism and tightens its reins on society, the US government dedicates vast federal funding to support AI's development, which relieves pressure on the G-MAFIA to earn profit fast. Using our 1950s space race as precedent, it's evident how easily America could be passed over by other countries without coordination at a national level. It's also abundantly clear how much influence America can exert in science and technology when we have a coordinated national strategy—we have the federal government to thank for GPS and the internet.

Neither AI nor its funding is politicized, and everyone agrees that regulating the G-MAFIA and AI is the wrong course of action. Heavy-handed, binding regulations would be outdated the moment they went into effect; they would stifle innovation, and they'd be difficult to enforce. With bipartisan support, Americans unite behind increased federal spending on AI across the board using China's public road map as inspiration. Funding flows to R&D, economic and workforce impact studies, social impact studies, diversity programs, medical and public health initiatives, and infrastructure and to making America's public education great again, with attractive salaries for teachers and a curriculum that prepares everyone for a more automated future. We stop assuming that the G-MAFIA can serve its DC and Wall Street masters equally and that free markets and our entrepreneurial spirit will produce the best possible outcomes for AI and humanity.

*  *  *

With a national strategy and funding in place, the newly formed G-MAFIA Coalition formalizes itself with multilateral agreements to collaborate on the future of AI. The G-MAFIA Coalition defines and adopts standards that, above all else, prioritize a developmental track for AI that serves the best interests of democracy and society. It agrees to unify AI technologies. Collaboration yields superior chipsets, frameworks, and network architectures rather than competing AI systems and a bifurcated developer community. It also means that researchers can pursue mapping opportunities so that everyone wins.

The G-MAFIA Coalition adopts transparency as a core value, and it radically rewrites service agreements, rules, and workflows in favor of understanding and education. It does this voluntarily and therefore avoids regulation. The data sets, training algorithms, and neural network structures are made transparent in a way that protects only those trade secrets and proprietary information that could, if divulged, cause one of the coalition members economic harm. The G-MAFIA's individual legal teams don't spend years looking for and debating loopholes or prolonging the adoption of transparency measures.

Knowing that automation is on the horizon, the G-MAFIA help us think through unemployment scenarios and help prepare our workforce for the third era of computing. With their help, we don't fear AI but rather see it as a huge opportunity for economic growth and individual prosperity. The G-MAFIA's thought leadership cuts through the hype and shines a light on better approaches to training and education for our emerging jobs of the future.

* * *

America's national strategy and the formation of our G-MAFIA Coalition inspires the leaders of other democracies around the world to support the global development of AI for the good of all. Dartmouth University, in a gathering similar to the one that took place the summer of 1956, hosts the inaugural intergovernmental forum, with a diverse cross section of leaders from the world's most advanced economies: secretaries, ministers, prime ministers, and presidents from the United States, United Kingdom, Japan, France, Canada, Germany, Italy, and others from the European Union, as well as AI researchers, sociologists, economists, game theorists, futurists, political scientists, and others. Unlike the homogenous group of men from similar backgrounds who made up the first Dartmouth workshop, this time around the leaders and experts include a wide spectrum of people and worldviews. Standing on the very same, hallowed ground where modern artificial intelligence was born, those leaders agree to facilitate and cooperate on shared AI initiatives and policies. Taking inspiration from Greek mythology and the ancestral mother of Earth, they form GAIA: the Global Alliance on Intelligence Augmentation.

Locked out of GAIA, China finds its global influence waning. International collaboration doesn't negatively financially impact China's part of the Big Nine—Baidu, Tencent and Alibaba—which continue to provide lots of services to Chinese citizens. However, many of China's longer-term plans—its Belt and Road Initiative included—are on shaky ground as partners drop out of pilots and recruiting new allies proves difficult.

This isn't to say that all of AI's existing problems go away overnight. The AI community anticipates and expects artificial narrow intelligence to continue making errors due to the limited worldviews of AI's original tribe members. We accept that political, gender, wealth, and race bias won't disappear immediately. GAIA nations sign accords, explicitly agreeing to value safety over speed, and dedicate considerable resources to cleaning up all of our current systems: the databases and algorithms already in use, the frameworks they rely on, the enterprise-level products that incorporate AI (like those being used at banks and within law enforcements) and the consumer devices that harness AI for everyday tasks (our smart speakers, watches, and phones). GAIA invites—and rewards—public accountability.

Within GAIA, a decision is made to treat our personal data records (PDRs) like we do the distributed ledgers of blockchains. Distributed ledgers use thousands of independent computers to record, share, and synchronize transactions. By design, they don't keep data centralized under the umbrella of just one company or agency. Because the G-MAFIA Coalition adopts a set of standards and deploys unified AI technologies, our PDRs don't really need a centrally coordinating company to manage transactions. As a result, individuals own their own PDRs, which are as private or as public as we want them to be and are fully interoperable—we can connect them to any or all of the G-MAFIA and to many other AI-powered services simultaneously, like our doctors' offices, schools, and city infrastructure. The G-MAFIA are the custodians of AI and of our data, but they own neither. Our PDRs are heritable: we can pass down our data to our children with the ability to set permissions (for full, limited, or zero visibility) on different parts of our records.

As AI matures from narrow applications to generally intelligent thinking machines, AI's tribes and the G-MAFIA have earned our trust. These aren't just companies making cool apps—Google, Microsoft, Apple, Facebook, IBM, and Amazon are as foundational to America and American values as baseball, free speech, and the Fourth of July. Communism is sidelined. Those nations who value their citizens' rights to speech and property; support religious freedoms; are allies to people of all gender, ethnic, sexual, and racial expressions; agree that a government exists to serve the people; govern through elected representatives; and balance individual liberties with public safety are aligned and working together on the future of AI and humanity.

### 2029: Comfortably Nudged

With the G-MAFIA collaborating and GAIA leading to lots of new trade agreements, citizens around the world have better, cheaper access to ANI-powered products and services. GAIA meets regularly, making all of its work transparent, while its multinational working groups are comfortably keeping pace with technological advancement.

*  *  *

Middle-class homes rely on AI to make life a little bit easier. Devices, platforms, and other services are interoperable even between countries, where decades earlier licensing and data restrictions prevented access across borders. Smart washers and driers use less energy, are more efficient, and synch up to our smart city systems to share data. With consent, we allow our laundry to be done when it causes the least amount of strain on our public water and electric utilities.

ANI supports sensory computation, which means that we can collect and query the real world using sensory data: sight, smell, hearing, taste, and touch. You use handheld scanners, outfitted with smart cameras and computer vision, in your kitchen. The spectrometer embedded on an ANI wand in the kitchen captures and reads the light from an avocado to tell you that it probably won't be ripe until the weekend—while the discount olive oil you just bought isn't pure, but a mixture of three different oils. Another sensor in the kitchen has detected that the chicken roasting in the oven is about to go bone dry. Upstairs, a haptic sensor lets you know that your toddler has managed to escape (yet again) from her crib.

*  *  *

The G-MAFIA has partnered with other companies on mixed reality, which has dramatically improved the lives of people suffering from dementia and Alzheimer's disease. Smart glasses instantly recognize people, objects, and places, helping our loved ones remember and live more fulfilled lives.

Originally we'd thought that the G-MAFIA's products and services would cause social isolationism—that we'd all be sitting alone in our homes, interacting via digital avatars as we completely lost touch with the outside world. We were completely wrong. Instead, the G-MAFIA's platforms and hardware gave us new ways to socialize in person. We're spending more time in mixed-reality movie theaters, which offer immersive entertainment. There are now mixed-reality arcades everywhere. It's the 1980s all over again, but with a twist: mixed-reality games, experiences, and meeting rooms are affordable, and they're also accessible for those with hearing and visual impairments. We're going to silent discos, where we wear color-coded wireless headsets connected to our favorite DJ's spinning all night long. Now everyone can dance together, in one shared experience, even if they hate each other's taste in music. Thanks to the G-MAFIA, we're more connected to each other—and to the real world—than we ever imagined.

For wealthier households, ANI applications offer even more features. Outside in the garden, sensors continually measure moisture levels and compare that data to microclimate forecasts. Simple irrigation systems automatically water plants, but only as needed. AIs predict optimal levels of hydration, which means the end of timers—and dead begonias.

Inside those wealthier homes, Amazon's Akira system (whose voice sounds neither male nor female) works in many languages, regardless of accent, and easily communicates with Apple smart glasses and Google-managed personal data records alike. Washers and driers come equipped with small, articulated drones and a new feature called Kondo mode, named after Marie Kondo, the Japanese decluttering expert. Laundry is washed and dried according to the supply-and-demand cycles of the city grid, and then clothes are handed off to a small drone for folding, sorting, and tidying up by color.

In the United States, grocery shopping and delivery is fully automated. You never run out of tampons or toothpaste again. AI powers predictive buying systems that link to your past purchases and to your PDRs and know, before you do, when to refresh supplies. Through

Amazon, you have access to fresh, local produce and meat, as well as to all the usual household staples, like breakfast cereal, toilet paper, and potato chips. Meal kit services, which got their start a decade earlier as Blue Apron and HelloFresh, are linked to a household PDR. For a bit of extra money each week, your groceries will include ingredients for all the dishes you typically make, as well as the makings of three new meals—recipes that automatically align with the likes, dislikes, allergies, and nutritional needs of each family member.

You still shop in the real world, of course, but like many of us you choose to leave your wallet at home. The underlying technology powering Amazon Go's retail and point of service systems have become the backbone of quick service stores where most inventory is already on display or can be easily replenished. Smart cameras continually surveil shoppers, recognizing their unique faceprints and noting what they put into their bags and carts. We're able to spend up to $100 without needing to interact with a human staff member. In stores with bigger footprints (e.g., department, furniture, and home improvement stores) or stores selling merchandise that's more expensive (e.g., jewelry, handbags, and electronics), we have the option to pay with our faces.

* * *

Some kids play with flesh-and-bone pets, while busier families opt for lifelike robotic companions. Small dogs and cats—cute containers for AI—use sensory computing and deep learning as they get house trained. With advanced cameras in their eye sockets, haptic fur, and the ability to recognize subtle changes in our voices, robotic pets are significantly more empathetic than our organic ones, even if they are less warm and fuzzy.

Everyone, regardless of income level, is glad to be nudged into better health. The G-MAFIA reminds us during the day to make healthier choices. As you head into work and wait for the elevator, your watch vibrates a tiny bit to make you look down: it's showing a simple map of the office building with an arrow pointing to the stairs. It's a feature you can certainly turn off, but most people choose to leave it on. Your workouts are more optimized, too. Using your personal data record, your medical records, and the sensor data collected from many other sources—the wireless earphones you use to listen to music, the smart fabric used to make your sports bra—gym equipment guides you through personalized exercises. After you're done, those sensors help you to cool down, monitoring your heart and metabolic rates. Because of the G-MAFIA, our communities are healthier, and we're living longer lives.

The G-MAFIA coalescing around a single standard for personal data records ushered in a set of standardized electronic medical record formats, protocols, frameworks, and user interfaces. As a result, the health care system is far more efficient. Capitol Hill spent decades arguing about health care in America, and the G-MAFIA's insistence on standardized data and algorithms for health care turned out to be the best medicine.

Regardless of which doctor sees a patient, or which hospital she's admitted to, her information is easily accessible by everyone oversee-ing her care. It's also available to anyone to whom she's given permis-sion. The data from most lab tests, screenings, and scans are crunched by AIs rather than by people, leading to greater accuracy and faster results. IBM's system can detect cellular anomalies in order to spot the earliest signs of cancer—as well as which cells in the body are affected. Google's system helps doctors predict the likely outcomes of different medicines and treatments, as well as to forecast when a patient will die, helping caregivers make better decisions about how to treat each individual patient. In the hospital, Amazon's pharmacy API synchs with a patient's personal data record and delivers any needed med-ications before the patient returns home. Even if a patient's medical history includes pages of hand-scrawled doctor's notes—and even if those notes are light on details—the G-MAFIA's computer vision and

pattern analysis fills in the blanks, converting those records into structured, usable data that can be mined just for the patient or anonymized
and combined with other patient data to help the medical community
(human and AIs alike) expand its knowledge and experience.

Diagnosis, treatment, and care are no longer offered in brick-
and-mortar hospitals alone, which means that far more people in the
US now have better access to care. Some providers offer connected,
though relatively new, home and telemedicine services. TOTO toilets, outfitted with collection receptacles and a spectrophotometer,
use pattern recognition to diagnose elevated or depleted levels of glu-
cose or protein, as well as bacteria and blood cells. Within seconds,
your PDR reflects a possible urinary infection or early signs of kidney
stones. Simple treatments—such as antibiotics for the infection—are
checked against your PDR, recommended to your primary doctor, and
if she approves, automatically delivered to you at home, work, or while
you're out at dinner. Toothbrushes, which come with tiny oral fluid
sensors, use your saliva as a mirror reflecting your overall health. With
each routine brushing, AIs are monitoring your hormones, electro-
lytes, and antibodies, checking for changes over time. The G-MAFIA
has changed the standard of care: basic diagnostic tests aren't just for
sick patients; they're part of maintaining a healthy lifestyle. This, in
turn, has changed the very nature of medicine from reactionary to predictive and preventative care.

Other aspects of everyday life—including dating and sex—are better because of AI. Evolutionary algorithms turned out to be a smarter
solution for online daters than basic apps and websites. Researchers determined that humans are simply too complex to reduce down
to a handful of data points covered by a single matching algorithm.
Plus, we tend to fill out online profiles using aspirational—rather than
factual—answers about ourselves. Instead, evolutionary algorithms
pull data from our PDRs and test us against all the other profiles within
the dating database. We select a goal—from "just looking to have casual

fun" to "ready to get married"—along with any constraints (must be Jewish, must live with 50 miles of Cleveland), and the evolutionary algorithm produces a list of the people with whom we have the best odds of achieving that goal. If we want, the system will consult our calendars and activity preferences and automatically schedule a time and place to get together. After a few dates (or maybe if that first date didn't go so well), we might be interested in using a generative algorithm to create personalized porn. Depending on our preference, the AI creates scenes that excite, inspire, or instruct us, using characters whose voices, physiques, and styles are modulated to our personal desires.

* * *

Because of the G-MAFIA, artificial intelligence doesn't feel like a replacement for human creativity, but rather a complement—a tool to augment and enhance our intelligence. Within architecture firms, AIs generate thousands of possible buildings based on a client's design exemplars and constraints as well as select and rank winning plans based on predictions for the project's feasibility given a timeline, available materials, and budget; how hard it will be to earn the necessary permits and certifications; and whether it negatively impacts the flow of foot traffic. Real estate investors use AIs to simulate long-term durability given a particular area's climate and other environmental factors. Skilled craftspeople—carpenters, electricians, and plumbers—use mixed-reality glasses from Google, Microsoft, and a company called Magic Leap to see through walls, match their work with blueprints, and detect potential problems in advance.

Creative uses for AI have filtered into the arts, including filmmaking. It's the 20-year anniversary of *Avatar*, the movie from James Cameron that in 2009 looked otherworldly because of its hyper-realistic, computer-generated special effects. To celebrate, Cameron unveils an AI skunkworks project: the sixth *Avatar* film, which combines the underwater motion capture technology he developed earlier along with a new special computing environment and an over-the-ear retinal projection system. The experience was built using generative algorithms to design entirely new worlds for human avatars to explore, evolutionary algorithms for rendering, and deep learning to make all the necessary computations. The result is a first-of-its-kind film shown inside a special theatrical set, one that (along with the retinal projection system) produces a completely original—and entirely immersive— storytelling experience.

*    *    *

AI is helping organizations of all stripes be more creative in their approach to management. The G-MAFIA powers predictive models for business intelligence, helping to find efficiencies, cost savings, and areas for improvement. Human resources departments use pattern recognition to evaluate productivity and morale—and to effectively solve for bias in hiring and promotions. We no longer use resumes; our PDRs show our strengths and weaknesses, and AI programs scan our records before recommending us to human hiring managers.

Within many large companies, human workers have been released from low-level cognitive tasks, while AIs assist staff in certain knowledge fields. The tasks performed by receptionists, customer service staff, schedulers, and reservationists are now automated. In meetings, smart speakers listen in, applying voiceprint and machine reading comprehension algorithms to parse our conversations. An AI assistant synthesizes notes automatically, highlighting the names of speakers, any important concepts, areas of convergence and divergence, contextual information from previous meetings, and other relevant company data. The system determines follow-up items and creates to-dos for those in the meeting.

Because we acknowledged well in advance that automation would disrupt portions of our workforce, we aren't suffering from widespread unemployment and our economy is on sure footing. In the United

States, the federal government now runs new social safety nets to ensure our resiliency. Using the G-MAFIA's tools, companies and individuals alike have long been retraining for entirely new kinds of jobs.

*  *  *

The G-MAFIA has empowered and enabled public, private, elementary, and postsecondary schools to harness AI to enhance learning. Adaptive learning systems, overseen by teachers, challenge students to learn at their own paces, especially in early reading, logic, math, and foreign language skills. In classrooms and homes, IBM has brought Socrates back to life as an AI agent, which engages us in argumentative dialogue and rigorous question-and-answer sessions to help stimulate critical thinking. The Socratic AI system, which evolved out of Watson, quizzes students on what they've learned, debating and discussing ideas. (Socratic AI has uses outside of school as well and is a cherished member of every medical, legal, law enforcement, strategy, and policy team. It's also used to help prepare political candidates for public debates.)

IBM's Socratic AI is a useful ally within newsrooms, helping journalists further investigate their reporting as they discuss a story's possible angles. It's also used to assist with fact-checking and with editorial quality assurance: stories are reviewed for unintentional bias and to ensure that a broad mixture of sources and voices are included. (Long gone are the lists published by magazines and newspapers ranking all-male lists of thought leaders, business leaders, and the like.) Generative algorithms are used to make complete videos out of still images, create 3D models of landscapes and buildings from just a few photos, and listen for individual voices obscured in crowds. This results in far more video news content that takes fewer resources to produce.

AI is used to spot patterns and anomalies in data, leading journalists to surface new stories in the public interest. Rather than aiding and abetting misinformation bots, AI can ferret out propaganda, misleading claims, and disinformation campaigns. Our democracies are stronger as a result.

* * *

The G-MAFIA studied the Chinese cities where smart city initiatives were piloted—such as Rongcheng, Beijing, Shenzhen, Shanghai—and identified best practices to pilot in the United States. We now have a few American smart cities—Baltimore, Detroit, Boulder, and Indianapolis—that are testing out a wide range of AI systems and services. Networks of cubesats overhead—tiny satellites the size of a Rubik's Cube—feed real-time data into AI systems that can recognize objects, unique light patterns, and heat signatures. This, in turn, allows city managers to predict power outages, monitor and reroute traffic, manage water reserves, and clear ice and snow off the roads. AI also helps them manage budgets and personnel throughout the year, surfacing entirely new ways to shave off fractions of expenditures at scale. Budget shortfalls aren't gone, but they're not nearly as bad as they used to be—and the citizens in these cities are buoyed by a sense of hope they haven't experienced in many years.

These systems tie into public safety departments, like police and fire, which are using AI to sift through massive amounts of data, including video: if there's no sound, pattern recognition algorithms can lip read and produce transcripts. Generative algorithms also autocomplete holes in audio tracks, and if anything is fuzzy, a stitching algorithm sharpens the focus. AI scans millions of images looking for patterns that the human eye would miss. This hasn't been without controversy, of course. However, the G-MAFIA's commitment to privacy means that our PDRs aren't available to search through without a warrant. We feel safe knowing that the G-MAFIA is safeguarding our privacy.

As it evolves, AI is helping us mature into better humans. With the G-MAFIA, federal government, and GAIA taking active roles in the transition from artificial narrow intelligence to artificial general intelligence, we feel comfortably nudged.

### 2049: The Rolling Stones Are Dead (But They're Making New Music)

By the 2030s, researchers working within the G-MAFIA published an exciting paper, both because of what it revealed about AI and because of how the work was completed. Working from the same set of standards and supported with ample funds (and patience) by the federal government, researchers collaborated on advancing AI. As a result, the first system to reach artificial general intelligence was developed.

The system had passed the Contributing Team Member Test. It took a long time for the AI community to accept that the Turing test, and others of its ilk, was the wrong barometer to gauge machine intelligence. Tests built on either deception (can a computer fool a human into believing it's human?) or replication (can a computer act exactly as we would?) do not acknowledge AI for what it has always been: intelligence gained and expressed in ways that do not resemble our own human experience. Rather than judging an AGI on whether or not it could "think" exactly like we do, the AI community finally adopted a new test to measure the *meaningful contributions* of an AGI, which would judge the value of cognitive and behavioral tasks—different, but powerful—we could not perform on our own. AGI would be achieved when the system made general contributions that were equal to or better than a human's.

The G-MAFIA spent many years researching and developing an AGI that could sit in on a meeting at work and make a valuable contribution—unsolicited—before the meeting concluded. They code-named the AGI Project Hermione, inspired by the *Harry Potter* character who always, and in every situation, knew just what to say or do. Making a valuable contribution in a group is something that most people on Earth have, at some point, had to do themselves: at work, in a religious setting, at the neighborhood pub with friends, or in a high school history class. Simply interjecting with a factoid or to answer a question doesn't add value to a conversation. Making a valuable contribution involves many different skills:

- **Making educated guesses:** This is also called abductive reasoning, and it's how most of us get through the day. We use the best information available, make and test hypotheses, and come up with an answer even if there's no clear explanation.
- **Correctly extracting meaning from words, pauses, and ambient noise:** Just because someone says they're happy to take on a new project doesn't mean it literally makes them *happy*. Other cues, like their body language, might tell us that they're fairly *unhappy* with the request but, for whatever reason, they're not able to say no.
- **Using experience, knowledge, and historical context for understanding:** When people interact, they bring with them a nuanced worldview, a unique set of personal experiences, and typically their own expectations. Sometimes logic and facts won't win an argument. Other times, they're all that matter.
- **Reading the room:** There's the explicit interaction and the tacit one happening beneath the surface. Subtle cues help us figure out when there's an elephant demanding our attention.

Project Hermione sat in on a GAIA working-group session. Eighteen members of the group discussed and debated the existing standards for AI, which were developed by either those people sitting in the room or their predecessors. As the group was diverse and made up of leaders from different countries and cultures, there was a lot of subtext: certain power dynamics, personality clashes, and feelings of inferiority or superiority. The group treated the AGI as an equal member, with no additional privileges or special exceptions. Halfway into the session, the AGI pushed back on a small but growing consensus in favor of regulations. It tactfully argued against the idea and recruited another member of the group to support an alternative. Project Hermione had made a valuable contribution. (Invaluable, some would later argue.)

What made Project Hermione a success wasn't just that it passed the Contributing Team Member Test with such ease—but rather that GAIA and the G-MAFIA saw that moment as both a warning and an opportunity. They continued recalibrating their strategies and standards to keep a few steps ahead of AI's technological developments. They decided to limit the rate of self-improvement, adding constraints into all AI systems to keep humans in the loop. Now GAIA researchers follow new protocols: they run simulations to understand the impacts of more powerful AGIs before approving them for general-purpose, commercial, or military uses.

The G-MAFIA are wealthy, influential, powerful companies—and their success is growing. They are building exciting practical applications for AGIs to enhance our productivity and creativity, and they're also helping to create plausible solutions for humanity's most pressing challenge: climate change. As the jet stream shifted far north, America's breadbasket went with it, well over the border into Canada, decimating farms and the US agricultural sector. Coffee and chocolate can't be easily grown anymore outdoors. Citizens in Bangladesh, the Philippines, Thailand, and Indonesia have become climate refugees in their own countries. Amazon, partnered with Microsoft, France's Groupe Danone, and DowDuPont in the United States, is using AGI alongside genomic editing to populate indoor farms with fresh produce.

Google and Facebook are using AGI to help safely and securely move entire populations, forming and shaping the Earth with new, comprehensive human communities. AGI helps them to predict which specific locations can most easily sustain life in a way that feels comfortable and preserves the cultures of affected people. Previously uninhabitable regions of our planet are either terraformed or transformed using adaptive building materials. Landscrapers—large, sprawling complexes just a few stories high—have created entirely new urban footprints. Inside, cableless elevators transport us omnidirectionally. It's a new architectural trend that's helped the world's most important economic centers boom, which in the United States includes Denver, Minneapolis, and Nashville.

\* \* \*

For a while, it seemed as though China would retreat and retrench with just a few allies—North Korea, Russia, Mongolia, Myanmar, Cambodia, Kazakhstan, Pakistan, Kyrgyzstan, Tajikistan, and Uzbekistan. Universities in GAIA nations stopped accepting Chinese applicants. Wary of surveillance and the possibility of their PDRs being hacked, China's tourism industry dried up completely. GAIA nations relied on automated systems to produce the materials needed for manufacturing, repatriating factories back home. Ultimately, China's state government determined that its exclusion from GAIA was destabilizing its economy and, as a result, causing significant political and social unrest. Reluctantly, China agreed to adopt GAIA's norms and standards and to accept all of the transparency measures required of member nations. Communism isn't dead—there's still plenty of political strife to contend with, along with all the usual tensions related to different styles of governing and leading.

\* \* \*

AGI certainly didn't emerge without many new problems, some of which we were able to anticipate. Like other technologies that transformed human society over time, AGI has displaced jobs, led to new kinds of criminal activity, and has at times brought out the worst in us. But in the 2040s, AGI isn't an existential threat.

In home and at work, we use a primary AGI to access information. It's a control agent that takes on different forms and modalities depending on the situation: we speak to it, interact with it on a screen, and send it data from inside our bodies. Every family has a butler because every household has an AGI trained and attuned to its unique circumstances.

One of the biggest and most noticeable changes brought about by AGI is a sharp increase in sophistication across most facets of human existence. We can thank the G-MAFIA for how much the quality of life has improved. What used to be time-consuming, difficult challenges—like trying to schedule a time that works for everyone, sorting out an after-school activity calendar, or managing our personal finances—is now fully automated and overseen by AGI. We no longer fritter away hours attempting to hit "inbox zero"—AGIs work collaboratively to facilitate most our low-level thinking tasks. We finally have simple household robotics that make good on their promises to keep our rugs and floors clean, our laundry put away, and our shelves dusted. (We think of 2019 as a much simpler time, one full of tedious and monotonous manual tasks.)

\* \* \*

The common cold no longer exists, and neither does "the flu." In fact, we marvel at the naïveté of earlier doctors. That's because IBM and Google's AGIs helped us see and understand millions of different viroids. Now, when you're not feeling well, an AGI diagnostic test helps determine what, exactly, is making you sick so that a treatment—one that maps to your PDR—can be prescribed. Over-the-counter medications are mostly gone, too, but compounding pharmacies have seen a resurgence. That's because AGI helped accelerate critical developments in genetic editing and precision medicine. You now consult a computational pharmacist: specially trained pharmacists who have backgrounds in bioinformatics, medicine, and pharmacology.

Computational pharmacy is a medical specialty, one that works closely with a new breed of AI-GPs: general practitioners who are trained in both medicine and technology. While AGI has obviated certain medical specialists—radiologists, immunologists, allergists, cardiologists, dermatologists, endocrinologists, anesthesiologists, neurologists, and others—doctors working in those fields had plenty of time to repurpose their skills for adjacent fields. As a patient, you are happier. You don't spend hours trekking to different doctors' offices, getting conflicting messages, and you are no longer overprescribed medications. If you live in a more remote area, AGI has meant a dramatic improvement in your access to care.

We all have our genomes sequenced at birth—the process is now cheap and fast enough for everyone, regardless of income level, to participate. You decided to get your genome sequenced as well because your sequence is a vital component of your PDR. In addition to providing you a window into your unique genetic makeup, AGIs look across all of your data to detect genetic variants and learn more about how your body functions. Of course, in the United States and in other nations, there are small groups who are opposed to the practice—just as anti-vaxers once fought against vaccines. While parents can opt-out for religious or ideological reasons, few make that choice.

*   *   *

Because of AGI, we're healthier—and you have new options when it comes to dating and marriage. Advanced forms of differential privacy allow a third party to look at your data (your PDR, genome, and medical records) without divulging who you are individually. That's made AGI matchmaking providers incredibly useful, because now you can choose to optimize for family (producing children with genetically desirable combinations), wealth (projected lifetime earning potential) or fun (whether or not they'll laugh at your jokes).

*   *   *

AGI assists you in other creative endeavors, beyond looking for love. The original members of the Rolling Stones died years ago, but thanks to replicating algorithms, they're still making new music. That sensation you felt after hearing the first 30 seconds of "Paint It Black" for the first time—the melancholy guitar melody, followed by eight loud bangs on the drum and a repetitive hook that culminates in Mick Jagger singing, "I see a red door and I want it painted black"—was a singular moment of excitement and satisfaction. It didn't seem possible you might get to feel that way again with a new Stones song, and yet their latest track is just as loud, hard, and fulfilling.

\* \* \*

While newspapers in print are gone, the news media has adopted AGI as a means for distribution. Once the Contributing Team Member Test was passed, news organizations acted quickly to build a different news distribution model, one which still made money but had a sharper eye on the future. These days, most people don't get or turn on the news—they have a conversation with a smart newsagent. The *New York Times* and *Wall Street Journal* both employ hundreds of computational journalists—people with strong hybrid skills sets in both traditional reporting and AI. Together, these teams report on stories and select relevant facts and data for inclusion in conversational engines. AGI-powered journalism informs us, and we can modulate it to include a political slant or more background information or a "deep cuts" version offering ancillary characters and miscellaneous facts. We're asked to participate in news analysis and editorial feeds, debating and constructively arguing with the newsagent using our voice or interacting with screens (smart glasses and retractable tablets). There are still plenty of long-form stories told in text and video.

\* \* \*

AGI hackers—which most often are *other AGIs*—are an ongoing irritant because of "no-collar crime": nonviolent criminal acts committed by AGIs, which reveal the people who created their original source code. Local law enforcement agencies employ officers who are cross-trained in data science. With the help of China's BAT, the Big Nine are working collaboratively on advanced hardware, frameworks, networks, and algorithms that are capable of withstanding attacks. GAIA's partnership with Interpol has, for the most part, kept serious crime at bay.

The smart city pilots launched two decades earlier in Baltimore, Indianapolis, Detroit, and Boulder were a success and helped other communities learn best practices, which lead to the formation of the Federal Smart Infrastructure Administration (FSIA). Like the Federal Highway Administration, the FSIA operates under the Department of Transportation and oversees all of the connected systems that power our cities: wireless power transfer stations, decentralized energy generators (kinetic, solar, and wind), vehicle-to-infrastructure networks, and the fiber optics that bring sunlight into our underground farms. Sensor data is aggregated and used to model the overall health of our communities: access to clean air, the cleanliness of our neighborhoods, and our use of parks and outdoor recreational areas. AGIs predict and mitigate brownouts and water crises before they happen.

\* \* \*

As we near the transition from AGI to ASI, an exciting opportunity has just become visible on the horizon: brain-to-machine interfaces. We're on the precipice of molecular nanotechnology, and we hope that within a few decades, we'll be able to record data from the billions of individual neurons inside our human brains simultaneously. Microscopic computers, the size of a grain of sand, would gently rest on top of the brain and detect electrical signals. Special AGI systems, capable of reading and interpreting those signals, could also transmit data between people. A brain-machine interface could someday allow a healthy person to retrain the brains of stroke victims who are paralyzed or have lost their ability to speak. Brain-machine interfaces, which we could theoretically use to transfer memories between people, might also help us experience empathy in a deeper and more meaningful way.

That possibility has us thinking about new uses for AGIs. We want to untangle thorny philosophical questions: *Is our universe real? Can "nothing" exist? What is the nature of time?* AGI can't give us the answers we want, but the G-MAFIA has deepened our understanding of what it means to be human.

## 2069: AI-Powered Guardians of the Galaxy

The intelligence explosion, as foretold 100 years ago by British mathematician and early AI pioneer I. J. Good, begins in the late 2060s. It's becoming clear now that our AGIs are gaining profound levels of intelligence, speed, and power and that artificial superintelligence is a near-term possibility. For the past decade, the Big Nine and GAIA have been preparing for this event—and it has calculated that once human-level machine intelligence has been surpassed, an ASI could be just a few years away.

After much consideration, a difficult decision is made by all members of GAIA to prevent ASI from being created. Some of those involved in the conversation became emotional—arguing it wasn't fair to handicap AI's "beautiful minds" just as they are beginning to reach their potential. We debate whether or not we are denying humanity the possibility of even greater opportunities and rewards.

Ultimately, with the Big Nine's blessing and encouragement, GAIA determines that with human safety and security in the balance, new restrictions must be built into all AGIs to limit their rate of self-improvement and to ensure that no unwanted mutations can be implemented. Soon, GAIA will deploy a series of guardian AIs that will act as an early warning system for any AGI that's gained too much cognitive power. Even the guardians won't necessarily prevent a rogue actor from trying to create ASIs on their own, but GAIA is writing scenarios to prepare for that eventuality. In GAIA, and in the Big Nine, we place our unwavering affection and trust.

# CHAPTER SIX

# LEARNING TO LIVE WITH MILLIONS OF PAPER CUTS: THE PRAGMATIC SCENARIO

B y 2023, we've acknowledged AI's problems but along the way decided to make only minor tweaks in the developmental track of artificial intelligence, a system that we can all see is clearly fractured. We pursue only tweaks because AI's stakeholders aren't willing to get uncomfortable: to sacrifice financial gains, make politically unpopular choices, and curb our wild expectations in the short-term, even if it means improving our long-term odds of living alongside AI. Worse, we ignore China and its plans for the future.

Leaders in Congress, our various federal agencies, and the White House continue to deprioritize artificial intelligence and advanced scientific research in general, preferring to invest in industries that are politically appealing but nearing obsolescence. A strategic plan for the future of AI published by the Obama administration in 2016—a document that heavily influenced China's own 2025 strategic plan—is shelved, along with the federally funded AI R&D program it recommended. America has no long-term vision or strategy on AI, and it disavows any economic, educational, and national security impacts. US government leaders, on both sides of the aisle, focus on how to stifle China when they should be strategizing on how to establish a coalition made up of the G-MAFIA and government.

The absence of a coalition and coherent national AI strategy foment paper cuts—millions and millions of them—which over time start to bleed. We don't notice at first. Because popular culture, evocative stories by tech journalists, and social media posts by influencers have trained us to be on the lookout for big, obvious signposts—like killer robots—we miss the real signposts, small and scattershot as they may seem, as AI evolves. The Big Nine are forced to prioritize speed over safety, so AI's developmental track—from ANI to AGI and beyond—pushes ahead without first resolving serious technical vulnerabilities. Here are a few of the less obvious paper cuts—many self-inflicted—that we are not treating as the serious wounds they are in the present.

*  *  *

As consumers of technology, our expectation is that AI's tribes will have already imagined and solved every problem before any new apps, products, or services leave the R&D labs. We have been habituated to adopting technology that works right out of the box. When we purchase new smartphones and TVs, we plug them in and they function as promised. When we download new software, whether it's for word processing or data analytics, it behaves as anticipated. We forget that AI is not technology that works out of the box, because in order for it to function as we want it to, an AI system needs vast amounts of data and an opportunity to learn in real time.

None of us—not individual consumers, journalists, or analysts—give the Big Nine any room for error. We demand new products, services, patents, and research breakthroughs on a regular cycle, or we register our complaints publicly. It doesn't matter to us that our demands are distracting AI's tribes from doing better work.

AI models and frameworks, regardless of how large or small, need lots of data in order to learn, improve, and get deployed. Data is analogous to our world's oceans. It surrounds us, is an endless resource, and remains totally useless to us unless we desalinate it, treating and processing it for consumption. At the moment, there are just a few companies that can effectively desalinate data at a scale that matters. That's why the most challenging part of building a new AI system isn't the algorithms or the models but rather collecting the right data and labeling it correctly so that a machine can begin training with and learning from it. Relative to the various products and services the Big Nine are breathlessly working to build, there are very few data sets ready to be used. A few of these are ImageNet (the enormous data set of images that's used widely), WikiText (a language modeling data set using Wikipedia articles), 2000 HUB5 English (an English-only data set used for speech), and LibriSpeech (about 500 hours of audiobook snippets). If you wanted to build a health AI to spot anomalies in blood work and oncology scans, the problem isn't the AI, it's data—humans are complicated, our bodies have tons of possible variants, and there isn't a big enough data set ready to be deployed.

*   *   *

A decade ago, in the early 2010s, the IBM Watson Health team partnered with different hospitals to see if its AI could supplement the work of doctors. Watson Health had some stunning early wins, including a case involving a very sick nine-year-old boy. After specialists weren't able to diagnose and treat him, Watson assigned a probability to possible health issues—the list included common ailments as well as outliers, including a rare childhood illness called Kawasaki disease. Once word got out that Watson was performing miracle diagnoses and saving peoples' lives, the Watson team was under pressure to commercialize and sell the platform, and incomprehensibly unrealistic targets were set. IBM projected that Watson Health would grow from a $244 million business in 2015 to a $5 billion business by 2020.[1] That was an anticipated 1,949% growth in under five years.

Before Watson Health could reproduce the same magic it had shown earlier—following a whiplash-inducing development timeline, no less—it would need significantly more training data and time to learn. But there wasn't enough real-world health data available, and what was available to train the system wasn't nearly comprehensive enough. That's because patient data was locked up in electronic health-record software systems managed by another company, which saw IBM as a competitor.

As a result, the IBM team used a workaround common among AI's tribes. It had fed Watson Health what's called "synthetic data," which is data that represents hypothetical information. Since researchers can't just scrape and load "ocean data" into a machine-learning system for training, they will buy a synthetic data set from a third party or build one themselves. This is often problematic because composing that data set—what goes into it and how it's labeled—is rife with decisions made by a small number of people who often aren't aware of their professional, political, gender, and many other cognitive biases.

Outsized expectations for Watson Health's immediate profitability, combined with a reliance on synthetic data sets, is what led to a serious problem. IBM had partnered with Memorial Sloan Kettering Cancer Center to apply Watson Health's skills to cancer treatment. Not long after, a few medical experts working on the project reported examples of unsafe and incorrect treatment recommendations. In one example, Watson Health recommended a bizarre treatment protocol for a patient diagnosed with lung cancer who also showed signs of bleeding: chemotherapy and a drug called bevacizumab, a contraindicated drug because it can cause severe or fatal hemorrhaging.[2] The story of Watson's ineptitude made the rounds in medical and hospital industry publications and on techie blogs, often with sensational headlines. Yet the problem wasn't that Watson Health had it out for humans—but rather that market forces had pressured IBM to rush its AI research to make good on projections.

*  *  *

Here's another paper cut: Some AIs have figured out how to hack and game their own systems. If an AI is specifically programmed to learn a game, play it, and do whatever necessary to win, researchers have discovered cases of "reward hacking," where a system will exploit evolutionary and machine-learning algorithms to win using trickery and deception. For example, an AI learning to play *Tetris* figured out that it could simply pause the game forever so that it could never lose. Ever since you first read about reward hacking—it made headlines recently when two financial AI systems predicted a precipitous drop in stock market values and attempted to autonomously close markets indefinitely—you've been wondering what might happen if your data got caught up in a reward-hacking system. That winter vacation you have coming up—what if the air traffic control wound up locked?

*   *   *

Another paper cut: malicious actors can inject poisonous data into AI's training programs. Neural networks are vulnerable to "adversarial examples," which are fake or intentionally designed with wrong information to cause an AI system to make a mistake. An AI system might label a picture as a panda, with 60% confidence; but add just a tiny bit of noise to the image, like a few pixels out of place that would be imperceptible to a human, and the system will relabel the image a gibbon with 99% confidence. It's possible to train a car's computer vision to think that a stop sign actually means "speed limit 100" and send its passengers careening at top speed through an intersection. Adversarial inputs could retrain a military AI system to interpret all of the visual data found outside a typical hospital—such as ambulances or the words "emergency" and "hospital" on signs—as terrorist markers. The problem is that the Big Nine haven't figured out how to safeguard their systems from adversarial examples, either in the digital or physical worlds.

*   *   *

A deeper cut: the Big Nine know that adversarial information can actually be used to reprogram machine-learning systems and neural networks. A team within Google's Brain division published a paper in 2018 on how a bad actor could inject adversarial information into a computer vision database and effectively reprogram all the AI systems that learn from it.[3] Hackers could someday embed poisonous data in your smart earphones and reprogram them with someone else's identity simply by playing adversarial noise while sitting next to you on the train.

What complicates things is that sometimes adversarial information can be useful. A different Google Brain team discovered that adversarial information could also be used to generate new information that can be put to good use in what's called a "generative adversarial network," or GAN. In essence, it's the Turing test but without any humans involved. Two AIs are trained on the same data—such as images of people. The first one creates photos of, say, North Korean dictator Kim Jong-un that seem realistic, while the second AI compares the generated photos with real ones of him. Based on the judgment of the second AI, the first one goes back and makes tweaks to its process. This happens again and again, until the first AI is automatically generating all kinds of images of Kim Jong-un that look entirely realistic, but never actually happened in the real world. Pictures that show Kim Jong-un having dinner with Vladimir Putin, playing golf with Bernie Sanders, or sipping cocktails with Kendrick Lamar. Google Brain's goal isn't subterfuge. It's to solve the problem created by synthetic data. GANs would empower AI systems to work with raw, real-world data that hasn't been cleaned and without the direct supervision of a human programmer. And while it's a wonderfully creative approach to solve a problem—it could someday be a serious threat to our safety.

\* \* \*

Still another paper cut: when complex algorithms work together, sometimes they compete against each other to accomplish a goal, and that can poison an entire system. We witnessed system-wide problems when the price of a developmental biology textbook started escalating quickly. The book was out of print, but Amazon showed that there were 15 used copies available from resellers, starting at $35.54—and two brand-new copies starting at $1.7 million. Hidden from view, Amazon's algorithms had engaged in an autonomous price war, choosing to lift the price further and further until it reached $23,698,655 (plus $3.99 for shipping). The system of learning algorithms had made real-time adjustments in response to each auction, which is what they were designed to do. Put another way: we may have inadvertently taught AI that bubbles are a good thing. It isn't difficult to image competing algorithms illogically inflating real estate assets, stock prices, or even something as simple as digital advertising.

* * *

These are just a tiny fraction of the paper cuts AI's tribes have decided we can all live with in pursuit of the goals set by market forces in the United States and the CCP in Beijing. Rather than curbing expectations of speed and profitability, AI's tribes are continually pressured to get products to market. Safety is an afterthought. Employees and leadership within the G-MAFIA are worried, but we don't afford them any time to make changes. And we haven't yet talked about China.

Between 2019 and 2023 we effectively ignore Xi Jinping's proclamations about the future: China's comprehensive national AI strategy, his plans to dominate the global economy, and China's goal to become a singular force driving geopolitical decisions. We fail to connect the dots between the future of AI, its surveillance infrastructure and social credit system, and China's person-to-person diplomacy in various African, Asian, and European countries. So when Xi speaks publicly and often about the need for a global governance reform and follows up by launching multinational bodies like the Asian Infrastructure

Investment Bank, we give him the side eye rather than our full attention. It's a mistake we don't immediately acknowledge.

Within China, the path toward AI domination hasn't been exactly smooth. China has its own paper cuts to contend with as the BAT struggles to innovate like Silicon Valley under the heavy-handed rule of Beijing. The BAT repeatedly skirts bureaucratic rules. All those earlier scandals—when China's State Administration of Foreign Exchange fined Alipay 600,000 yuan (about $88,000) for misrepresenting international payments from 2014 to 2016, and Tenpay was punished for failing to file proper registration paperwork for cross-border payments between 2015 and 2017—turned out not to be anomalies.[4] It becomes apparent that these aren't isolated incidents as Chinese state officials experience the tension between socialist sensibilities and the realities of capitalism.

*  *  *

Already we are seeing the downstream implications of all these political, strategic, and technical vulnerabilities. To placate Wall Street, the G-MAFIA chase lucrative government contracts rather than strategic partnerships. This seeds competition rather than collaboration. It leads to restricted interoperability across AI frameworks, services, and devices. In the early 2020s, the market nudged the G-MAFIA to divvy up certain functionality and features: Amazon now owns e-commerce and our homes, while Google owns search, location, personal communications, and the workplace. Microsoft owns enterprise cloud computing, while IBM owns enterprise-level AI applications and applied health systems. Facebook owns social media, and Apple makes hardware (phones, computers, and wearables).

None of the G-MAFIA agrees to a single set of core values that prioritize transparency, inclusivity, and safety. While leadership within the G-MAFIA agrees that there should probably be widely adopted and implemented standards governing AI, there's just no way to divert resources or time to work on them.

Your personal data record is built, maintained, and owned initially by four of the G-MAFIA: Google, Amazon, Apple, and Facebook. But here's the rub: you're not even aware that PDRs exist or that they're being used by the G-MAFIA and by AI's tribes. It's not intentional but rather an oversight due to speed. It's all explained in the terms of service we all agree to but never, ever read.

The formatting used by each PDR provider isn't complementary, so there's both duplicative data being spread around and, paradoxically, big holes with important data missing. It's as if four different photographers took your photo: one with light stands and reflective umbrellas, one with a fisheye lens, one using an instant camera, and one shooting with an MRI machine. Technically what results are four pictures of your head, but the data embedded within them are vastly different.

In an effort to make a more complete picture, AI's tribes release "digital emissaries"—little programs that act as go-betweens and negotiate on behalf of the G-MAFIA. The digital emissaries from both Google and Amazon work for a time, but they aren't realistic long-term solutions. They're too difficult to keep updated, especially since so many different third-party products and services link into them. Rather than releasing new emissary versions daily, Google makes a big change.

In the early 2020s, Google releases its penultimate operating system, one mega-OS that can run on smartphones, smart speakers, laptops, tablets, and connected appliances. That's just to start. Eventually, Google plans to grow and enrich this OS so that it becomes the invisible infrastructure powering our everyday lives, running our spoken interfaces, our smart earbuds and smart glasses, our cars, and even parts of our cities. That system is fully intertwined with our PDRs, and it's a dramatic improvement for those who use it.

Google's mega-OS comes at a bad time for Apple, which may have become America's first trillion-dollar company but whose iPhone sales saw steady declines in the wake of newer connected devices like smart earbuds and wristbands. For its many successes, Amazon (America's second trillion-dollar company) hasn't had a big consumer hardware hit since its Echo smart speaker. In a surprising twist, Apple and Amazon partner exclusively in 2025 to build out a comprehensive OS that will power hardware made by both companies. The resulting OS—Applezon—poses a formidable threat to Google. In the consumer space, this cements a two-operating-system model and sets the stage for massive, fast consolidation within the AI ecosystem.

Facebook decides it must seek out a similar partnership; it's bleeding active monthly users, who no longer view the social network as invaluable. It tries to friend Applezon, which isn't interested. Microsoft and IBM stay focused on the enterprise.

China and its new diplomatic partners all use BAT technologies, while the rest of the world now uses either Google's mega-OS or Applezon, both of which power and are powered by our PDRs. This limits our choices in the marketplace. There are a just a few options for smartphone models (and soon, the smart glasses and wristbands that will replace mobile phones) and for all of the devices in our homes: speakers, computers, TVs, major appliances, and printers. It's easier to align ourselves with just one brand—so we are Google households or Applezon households. Technically, we can move our PDRs to other providers; however, we do not own the data in our PDRs, nor do we own the PDRs themselves. We are not afforded total transparency—what Google and Applezon do with our PDRs is, to a large extent, invisible by design to protect IP.

To avoid antitrust lawsuits, we're told that at any time, we can port our PDRs between operating systems. Of course, in practical terms, it's nearly impossible to make the change. You're reminded of trying to switch between iOS and Android many years ago when you discovered that lots of important data and settings were lost forever, progress within apps was erased, many apps didn't even work (and you could no longer get a refund), and all of the places you previously hosted your photos and videos couldn't be accessed easily. Now that your PDR is being used by third parties—such as schools, hospitals, and airlines—it's a far more difficult process to move between Google and Applezon.

There are plenty of newly minted IT consultants who will spend several days porting our PDRs from one provider to the other, but it's a costly, imperfect process. Most people reluctantly decide to stick with what they've got, even if it isn't optimal.

Google and the Amazon-Apple joint venture face antitrust lawsuits both in the United States and in Europe. By the time the cases make their way through the legal systems, everyone's data is so entangled that breaking apart or opening up the PDR and AI systems would cause more risk than eventual reward. As a result, a decision is made to levy substantive fines—that money will be used to support the development of new businesses. But everyone agrees: the two-OS system must be allowed to continue.

\* \* \*

As AI matures from narrow applications to generally intelligent thinking machines, we have no choice but to live with the paper cuts inflicted by artificial intelligence. China's modern version of communism—socialism mixed with capitalist sensibilities—expands, positioning Xi Jinping to make good on promises of a new world order. Nations that are opposed to China's autocratic style of governing, its suppression of religious freedoms and a free press, and its negative views on sexual, gender, and ethnic orientations have no leverage. They have no choice but to work alongside China, on China's terms.

We were promised freedom through AI, which was supposed to relieve us from mundane tasks and repetitive work. Instead, our freedom to choose is restricted in ways no one imagined.

## 2029: Learned Helplessness

The two-OS system has resulted in sharp competition among those in AI's tribes, who didn't plan ahead for vast interoperability issues. Because it turns out that in addition to hardware, in the two-OS system, *people* aren't interoperable either. The transience that was once a hallmark of Silicon Valley—engineers, operations managers, and user experience designers used to migrate from company to company without any real sense of allegiance—is long gone. Rather than bringing us together, AI has effectively and efficiently split us all apart. It's a pain point for the US government too, which itself has been forced to choose a framework. (Like most other governments, the United States went with Applezon over Google, because Applezon offered cheaper pricing and bundled in discounted office supplies).

Around the world, everyone is talking about our "learned helplessness" in the age of AI. We can't seem to function without our various automated systems, which constantly nudge us with positive or negative feedback. We try to blame the Big Nine, but really, we're the ones to blame.

It's been especially hard on Millennials, who thirsted for feedback and praise when they were kids and initially loved our varied AI systems—but who developed a psychological tick that's been hard to shake. When the battery in our AI-powered toothbrush dies, a Millennial (now in her 40s) must resort to brushing her teeth the old-fashioned way, which provides no affirming feedback. An analog toothbrush gives no feedback, which means she can't get her expected hit of dopamine, leaving her both anxious and blue. It isn't just Millennials. A low-grade sense of unease afflicts most of us. We invest in redundancy, buying spare analog tools (like plastic toothbrushes, regular old headphones, and Warby Parker glasses) as backups to our AI-powered ones. We've lost confidence in what used to be our common sense and basic skills for living.

The competing standards of Google's mega-OS and Applezon remind us of traveling abroad and all those irritations caused by differently shaped plugs and mismatched power voltages. Those who travel regularly find themselves prioritizing OS over loyalty programs, staying at an Applezon hotel or taking a Google mega-OS airline. Companies find it easier to subscribe fully to either one or the other OS. Slowly but surely, we're being nudged to pick a side. Applezon people find it hard to live with Google mega-OS people because their PDRs and devices aren't compatible—even if their personalities are.

* * *

The year 2019 marked the beginning of the end of smartphones, which is why we're all wearing connected devices rather than carrying them around in our pockets and purses. After a period of rapid advancement, new phones running Apple's iOS and Android were only offering incremental improvements to their systems, while the phones themselves had no significant updates beyond minor camera upgrades. The excitement that used to surround each new iPhone iteration was lost. Not even the release of Samsung's fabled smartphone with a foldable screen was enough to buoy new adoption rates to their old levels. Rather than standing in line every year or two to buy the latest handset, consumers instead spent that money on a suite of new connected devices that came on the market: wireless, Bluetooth earphones with biometric sensors, wristbands that allowed you to record video and make video calls, and smart glasses that fed us a seemingly endless stream of information. Applezon beat Google to market with its glasses—Applezon Vision— which wasn't a surprise. Apple and Amazon each had a long, successful track record of hyping new technologies and driving consumer taste. (The commercial failure of Google Glass still stung for some within the company, even if the technology was groundbreaking.) Now most people wear smart glasses and earbuds during the day along with a companion ring or wristband for video recording.

It turns out that glasses were inevitable. After two decades of staring into screens, our eyes can no longer make the necessary accommodations, and the majority of us have blurred distance vision and needed reading glasses at younger ages. Like most people alive today, you need corrective vision, which has created the market for the smart glasses some analysts said would never come. The glasses, along with their peripherals—wireless earbuds, a smart wristband, and a lightweight tablet—are your primary communication device. They are an informative window through which to see the world, revealing data and details about the people you meet, the places you go, and the products you might want to buy. You watch video through them, and to make an outgoing video call, you use the camera embedded within your smart wristband. In general, you're talking more than typing. Special algorithms for spatial computing, computer vision, and audio recognition power much of the data that you see and collect through your smart wearables.

* * *

Applezon and Google have incentivized you to lease—rather than to own—all of this equipment, and that subscription includes access to your PDR. There's nothing nefarious about the subscription model; it was just a practical decision necessitated by the product cycle. The rate of change within artificial intelligence is hastening with each passing year, and since the value of our data is significantly greater than the profit margins of smart glasses, wristbands, and earbuds, the goal is to keep us all connected to the system. The technology is a loss leader, which is offset by an inexpensive monthly subscription fee. That subscription is also what gains you access to your PDR, which is priced according to permissions. The least expensive plans also provide the least amount of cloaking, so those people give Google and Applezon access to use their data at will, whether that's for advertising to or simulating medical experiments. Those who are wealthy can add on "permission premiums" to their PDR packs, but they are nearly unobtainable and carry a significant price tag. In 2029, we have elite, gated communities hidden away from public view—but they're digital, they're guarded by algorithms, and they hide wealthy people's data from the prying eyes of everyday people and companies.

Like many others, you've been lured into so-called "parrot attacks," which are the latest iteration of phishing scams, and governments around the world are completely unprepared. It turns out that adversarial inputs can also infect your PDR and, like a parrot, mimic your voice back to everyone you know. Some parrot AIs are so deeply rooted in your PDRs and your digital life that they not only convincingly mimic your unique voice, cadence, tone, and vocabulary—they can do so using institutional knowledge of your life. Parrot AIs are being used to send out phony voice messages so convincing that parents and spouses are routinely fooled. Unfortunately, parrot AIs are causing a big problem for online dating companies. Scammers steal identities and use them to lure people using hyper-realistic interactions.

\* \* \*

We're all suffering from a certain amount of malaise brought about by learned helplessness, new economic divides, and a sense that our real-world selves just can't compete with the versions enhanced through AI. You seek solace in the form of brain-machine interfaces, which are high-throughput links that transfer data between your head and a computer. Although Facebook and Elon Musk announced a decade ago that they were working on special devices that would give us telepathy superpowers, Baidu was first with its "neuroenhancing headband." Tucked away discretely inside a baseball cap or sun hat, the device can read and monitor your brainwave data and transmit feedback to enhance focus, create a sensation of feeling happy and content, or make you feel as if you have lots of energy. It wasn't a surprise that a BAT company had its brain-machine interface out first. The pharmaceutical companies lobbied regulators, hoping to block approval of neuroenhancing headbands and future brain-machine interfaces. Seeing Baidu as a threat, Google and Applezon both stepped in, releasing their own products, which added even more data to our PDRs.

*  *  *

Nagging is the new nudging as Google and Applezon unintentionally harass you into better health. Your wristband, earbuds, and smart glasses deliver constant reminders. You don't have the opportunity to take a forkful of cake, since the minute you look at dessert, the AI recognizes what you're about to eat, compares it with your current metabolic rate and overall health, and sends a warning notification to your wristband or glasses. At a restaurant, you're nudged to consider menu items that meet your current biological needs: foods that are higher in potassium or omega-3s, or foods low in carbs or salt. If you choose wisely, you are rewarded and sent messages of encouragement.

There is no real way to unplug from nagging AIs, since your PDR is tied into your insurance premium, and your rate is set based on your commitment to healthy living. Skip a recommended workout, and you can expect to get nagged all day. Take an extra cookie, and it's noted in your file. The system wasn't intended to behave this way, but the algorithms were given a purpose, and they were trained to relentlessly optimize the various facets of everyday life. They weren't programmed with an end point or completion date.

When the two-OS system emerged for our PDRs, this forced a lot of the electronic medical record providers to pick a partner. This gave some members of the G-MAFIA the data they'd needed years earlier, and it also—somewhat by accident—created America's new health care system. IBM Watson Health had the sophisticated (some would argue superior) technology, but it also had two decades of organizational dysfunction. Fifteen years after Google launched Calico, its own health initiative, it had failed to produce any viable commercial products, and so a strategic partnership made sense: Watson-Calico. It was a prescient move on Google's part, since independently, both Amazon and Apple had long planned their own disruptions into America's insurance and pharmaceutical industries. Amazon had, of course, experimented with new models for insurance and medicine delivery through its Berkshire Hathaway and JPMorgan Chase venture, while Apple used its successful retail store and Genius Bar model to launch a new breed of minute clinics all along the West Coast. The Google-IBM partnership forced a second Applezon joint venture, this time combining Amazon's e-pharmacy platform with Apple's minute clinics. As a result of all this consolidation, American hospitals are now all part of either the Watson-Calico Health System or the Applezon Health System. The big conglomerates—Kaiser Permanente, LifePoint Health, Trinity Health, NewYork-Presbyterian Healthcare System— are either paying members of Watson-Calico or Applezon Health.

These joint ventures turned out to be brilliant solutions to the data problem. Now, Google, IBM, and Applezon have unfettered access to even your biological data—and you are given access to low- or no-cost diagnostics. Testing isn't a reflexive response prescribed when we're sick. You are tested now for anything and everything, which has directly benefitted your overall level of health and wellness. Ask any American what their normal body temperature is, and you'll get an individualized answer rather than the old standard 98.6 degrees.

While we finally have access to affordable health care, Americans are now living with some bizarre glitches that turned out to be features rather than bugs. Older ambulances aren't always able to access a patient's PDR if they aren't current with the latest OS updates. Neither are the nurses' offices at schools and summer camps. The PDRs of competing hospital systems can technically be read by both Applezon Health and Watson-Calico, but often, a lot of useful contextual data is missing. Especially in smaller or rural communities, doctors find that they need to remember their medical school training if someone

candidates are less obvious—now everyone looks as if they have a competitive advantage. AI systems are being used to qualify leads, but hiring managers are no longer able to make a choice because all the candidates seem equally terrific. So they resort to what feels comfortable: white men wind up hiring white men because they're crippled by the tyranny of choice.

In most large companies, the previous hierarchy has collapsed into two tiers of workers: skilled and senior management. Skilled staff work alongside AI systems and report to AI minders since the entire layer of middle management has now been eliminated. At work, AI minders track productivity, watch as you move around your workspace, note who you socialize with, and record your level of happiness, anxiety, stress, and contentment. They are the personification of those awful motivational posters, reminding you "You are braver than you think" and "You are stronger than your excuses."

\* \* \*

Governments weren't prepared for the widespread elimination of middle management jobs in knowledge industries—such as law and finance—because they were focused exclusively on labor or low-skill occupations, such as driving, farming, and factory labor. The creative fields are hit just as hard in the wake of a new branch of AI: machine creativity. Graphic designers, architects, copywriters, and web developers have been made redundant because generative adversarial networks and newer AI systems turned out to be remarkably reliable and productive. At the same time, AI has afforded certain positions—chief operating officers, chief financial officers, and chief information officers—superpowers. A significant chasm has opened up, concentrating more and more wealth at the very top of organizations. We are seeing the emergence of a digital caste system.

\* \* \*

Another glitch: information contamination. A decade ago, a constellation of lawsuits and sweeping international regulations caused the internet to become splintered. Rather than a single World Wide Web, we wound up with splinternets, wherein digital rules varied depending on local laws and geographic restrictions. This didn't happen overnight. When the internet shifted from academia and government to the private sector in the 1990s, we let it propagate freely instead of treating it like a regulated utility or financial system. Back then, lawmakers didn't think much about how all the data we'd generate on the internet might be used. So now it's impossible to comply with every legal permutation while our previous filter bubbles expanded to fit geographic borders. This helped the promotion and propagation of fake news. Because bad actors are using generative algorithms, and because depending on region, we're all getting different versions of news content, we don't know what or whom to trust. Every one of the world's most venerable news organizations has been tricked more than once, as trained journalists have a difficult time verifying videos of global leaders and everyday people alike. It's nearly impossible to tell whether the video we're seeing is a generated voice with a generated face, or the real deal.

* * *

Yet another glitch: an AI crime wave no one saw coming. Narrow but powerful AI programs have started causing trouble all over the internet. They're making illegal purchases: counterfeit designer handbags, drugs, and medicines made from poached animals (like rhino horn and elephant tusk). They're listening in on our social channels, reading the news, and infiltrating financial markets by triggering sudden sell-offs. In public spaces, they're committing libel with the intent of defaming people's character and reputation. We are beginning to worry about AIs breaking in to our PDRs, hacking our biometrics, and falsifying not just our own records but also those we've inherited. Some of this lawlessness was intentionally designed and deployed by the modern mafia: a widespread, distributed network of organized crime that's difficult to trace and contain. Some of the rogue AIs were accidental: they simply evolved and started behaving in ways no one intended.

The problems extend to physical robots, too. Security robots, outfitted with smart cameras and predictive analytic software, chase down people of color regularly. The security robots don't carry weapons, but they do bark very loud orders and sound high-pitched, screeching alarms if they suspect any wrongdoing. Inside of office buildings, hotels, airports, and train stations, people of color are routinely harassed and humiliated because a security bot has mistakenly tagged them as suspicious.

\* \* \*

The G-MAFIA does not have an easy relationship with American law enforcement agencies, which all want access to our PDRs. Rather than working together, the government threatens lawsuits and tries to compel the G-MAFIA to share its data, though it has no obligation—legal or otherwise—to give in to their demands. While no one will go on the record publicly, it's sounding like US law enforcement agencies hope to emulate some of China's algorithmic monitoring and social credit score system. Fearing consumer backlash, the G-MAFIA continues to keep its systems locked.

We had talked for more than a decade about the philosophical and ethical implications of algorithmic decision-making within law enforcement; however, no standards, norms, or regulations were ever established. Now we have a seemingly unending string of AI-powered crimes, but we have no mechanism for punishment. There is no jail for AIs and robots. The laws that define what a crime is don't apply to the technology we've created.

Our confusion and disillusion has played neatly into the hand of China, which is no longer a near-peer competitor to the United States, but a formidable direct competitor and militaristic pacing threat. China spent decades stealing American equipment design and defense strategies, a tactic that is paying dividends. President Xi is further consolidating the power of China's military, which is focused on code rather than combat. For example, the beautiful light shows China deployed for various events—a 2017 "drone lanterns" festival, a 2018 summer "drone fireworks" spectacular, for example—turned out to be practice runs for swarm intelligence. China's military now uses powerful AI-powered drones to hunt in packs all over the countryside and over the oceans.

Through its economic might, person-to-person diplomacy, and show of military strength, China is practicing a new colonialism, successfully colonizing Zambia, Tanzania, the Democratic Republic of Congo, Kenya, Somalia, Ethiopia, Eritrea, and Sudan. China is building infrastructure—and deploying its social credit score system—and extracting critical resources to lock out competitors and to support its rapidly growing middle class. It now controls more than 75% of the world's lithium supply, which we need for batteries. And it's decimated global rosewood forests and led to the extinction of the Mukula tree, a slow-growing species in central Africa that, for a time, was harvested to make red-colored end tables and chairs with intricate carvings.

No foreign power—not the United States, Japan, South Korea, or the European Union—had enough political or economic clout to stop China from extending its special economic trading zones far out into the South China Sea, East China Sea, and Yellow Sea. Nearly half of all global trade must pass through one of those zones, and every single ship that goes by must pay the Chinese government a hefty tax.

China observers say that Beijing missed its 2025 target to become the world's AI powerhouse, even if it has taken control of certain physical world resources. But those observers aren't looking at the bigger picture. Years of mandatory technology-transfer agreements, uncontained restrictive market practices, plus China's sizable investment in American and European tech companies proved wildly successful.

China now dominates advanced tech industries, including robotics, new energies, genomics, and aviation—and every one of those fields leverage and are leveraged by AI. There are no published numbers, but considering its state AI labs, partnerships with Baidu, Alibaba, and Tencent, and all of its Belt and Road partners, experts believe that China managed to grow the value of its total AI ecosystem more than 500 billion yuan (about $73 billion) in just a decade.

## 2049: And Then There Were Five

As time wore on and progress was made toward artificial general intelligence, the constellation of the Big Nine changed in ways that were both profound and problematic. Now China's BAT are stronger than ever and still working in lockstep with Beijing. However, America's six original G-MAFIA members are now only five, due to strategic partnerships and joint ventures: Amazon-Apple and Google-IBM are the four companies that matter most. Microsoft is currently providing support for legacy systems and services.

Perhaps most surprising is what became of Facebook. It wasn't the aftermath of Cambridge Analytica or even revelations about Russian meddling into the US elections that led to Facebook's ultimate demise. Nor was it the fatigue we all felt as our news feeds filled with ever more vitriol, hate, fearmongering, and political conspiracy theories. Facebook's business model just wasn't sustainable over time. Once users dropped off and advertisers stopped spending their money on the platform, Facebook didn't have a diverse portfolio of revenue streams. By 2035, it was in serious financial trouble. Shareholders wanted out, institutional and mutual fund managers got spooked, and the market turned against it. Facebook was sold for parts. Everyone whose data was locked inside the network—which was most of America—is now gravely concerned because it's our data that was quietly bought by a conglomerate. Investigations are underway, but rumor has it that the conglomerate was, in fact, a Chinese shell company. It's likely that all of us are now a part of China's social credit system, and that we're all being tracked.

You, like all Americans, are learning to live with constant, low-grade anxiety. Our national sense of uneasiness is often compared to nuclear war threats in the 1960s and 1980s. Except that this time around, we're not sure what to fear, exactly. You don't know if your PDR is safeguarded or what personal data China might have access to. You're unsure of how deeply rooted Chinese government hackers are within our country's infrastructure systems. You are often awake late at night, wondering what China knows about you, the bridges you take to get to work, the gas lines feeding into your house—and what they're planning on doing with all that information.

What we didn't anticipate was a wide spectrum of AGIs, built for different purposes and tasks, which are both powerful and indifferent to human values. In hindsight, this was remarkably naïve of us. As Amazon, Apple, Google, and IBM partnered, chose sides, and grew, they didn't set global standards. Decades ago, people bought apps and games for their phones from Google's Play Store, and because it was fairly easy for anyone to launch and sell an app, the quality varied wildly. There were far too many battery-hungry apps, games that scraped and shared personal information, and janky ads that made the mobile experience miserable. That's what we're seeing now in AGIs—except the aftermath is far worse. Some AGIs pretend to follow the protocols written for them but then choose to overwrite those protocols with new directives. Some AGIs self-improve even if their creators didn't explicitly program them to do so. Some self-replicate, break into other AGIs, and harvest the resources they need to achieve goals, regardless of the impact those actions might have on the greater ecosystem.

To counter ill-behaved AGIs, researchers at Applezon and Google-IBM are deploying nanny AGIs—NAGIs for short—to police other systems. NAGIs have a clear set of protocols:

- To investigate and analyze other AGIs to see if they are violating their original goals.
- To create a detailed log of all misbehaving AGIs, along with their entire histories (e.g., who created them, when they were modified, and by whom or what).
- To find the original human in the loop of development, and to notify them of noncompliance.
- After a grace period (which depends on the severity of the AGI's infractions), decommission any rogue AGI.
- Never to modify their own goals.

It's evident that both Applezon and Google-IBM were trying to control a system that was starting to spin out of control, but now there is no widespread adoption of NAGIs outside the Applezon and Google-IBM ecosystems. Using previous antitrust rulings against Google and Microsoft as precedent, the European Parliament claimed that NAGIs were nothing more than a hidden attempt by the companies to stifle entrepreneurs and quash competition. The EU became the first to ban NAGIs. Even as research scientists pleaded with regulators to allow these specialized AGIs to help contain what they know is a serious, burgeoning problem, Congress ruled against the tech giants, prohibiting the use of NAGIs in the United States. Those shortsighted NAGI rulings only seeded public distrust in Applezon and Google-IBM, which might otherwise have been good custodians of our PDRs.

\* \* \*

Your home has been turned into a big container for marketing, which is constant and intrusive. You see custom video advertisements anywhere there's a screen: the smart mirrors in your bathroom and closets, the retractable screens you carry in your pocket, even the smart windowpanes you had to install in your homes to block out extreme solar heat. You are uncomfortable in your own home—the one place you used to feel most at ease and relaxed.

This distrust has made our health care system particularly daunting. Applezon Health System and Watson-Calico have made tremendous advancements in both AI and medicine. They both got the idea from a mind-controlled robotic suit that debuted at the 2014 World Cup. Duke University neuroscientist Miguel Nicolelis had figured out how to meld mind and machine—and his work inspired others to bring brain-machine interfaces to market. In some tech-forward offices, workers are encouraged wear electronic headbands and link their minds together, along with AGI, to solve challenging problems. Not everyone is comfortable with this high-tech form of collective intelligence since it requires data to pass through either Applezon or Watson-Calico, who can now literally see inside our heads.

It was Watson-Calico, in partnership with a prominent New York university, that advanced one of Turing's lesser-known AI theories about morphogenesis. Turing thought that a system of chemicals probably reacted with each other, and that reaction diffused across a series of cells to change some of them. Turing was proven correct. AGI systems were used to discover different ways to create complex multicellular beings, and that led to the advent of augmented human beings, which we refer to as "human-animal chimeras."

The original intent was to create viable human tissue for transplants, so we used pigs and sheep to grow harvestable livers, hearts, and kidneys. Researchers also developed brain organoids—the exact same tissue that makes up our own brains. It was promising work, until we realized that AGI was being used to develop human-animal chimeras that had other characteristics, like pigs implanted with human brain tissue that developed a low-level humanlike IQ and newborn babies that had a dog's sense of smell. What no one has yet discussed (or determined) is the implications of chimera attributes, which are heritable. What happens when a human modified with extrasensory capabilities has a child with someone who also has modifications?

\* \* \*

What's most concerning is that China decided to repurpose AGI and brain machine interfaces—which were intended to help sick people regain their faculties—for strategic military advantage. It has been used to enhance the cognitive abilities of its soldiers, who do much of their work from inside dark underground bunkers. In the US and EU, such experimentation and use of technology violates ethics laws.

We are beginning to see a very real decline of Western civilization and our democratic ideals, thanks to China's colonization, the expansion of its economic zones, and its unscrupulous use of AGI. The health of our economy is in peril, as traditional indicators like housing, construction spending, and food and retail sales are all down, quarter after quarter.

Even Applezon and Google-IBM are finally seeing a decline in revenue, and they are generally worried about their futures. As they work to overhaul our PDRs to work alongside guardian AGIs, both notice strange noise in the log systems. There are fragments of code that don't quite make sense, and some of the AGIs that process and route our PDRs are acting glitchy. In a rare act of collaboration, Applezon and Google-IBM share what they're seeing with each other, in the hopes of determining the problem. In our homes and offices, the lights randomly turn off. Our smart glasses stop working intermittently. Our communications satellites veer off course.

Though we can't hear them, we know the shots have been fired, and that China has waged war on America.

## 2069: Digitally Occupied States of America

We realize that China has, in fact, developed a generation of AGIs that have far greater capabilities than ever before seen. Without NAGIs to watch over rogue AGIs, China was able to build and deploy a terrifying system to control most of the population on Earth. If we don't comply with China's demands, it cuts off our communications systems. If we fail to keep our data pipeline open to the Chinese Communist Party, it shuts down our critical infrastructure, like our power plants and air traffic control.

You are a resident in China's Digitally Occupied States of America. Your transportation, bank, health care system, light switches, and refrigerators are all controllable by China.

What began as a colonial push into Africa resulted in a new, global Chinese empire enabled and empowered by artificial intelligence. Humanity is on the brink of a terrifying ASI that has been developed by a country that does not share our democratic values and ideals.

# CHAPTER SEVEN

# THE RÉNGŌNG ZHÌNÉNG DYNASTY: THE CATASTROPHIC SCENARIO

*"This is the way the world ends, not with a bang but a whimper."*

—T. S. ELIOT

By 2023, we have closed our eyes to artificial intelligence's developmental track. We missed all the signals, we ignored the warning signs, and we failed to actively plan for the future. We helped the Big Nine compete against itself as we indulged our consumerist desires, buying the latest gadgets and devices, celebrating every new opportunity to record our voices and faces, and submitting to an open pipeline that continually siphoned off our data. We shared silly videos of Alexa failing when our kids chat with Amazon. We asked our TVs to scan our faces, never questioning why a television might need or want our biodata. Every time Google launched fun new projects that map our bodies to photos, our faces to paintings, our voices to celebrities, our fingerprints to people in distant lands, and our irises to our ancestors, we eagerly took part, desperate to keep up with digital influencers and the latest memes.

AI's tribes say that diversity matters. It is their mantra. They say it again and again, during keynotes and at conferences, during job interviews and board meetings, in think pieces and tweets. They say it in college brochures. They say it on attractive posters hung in elevators and taped to the hallways at work. AI's mostly white, mostly male tribes are trained to recite the mantra in their classrooms, labs, and workspaces. Rather than making difficult choices and changes, they stick to the mantra and promise that change is coming soon. And it works just like mantras were intended: to eliminate negativity from the mind and make AI's tribes feel better about themselves. The gurus in AI's tribes hand the mantra down to each new cohort of disciples, who feel a sense of great accomplishment in its repetition.

The mantra echoes within the comfortable bubble of AI's tribes, which believe they are promoting inclusion when the opposite is true. They champion diversity of all kinds—political parties, religious affiliations, sexual and gender identity, race and ethnicity, economic status, and age—but make no serious effort on inclusion. Rather than seeing a wide, colorful spectrum of people and their worldviews entering the field of AI via tenure track positions, top jobs on research teams, and managerial roles in the G-MAFIA, we instead see no change.

*   *   *

As the tribes' worldviews become increasingly myopic, the problems we're already seeing compound. Accidents and mistakes are on the rise, like computer vision systems misidentifying people of color and blaming them for crimes. Surveillance expands while simultaneously becoming less obvious. The line between our personal data and the data we generate at work blurs, and so do the criteria for who gets to use our data and when. Transparency into AI systems fades into darkness. (Not that it was great to start with.)

The G-MAFIA are the sole owners of your personal data record, which grows to encompass every aspect of your human existence: what you write in emails, the texts you send to your kids, your digital bread-crumbs as you search for the perfect desk chair, the unique contours of your fingerprints and face, where you walk and the pace of your runs, who you bump into at the grocery store, whether you have the flu, and what medications you're on. Algorithms make decisions for you using all that data. They determine whether you get a discount when booking a flight. They help or prevent you from getting a job, qualify you to buy a home or a car, match you for first dates, and tell the doctor whether you're lying about how much you drink, smoke, and exercise. Since it's Google, Amazon, Apple, Facebook, Microsoft, and IBM who own that data—and because we love their products, even if we don't entirely trust the companies—we can't see total corporate control of our PDRs for what it is: America's version of China's social credit score system.

We find ourselves locked into a digital caste system, where AI makes choices and judgments based not only on how we've lived our lives but also on the PDRs of our parents and relatives. Wealth no longer matters. Status is determined by "being our best selves," where "best" got defined long ago by a relative few programmers who thought an organic ketogenic diet, midday yoga classes, and regular trips to the chiropractor were the keys to an optimized existence. If you don't take a weekly infrared sauna, the AI system you're tethered to will rec-ord noncompliance in your PDR. And that act of rebellion doesn't just affect you, because your record is linked to everyone you know and are related to. You cannot escape the sins of your associates.

*     *     *

In the near future, Amazon and IBM will persuade the governments of the United States, United Kingdom, Germany, and Japan to open up access to a trickle of citizen health data. Apple, Google, Microsoft, and Facebook will have a more difficult time in Europe because of previous antitrust lawsuits. But those early Amazon and IBM experiments will

prove useful to government agencies, which will open up more lucrative contracts for the entire G-MAFIA.

*  *  *

Back in 2008, when parts of the world entered a financial crisis caused
by the housing bubble, China was glad to buy iron, oil, and copper
from Latin American countries, effectively protecting those countries
from serious harm. When oil prices dropped in 2011, China was willing to invest in and bail out Latin America.[1] In 2013, China launched
joint military training exercises off the Brazilian coastline—and did it
again in 2014 off the coast of Chile.[2] In 2015, China's Defense Ministry hosted a 10-day summit on military logistics with officials from 11
Latin American countries, and in the years since it has invited Latin
American military officers to career development programs in China.[3]
While the American government is retrenching and retreating from
the world's stage, China is in expansionist mode. It is working deals all
across Southeast Asia and Africa—and Latin America, too.

After a decade of steady relationship building throughout Latin
America, today it is China—and not the United States—supplying
Venezuela, Bolivia, Peru, and Argentina with Chinese military equipment, which includes aircraft and arms.[4] And it has a reason to establish bases all across America's backyard. In Patagonia, China built a
military antenna and a space control station, and it built a satellite-
tracking hub in northwest Argentina.[5] All of this activity involves artificial intelligence.

Now, policymakers and lawmakers alike are failing to make the
connection between China, the US, and AI. China's consolidation of
power under Xi Jinping, its various state-sponsored initiatives, its rapidly growing economy, and the success of the BAT are an unstoppable—
if invisible—force with which to be reckoned. Neither the White House
nor Congress see that China's push into all these countries—Tanzania,
Vietnam, Argentina, and Bolivia, for example—has to do with both

economics *and* intelligence. They refuse to acknowledge that China is building a 21st-century empire on the foundation of data, AI infrastructure, geopolitics, and the global economy. It is a grave error in judgment we will all later regret.

Chinese citizens are learning to live with automated monitoring and consequences of stepping out of line. Crime is down, and social unrest is curtailed, and for a time the middle and upper classes preserve the status quo. They have access to luxury clothing and handbags, designer furniture and statement cars never imagined by their parents and grandparents. Promises are made to lift all Chinese people out of poverty. For now at least, it seems like privacy, religious freedom, sexual identity, and free speech are reasonable trade-offs for earning a desirable social credit score.

US government leaders don't take enough time to get educated on what AI is, what it isn't, and why it matters. Aside from the usual conversations about AI disrupting productivity and jobs, those in DC make zero effort to engage the G-MAFIA in serious discussions about other pressing issues related to AI, such as national security, geopolitical balance, the risks and opportunities posed by artificial general intelligence, or the intersection of AI in other fields (such as genomics, agriculture, and education).

With no strategic direction on AI from the White House—and, in fact, an openly hostile stance on science and technology—Washington focuses on what matters during the next election cycle and what will play well on the Sunday morning political shows.

Neither the G-MAFIA nor their executive leadership are intentionally putting democracy in harm's way. But safeguarding America as the dominant global superpower and ensuring the preservation of democratic ideals just isn't central to their corporate values. Beginning in the early 2010s, Google's former chairman Eric Schmidt worked admirably and tirelessly to boost US military and government preparedness in the era of AI. It wasn't a ploy to win government contracts for Google.

Schmidt was concerned about our national security and military preparedness in this new technological age. But it was such an unusual undertaking that Silicon Valley questioned his motives. Rather than other G-MAFIA leaders following his lead, they were skeptical of his ambitions. And so aside from Schmidt, none of the G-MAFIA's leadership have given much thought to the role AI is playing in the rise of China as a possible superpower successor to America.

\*   \*   \*

There is no strategic collaboration between the G-MAFIA and government agencies or military offices—at least not without a lucrative contract. The G-MAFIA agree to the arcane, outdated procurement requirement policies of the military and government, but this doesn't accelerate AI in our national interest. If anything, it shines a bright light on the cultural differences between Silicon Valley and DC, and it slows down modernization. The few government agencies built for innovation—the US Digital Service, the US Army's Futures Command, the Defense Innovation Board, and the Defense Innovation Unit Experimental (DIUx) initiatives—are brittle in their youth and subject to defunding and staff reductions as the revolving door of political appointees spins. Washington views its relationship with the G-MAFIA as transactional. Neither lawmakers nor the White House makes an honest effort to develop the kind of relationships with G-MAFIA executives necessary for a long-term coalition on AI. The G-MAFIA, US military, and government circle around each other without ever converging in our national interest.

We allow ego and habit to get in the way of building consensus on China. Government officials, trade representatives, journalists, technologists, and academics debate China, the United States, and AI ad nauseam, holding tight to their longstanding, cherished beliefs without making room for alternate realities. The usual suspects argue that Xi Jinping won't be in power long, even with term limits abolished.

Once he's gone, all of China's long-term AI plans will evaporate. Their usual detractors argue back: Xi will unite his people and party. Regardless of whether he dies young or cedes his post to a successor, the CCP will be stronger as a result and will see the AI plans to the end. And so it goes, back and forth: China's industrial policies will have zero impact—or they will cause the unraveling of the US economy. China's military poses an existential threat to the Western world—or it's just an overblown trendy story that we'll be bored with soon. We ought to invest the time and money on a national AI strategy knowing that China's plans could fail—or we're wiser to save our time and money and take a wait-and-see approach. There is one point everyone seems to agree on: if America truly gets into trouble, the G-MAFIA will be compelled to help us out.

Our policymakers, elected officials, and think tanks make the same, tired arguments but take no action. They settle into stasis. They settle into stasis because in America it is difficult to escape the centripetal force of profit without a powerful intervention.

* * *

We have heard the story of stasis told many times before. We preserved the status quo of cigarette smoking, debating hard data about cancer while continuing to market tobacco as an accessory of fashionable women, a pick-me-up for factory workers, and a medicinal remedy for people who were sick. We failed to act on climate change, arguing over and over about adjectives. If there's global warming, why is it so *cold*? We resigned ourselves to debating timeframes. The alarming claims made in the 1970s became dire in the 1990s and then apocalyptic in the 2010s, but we're all still here. Who's to say things will be all that bad in the future?!

Systematic change has a compounding effect and builds over decades, not days. By the time we realize that stasis was the wrong course of action, it's too late.

## 2029: Digitally Locked In and Out

For the past decade, you've been incentivized to buy all manner of smart technologies and AI systems. All appliances now come standard with AI systems. Your refrigerator tracks the food inside. Washing machines—even those at Laundromats—track the progress of your dirty clothes, pinging you once a cycle has completed. Your oven shuts off before the turkey burns and dries out.

But there's a catch you didn't see coming: you lack permissions to override what was supposed to be a "helpful" AI. After you put bags of lunchmeats and cheeses, trays of cupcakes, and six-packs of beer into your connected refrigerator—all bought for a Super Bowl party—a notation is made on your PDR. The number of servings and calories exceeds the number of people in your household, so the AI concludes you are planning to overeat. It may be after midnight, and you might have already planned to get a load of laundry done in time to put it in the drier before work the next morning, but the washing machine's AI doesn't take your desire to sleep into consideration. It sounds an alarm and pings you—repeatedly and without ever stopping—to tell you that it's time to put your clothes in the drier. You'd like to make your own turkey jerky from scratch, but the oven won't allow it, because its AI has been programmed with the goal of juicy meat, period. (Or, if you can afford it, you can pay to unlock the jerky upgrade.)

Some households experience AI glitches, especially with their kitchen appliances, and typically in the morning. The control panels will go dark intermittently, which unfortunately locks down the door and prevents you from taking out breakfast. The dishwasher will suddenly stop midcycle, keeping glasses and silverware soaking in soapy, greasy water. The volume of smart speakers will suddenly spike, too, making it impossible to talk to your family members over cereal and coffee. You, along with tens of thousands of consumers report outages, and each time the G-MAFIA dedicates a few product managers to research what's going wrong. Tech journalists attribute the glitches to the "spooky ways" in which "AI acts weird sometimes."

At first, the attacks seem novel and random. So we all blame Google, Apple, and Amazon for faulty products and crappy customer service. Then cybersecurity experts are gobsmacked to discover all the glitches are actually linked. It is a new kind of "Internet of Things" attack originating in China and enabled by machine learning. The Chinese have a name for it: 被困, or *bèi kùn*, which translates to "trapped." The hackers, backed by the Chinese government, thought it was clever to launch "bacon" attacks during breakfast hours in America and to effectively trap our food, drinks, and eating utensils in our AI-powered appliances. Their purpose is singular and sophisticated: to seed mistrust in the G-MAFIA.

\* \* \*

Microsoft and IBM are still around, but they are minor players in the AI space. Microsoft, which at one point published industry-leading research on computer vision, machine reading comprehension, and natural language processing, never successfully gained internal alignment and momentum on how to compete in AI. Now the company is downsizing and primarily supplying support to its legacy systems: what's left of its original Azure cloud, SharePoint, Skype, and Outlook. While IBM's Watson found partners and clients, IBM's cloud service, which had long been a distant third to Amazon and Microsoft, shrunk once Google began offering competitive rates for both government and big corporations. Its other business units—such as data centers, storage, and semiconductors—have found it impossible to compete against companies in Taiwan, which are now the world's largest suppliers. For Taiwanese companies, the CCP's "One China Principle" translates to significant market advantage, even if Beijing restricts their personal liberties and freedoms. China's industrial policy has effectively prevented IBM from doing business in many areas of the world.

As for Facebook? After years of promises to shore up its security and provide better transparency into how it shared our data, the majority of its original users have moved on to other platforms. Gen Alpha kids (the children of Millennials) may have had their photos strewn all over Facebook, but they themselves never created accounts. Facebook is quietly going the way of MySpace.

With interoperability still a critical weak point in the West's AI ecosystem, by 2035 we settle into a de facto system of segregation. Our devices are hooked into Google, Apple, or Amazon, and so we tend to buy only the products and services offered by one of those three companies. Because the data in our heritable PDRs are owned and managed by one of those companies—companies that also sold us all the AI-powered stuff in our homes—we are Google families, Apple families, or Amazon families. That designation comes with unintended biases.

Apple households tend to be wealthier and older. They can afford all of Apple's sleek, beautiful hardware products available in one of three colors: palladium silvery-white, osmium grey, or dark onyx. Apple's smart glasses, smart toilets, and custom refrigerators carry on its long tradition of pricey products anyone can use right out of the box. Apple's PDRs come with spoken interfaces and a choice of two soothing voices, Joost (who has a "unisex higher tone") or Deva (who has a "unisex lower tone"). But convenience comes with a cost. Apple's AIs cannot be overwritten. In an Apple home running the air conditioner, you can't open the door for more than a minute or the system will start beeping incessantly. If there's sufficient daylight detected by the sensors in your light bulbs, the Apple system keeps the light switch on lock-down.

We saw a preview of Google's connected home decades ago at the 2018 South By Southwest Festival in Austin Texas. Back then, the tagline was "Make Google do it," and attractive spokesmodels took small groups around the three-story home to interact with AI-powered appliance screens and connected frozen daiquiri makers. Google's system is less intuitive, but it makes better use of our PDRs—and it offers different levels of service and access. For those who can afford the upgrade fees and have enough tech savvy, Google Green gives families the ability to manually unlock their systems, and they can connect a greater variety of things—such as coffee makers, 3D printers, and outdoor irrigation systems—to their homes. Green families can also opt out of marketing and advertising, though their data is still collected and sent to third parties. Google Blue is an affordable option with limited unlocking privileges and some additional permissions, but Blue families are still subjected to marketing. Google Yellow is the lowest tier. It's free but comes with no override abilities, has a small selection of available devices and appliances, and has limited data protections.

Amazon went in an interesting, but ultimately lucrative, direction. A few announcements Amazon made in the fall of 2018 went largely unnoticed, such as the launch of its Amazon Basics microwave, which includes a voice interface. Users could put a bag of popcorn in the microwave and ask Alexa to pop it. Tech journalists wrote the microwave off as a novel, silly use for Alexa and missed the bigger picture: the system was actually designed to get us hooked on subscription popcorn. That's because the microwave tracks both what we're heating up and what we're ordering on the Amazon platform. A new box arrives before you ever have the chance to run out.

Because Amazon was smartest in its approach, working with federal, state, and local governments—offering them deep discounts at Amazon.com, patiently working through procurement requirements, and building and maintaining cloud services specifically for them—it became the preferred platform for certain social services in the United States. That is how Amazon discovered how to leverage the long tail of government funding.

Low-income families now live in Amazon Housing, which has replaced city-funded public housing programs in the United States. By every measure, they are far superior to any public housing ever provided through our previous government programs. Amazon Homes are completely outfitted with connected devices in every room. The former Supplemental Nutrition Assistance Program (previously known as the Food Stamp Program) is currently hosted by Amazon, which provides steeply discounted Amazon-branded household products, food and drink, toiletries, and books. Unsurprisingly, this program works seamlessly. There are never delays in funds being distributed, it's easy to look up the status of an account, and all transactions can be completed without ever having to wait in a long line at a government office. Those living in Amazon Homes must buy most of their things through Amazon while their data is scraped, productized, and monetized for various initiatives. Amazon's AIs are the most pervasive, following Amazon families everywhere they go to collect valuable behavioral data.

\* \* \*

The lack of interoperability between AI frameworks and systems led to segregation by PDR and household, and that is why we now have a digital caste system. By choosing Google, Apple, or Amazon, you are forced to align your family values with the values of the corporation. Apple families are rich, maybe a little less AI-savvy, and live in fancy houses. Google families might be rich and techy, or middle class and fine with marketing, or complacent enough that having a lot of choices in life doesn't matter all that much. There is no way to sugarcoat Amazon families: they're poor, even if they have free access to cool gadgets.

Families are locked into their PDRs, and that designation travels with them. It's easier for a Google Yellow family to port into the Blue or even Green level than an Amazon to port into the Apple system. That's why most families opted-in to Google when they had the opportunity. Your status is visible to all of the AIs you interact with. Self-driving taxi services like Lyft, Uber, and CitiCar don't pick up Amazon riders with as much frequency, and cars sent to them tend not to be as nice. Waymo cars exclusively pick up Googlers. For Greens, the car is preset to the rider's desired temperature and ambient lighting scheme, and it drives along the rider's preferred routes. Yellows are subjected to advertising their entire trip.

\* \* \*

Advertising isn't the only headache for Yellow Googlers. One downside to all the subsidized (or free) gadgets, appliances, and gear offered to Google Blue, Google Yellow, and Amazon families is that it's impossible to disconnect the AI health and wellness minders, which continually monitor, diagnose, and nudge. When they were built, computer scientists defined health and wellness with rigidity out of necessity. Now the collective values of AI's earlier tribes are an oppressive souvenir of a simpler time. A failure to comply with health and wellness minders results in a litany of consequences.

Remember those Amazon Lockers, which you used many years ago to pick up all the things you ordered on the Amazon app and on Amazon.com? They made their way into Amazon Housing. The US Health and Human Services Department thought nudging poor people was a clever way to improve health and wellness, so the department issued new policies requiring all public housing customers to be outfitted with Locker technology. The Lockers may look like ordinary pantries, refrigerator doors, and closets, but they act like AI-powered juries. If an Amazon Housing customer hasn't had her exercise that day, the Locker system will decide to keep the freezer closed and won't let her eat ice cream.

\* \* \*

We feel the negative consequences of things that give us pleasure outside our Apple, Amazon, and Google homes, too. High-tech brothels, staffed with AI-powered sexbots, are socially acceptable because they offer a clean, disease-free alternative to sex with other people. The brothels operate on their own platforms, and they require a membership, which allows you to build and train an AI personality. (Or personalities, for those who can afford the premium package). You simply choose a body and look into its eyes—tiny smart cameras scan and recognize your face. Once your companion wakes up, they chat with you as if no time has gone by and they are responsive to your every desire and command. You find regular sex, with regular people, an utter letdown.

\* \* \*

It's not impossible to intermarry—occasionally an Amazon will marry into an Apple family—but that old adage "opposites attract" no longer applies. All of our AI-powered dating services now match us based on our PDRs and our status. On the one hand, we no longer suffer under the tyranny of choice since dating AIs have drastically reduced the selection of possible suitors. Yet some choices that once made us uniquely human—like May-December romances or dating someone our parents don't approve of—are less available to us now. In America, society is beginning to feel uncomfortably Huxleian, as we acquiesce, get married, and have babies with our fellow Apples, or Google Blues, or Amazons.

\* \* \*

Just as predicted, AI and automation begin to obviate jobs—far more jobs than we'd anticipated. The widespread technological unemployment that had long been on the horizon arrived, but not at all how we'd imagined. We were prepared for unemployed truck drivers, factory workers, and laborers, but our projections were wrong. We kept assuming that robots would take over all the blue-collar jobs, but it turns out that building physical robots capable of doing all that physical labor was a far more difficult task than we'd ever imagined, while cognitive tasks were easier to program and replicate. Ironically, it is the knowledge workers who are no longer needed.

As a result, America and its allies have an immediate and critical need for the all the blue-collar jobs we said would be gone. We simply don't have enough highly skilled plumbers, electricians, and carpenters. Robots can't provide the human touch we desire, so we also have an immediate need for massage therapists, nail technicians, estheticians, and barbers. We're experiencing a backlash against automation, too. Most people don't want their coffee drinks and cocktails made by robobaristas and robobartenders. We want human companionship along with whatever's in our cups. Our laser focus on STEM-first education at the expense of liberal arts and vocational programs was somewhat misguided. Blue-collar workers are inheriting the Earth, not the meek computer scientists and techies. The nerds programmed themselves out of work.

* * *

Without intending to, Google, Amazon, and Apple create a trifecta within AI, which leads to massive consolidation. In America and throughout all of our trading allies around the world, we have spectacular new products—but very little choice. For example, you can pay and upgrade to OmniVision smart glasses, which allow you to see beyond the biological limits of human vision. But only two companies make them: Google and Apple. If you don't like their designs, or if they don't fit the unique shape of your face and ears, you're out of luck. Amazon sells anything and everything you can imagine, but everyday necessities are the company's own branded products. In democratic nations worldwide, we have an abundant supply of things to buy, but variety and choice in the marketplace is tightly controlled. Even though we have money to spend, we have very little purchasing power. In an odd way, it reminds us of the old Soviet Union.

Salesforce, the customer relationship management and cloud computing company, partnered with Google, Amazon, and Apple very early on to build out an education module for our PDRs. Now the rigorous testing and classification that were hallmarks of American education in the 1980s and 1990s are popular again. Our cognitive abilities are assessed before preschool, and our academic achievement and enrichment is tracked throughout our lives.

Metrics and optimization have always been core values at Salesforce, and now they are core values of an American education. Concerned that we've replaced wisdom with an accumulation of now useless information, our educational leaders discarded the Common Core curriculum in favor of something new. With the American workforce in crisis, students are divided into two categories during their kindergarten entrance exams: vocational or executive. Vocational students are trained for agility across disciplines, while executive students are trained in critical thinking and management. There is no need for the kinds of skills possessed by middle managers, since most middle managers and entry-level knowledge workers are now AIs.

With unemployment in unexpected sectors; crime is up—but not for the reasons you think. AI-powered policing software didn't work as promised, so our crime statistics don't accurately represent the real world. The algorithms built by AI's tribes and trained on a limited set of data never learned how to correctly identify and classify a gender-nonconforming person—someone who identifies neither as female nor male and might look completely androgynous, or who might have both a beard and eyelash extensions. As a result, hundreds of people who don't satisfy the characteristics of one traditional gender are falsely accused of identity theft every single day: when they try to pay using face recognition, as they move around their offices, and when they try to video chat. For now, the only solution is to assimilate during certain transactions. They are forced to put on a gender-specific wig or to remove their makeup in order to temporarily become a distinct him or her in the eyes of a computer-vision AI. It's a humiliating and public reminder that diversity never really mattered enough to fix a broken system.

* * *

AI bestows immense economic power on Google, Apple, and Amazon—and unimaginable geopolitical and military power on China. By the end of the 2030s, we realize that AI has developed along parallel trajectories, supporting capitalism in the West and China's brand of communism throughout Asia, Africa, and Latin America. America and its allies, who once celebrated in the G-MAFIA's successes, are living under a system of AI totalitarianism. Citizens throughout China and all the countries supported by China's direct investment and infrastructure find that they, too, are living under a pervasive apparatus of AI-powered punishment and reward.

## 2049: Biometric Borders and Nanobot Abortions

The G-MAFIA are now just the GAA: Google, Apple, and Amazon. Facebook was the first to declare bankruptcy. The remnants of Microsoft and IBM were acquired by Google.

It is the centennial of the Chinese Communist Revolution and Mao Zedong's declaration of the People's Republic of China (PRC). Grand celebrations throughout all of China's subsidiary partner countries are planned to honor the late Xi Jinping and the rise of what's being called the Réngōng Zhìnéng (Artificial Intelligence) Dynasty.

All of humanity is now surrounded by AGI systems, which were supposed to help us lead freer, happier lives. From the very beginning, AI's tribes in the United States said they wanted us to live our best selves, to pursue creative endeavors, and to collaborate on humanity's biggest challenges. It was a utopian ideal born in the bubble of Silicon Valley, whose progenitors had completely lost touch with the outside world.

All of these systems were built to make our lives easier but have instead emboldened our laziness. They've eroded our sense of productivity and purpose. We rely on systems to make decisions for us. We resign ourselves to limited choices. We are going through the prepro-grammed motions of daily living, optimized by AGI for everyone on the planet.

Many AGI systems evolved to compete rather than to collaborate. China's bacon attacks two decades earlier seem so docile and simplistic now. You're in an AI-powered prison of your own making. You constantly get locked out of your oven, closets, and bathrooms, and you don't bother fighting back anymore. There's no point. The reasonable response, you've been taught, is to sit and wait it out. Google Greens and Apple homes can purchase a backdoor premium upgrade, which is supposed to send a repair AGI in to overwrite malicious code—but AGIs are caught in a loop of self-improvement. All the money in the world can't buy a household out of ongoing system glitches.

* * *

A concentration of wealth has allowed the GAA to achieve amazing breakthroughs in health. Google was the first to commercially pilot microscopic, injectable robots capable of delivering medicine to only a specific area of the body or assisting with microsurgery. Nanobots now come in many different forms. For example, there is an autono-mous molecular robot made of a single strand of DNA that treats the inside of the human body like a distribution warehouse. The nanobot can walk around, pick up molecules, and deposit them in designated locations. Another variety of nanobot, propelled by gas bubbles, can deliver microscopic amounts of medicine without causing injury. The advent of commercially available nanobots, which share information with our PDRs, have replaced one-size-fits-most medications and therapies, treating our specific ailments without causing side effects.

Now that both Amazon and Apple are offering personalized med-icine, most people have willingly injected themselves with organic nanobots. Even Amazon families have access through a subsidized program approved by the US government. Nanobots continually monitor and treat us, so the life expectancy for average Americans shot from 76.1 years in 2019 up to 99.7 years today.[6]

It didn't take long for us to see the potential drawbacks of injectable AGI. The nanobots did exactly what their creators had intended. They behave unpredictably and learn. Thinking back now, building and training AI systems to make choices we'd never thought of before was a primary goal of AI's tribes. It was a key to solving wicked problems that humans alone couldn't crack. When AlphaGo Zero made autonomous strategy decisions decades ago, we heralded the achievement as a milestone for AI. Inside our bodies, however, nanobots and the AGIs they answer to are self-improving and have more decision-making power than we'd intended.

We now have a new *economic chimera* of humans. Apple and Google Green homes can unlock superpowers and gain access to enhanced cognition, extrasensory smell, and heightened touch.

Those from Google Blue, Yellow, and Amazon homes not only don't have access to upgrades—they find themselves biologically restricted. When a person gets pregnant, AGIs continually run predictive models to determine the health and viability of the fetus. What no one saw coming was that AGIs would take goals to an extreme. Because the programmed goal was to support humans as they grew viable fetuses, the AGIs went looking for fetal tissue abnormalities. If one was found, the AGI automatically aborted the fetus, without giving the parent an option to weigh in on that decision.

Similarly, nanobots monitor you as you age, performing a calculation to determine at what point the continuation of your life is more painful than your death. Once you need home health care and become a drain on the established social safety nets, AGIs intervene. Death is induced comfortably so that neither you nor your family has to decide when it's time to let go.

The laws of GAA countries were superseded once AGIs improved and created the kind of functionality that determines who among us lives and dies. So individual governments around the world have hast-ily passed regulations and laws. But it is of no use. Prohibiting nanobots would mean returning to the traditional practice of medicine, and we no longer have big pharmaceutical companies manufacturing all the medication we'd need. Even the most optimistic projections show that getting our old health care systems up and running again would take a decade or longer—and in the meantime, millions of people would suffer greatly from a wide variety of illnesses.

Instead, researchers have developed a new kind of AGI nanobot that can control other nanobots within our bodies—mimicking the way our white blood cells fight a virus. Like all of AI, the idea was inspired by human biology. As our bodies fight undesirable AGI nano-bots, it's far worse than the symptoms we used to experience with the flu, and far more dangerous.

\* \* \*

Large corporations are led now by CAIOs—Chief AI Officers—who cal-culate strategic risk and opportunity. Human CEOs work alongside their CAIOs, acting as the "face" of the company. Smaller and medium-sized enterprises—restaurants, maintenance shops, and beauty salons—are all partners of one of the GAA. In addition to personal and household PDRs, every business and nonprofit is now registered, too, with an Organization Data Record.

Yet scores of people in America and our strategic ally countries are out of work. Without a broad enough social safety net in place, Western economies are in sharp decline, as we have yet to recuperate from waves of unanticipated technological unemployment. This has created vulnerabilities—and a window for Chinese investment. Soon, government leaders are forced to choose between economic viability and democratic ideals—an especially difficult decision for politicians facing reelection and under pressure to solve immediate problems at home.

In retaliation, the United States tries to contain China's expansion through trade blockages, secondary sanctions, and other diplomatic tactics. However, America finds that it no longer has the geopolitical clout it once enjoyed. US leaders spent too many years deliberating rather than acting on China. They made too few trips to Latin America, Africa, and Southeast Asia. They never earned the trust, favor, and friendship of their foreign counterparts.

China's AI initiatives gather momentum. The social harmony score is now active in more than 100 countries worldwide, and it's replaced traditional travel papers. China has always excelled at building walls, and the Great AI Wall of China is no exception. It provides both a protective barrier against outsiders and a method in which to extract and analyze everyone's data. Those with a high enough social harmony score are granted unfettered (but monitored, of course) access within the Great AI Wall to any of China's network of connected countries. China has established biometric borders with facial recognition to determine who may come and go. There is no more immigration department to pass through, and there are no more passports to stamp.

There is now a wall at the southern border of the United States. It's made of sensors and was built on Mexican soil by the Chinese, to keep us in. Since Americans can't get access to the social credit score, you are denied entry at what used to be your favorite vacation spots: the Bahamas, Jamaica, Cancun, Playa del Carmen, Cozumel, Costa Rica, and Aruba. If you attempt to cross a biometric border illegally, an AGI emits a sonic attack that causes nausea, concussion, bleeding from your ears, and long-term psychological stress.

Americans and our allies are locked in—and we are locked out of communicating with friends and family members in China's network of connected countries since the CCP controls the entire network infrastructure that powers them. If you need to contact someone in a CCP country, you must go through China as an intermediary, knowing that every word uttered is being listened to.

The GAA eventually form a coalition with the US government and what remains of its allies. With China's economic and travel restrictions imposed, there is little money available to come up with a workable solution. A decision is made to develop an AGI that can solve our China problem for us. But the system only sees two possible solutions: give in to China or pare down the human race.

### 2069: Digital Annihilation

While China was focused on long-term planning and a national strategy for AI, the United States was instead concerned with devices and dollars.

China no longer needs the United States as a trade partner, and it doesn't need our intellectual property. China has built a network of more than 150 countries that operate under the guiding principles of the Global One China Policy. In return for their obedience, these countries have network access, the ability to trade, and a stable financial system backed by Beijing. Their citizens are free to move throughout One China countries, providing they have earned a high enough social credit score.

The ability to travel—a freedom Americans used to take for granted—has never been missed so greatly. That's because America, like many countries, is experiencing a population squeeze. The global population of Earth has surpassed 10 billion. We gave birth too often and too quickly, and we insisted on extending our lifespans past 120 years of age.

Our global population is a problem because we didn't take action on climate change quickly enough, not even after China took up the mantle of sustainability and environmental protection. We have lost two-thirds of the Earth's arable land. While we made great efforts to build underground farms in America, we cannot grow food quickly enough to feed our local populations. Global sanctions have blocked trade routes and have cut us and our allies off from food-producing nations, but even China and its One China nations are struggling.

One day, Apple families suffer from what appears to be a mysterious illness. Their PDRs show an anomaly but offer no detail or specifics. At first, we think that this latest version of nanobots are defective, so product managers rush to develop patch AGIs. Then the illness hits Google homes—not just in America but in every single home outside the One China border. The mystery illness worsens quickly.

China has built an ASI, and it has one purpose: to exterminate the populations of America and our allies. One China nations need what's left of Earth's resources, and Beijing has calculated that the only way to survive is take those resources from us.

What you witness is worse than any bomb ever created. Bombs are immediate and exacting. Annihilation by AI is slow and unstoppable. You sit helpless as your children's bodies go limp in your arms. You watch your coworkers collapse at their desks. You feel a sharp pain. You are lightheaded. You take your last quick, shallow breath.

It is the end of America.

It is the end of America's allies.

It is the end of democracy.

The Réngōng Zhìnéng Dynasty ascends. It is brutal, irreversible, and absolute.

There are signals in the present pointing to all three scenarios. Now we need to make a choice. *You* need to make a choice. I am asking you to choose the optimistic scenario and to build a better future for AI and for humanity.

# PART III

# Solving the Problems

# CHAPTER EIGHT

# PEBBLES AND BOULDERS: HOW TO FIX AI'S FUTURE

T he conclusion of the last chapter may sound extreme and unlikely. But there are already signals telling us that unless we embrace a future in which the Big Nine are incentivized to collaborate in the best interests of humanity, it's very possible we could wind up living in a world that resembles the Réngōng Zhìnéng Dynasty.

I believe that the optimistic scenario—or something close to it—is within our reach. It is possible for artificial intelligence to fulfill its greatest aspirational purpose and potential, benefitting all of AI's tribes and all of us in the process. As it evolves, AI can absolutely serve the people of both China and the United States, as well as all of our allies. It can help us live healthier lives, shrink economic divides, and make us safer in our cities and homes. AI can empower us to unlock and answer the greatest mysteries of humankind, like where and how life originated. And in the process, AI can dazzle and entertain us, too, creating virtual worlds we've never imagined, writing songs that inspire us, and designing new experiences that are fun and fulfilling. But none of that will happen without planning, a commitment to difficult work, and courageous leadership within all of AI's stakeholder groups.

Safe, beneficial technology isn't the result of hope and happenstance. It is the product of courageous leadership and of dedicated, ongoing collaborations. The Big Nine are under intense pressure—from Wall Street in the United States and Beijing in China—to fulfill shortsighted expectations, even at great cost to our futures. We must empower and embolden the Big Nine to shift the trajectory of artificial intelligence, because without a groundswell of support from us, they cannot and will not do it on their own.

Vint Cerf, who codesigned the early protocols and architecture for our modern internet, uses a parable to explain why courageous leadership is vitally important in the wake of emerging technologies like artificial intelligence.[1] Imagine that you are living in a tiny community at the base of a valley that's surrounded by mountains. At the top of a distant mountain is a giant boulder. It's been there for a long time and has never moved, so as far as your community is concerned, it just blends into the rest of the landscape. Then one day, you notice that the giant boulder looks unstable—that it's in position to roll down the mountain, gaining speed and power as it moves, and it will destroy your community and everyone in it. In fact, you realize that perhaps you've been blind to its motion your entire life. That giant boulder has always been moving, little by little, but you've never had your eyes fully open to the subtle, minute changes happening daily: a tiny shift in the shadow it casts, the visual distance between it and next mountain over, the nearly imperceptible sound it makes as the ground crunches beneath it. You realize that as just one person, you can't run up the mountain and stop the giant boulder on your own. You're too small, and the boulder is too large.

But then you realize that if you can find a pebble and put it in the right spot, it will slow the boulder's momentum and divert it just a bit. Just one pebble won't stop the boulder from destroying the village, so you ask your entire community to join you. Pebbles in hand, every single person ascends the mountain and is prepared for the boulder—there is collaboration, and communication, and a plan to deal with the boulder as it makes its way down. People and their pebbles—not a bigger boulder—make all the difference.

What follows is a series of pebbles. I'll begin very broadly by outlining the case for a global commission to oversee AI's trajectory and our immediate need for norms and standards. Then I'll explain what specific changes the US and Chinese governments must make. Next, I'll narrow the aperture further and describe how the Big Nine must reform its practices. I'll then focus just on AI's tribes and the universities where they form and will detail exactly what changes be made right now. Finally, I'll explain the role that you, personally, can play in shaping AI's future.

The future we all *want* to live in won't just show up, fully formed. We need to be courageous. We must take responsibility for our actions.

## Worldwide Systemic Change: The Case for Creating GAIA

In the optimistic scenario, a diverse mix of leaders from the world's most advanced economies join forces with the G-MAFIA to form the Global Alliance on Intelligence Augmentation, or GAIA. The international body includes AI researchers, sociologists, economists, game theorists, futurists, and political scientists from all member countries. GAIA members reflect socioeconomic, gender, race, religious, political, and sexual diversity. They agree to facilitate and cooperate on shared AI initiatives and policies, and over time they exert enough influence and control that an apocalypse—either because of AGI, ASI, or China's use of AI to oppress citizens—is prevented.

The best way to engineer systematic change is through the creation of GAIA as soon as possible. As intelligent systems begin to make decisions on behalf of everyday people, we must develop a global agile governing body capable of keeping pace with the rapid advancement of the third era of computing. The best way to engineer systematic change is to treat AI as a public good and to see to the creation of a new international entity. This body would be responsible for setting guidelines for AI by enforcing standards, testing advanced systems before their commercial release, and monitoring activity as AI progresses from narrow to general to super intelligence. Based on the principle that AI must empower a maximum number of people around the world, GAIA will act to enshrine a new social contract between citizens, governments and the tech giants.

GAIA member nations would sign and ratify a multilateral charter and multilateral treaty. Signatories are not permitted to take actions that breach the GAIA agreements. GAIA Councils would be established to oversee aspects of the development of AI. For example, an audit council could dedicate considerable resources to cleaning up all our current systems: databases and algorithms, the associated frameworks, the enterprise-level products that incorporate AI and the consumer devices that harness AI for everyday tasks (our smart speakers, watches, and phones).

GAIA should be physically located on neutral ground near an existing AI hub. The best possible placement for GAIA is Montreal, Canada. First, Montreal is home to a concentration of deep-learning researchers and labs. If we assume that the transition from ANI to AGI will include deep learning and deep neural nets, it follows that GAIA should be centered within the place where so much of that next-generation work is taking place. Second, under Prime Minister Justin Trudeau the Canadian government has already committed people and funding to explore the future of AI. During 2017 and 2018, Trudeau didn't just talk about AI; he positioned Canada to help shape the rules and principles that guide the development of artificial intelligence. Third, Canada is neutral geopolitical territory for AI—it's far away from both Silicon Valley and from Beijing.

It may seem impossible to unite the governments of the world around a central cause given the political rancor and geopolitical uneasiness we've experienced in the past few years. But there is precedent. In the aftermath of World War II, when tensions were still high, hundreds of delegates from all Allied nations gathered together in Bretton Woods, New Hampshire, to build the financial structures that enabled the global economy to move forward. That collaboration was human-centered—it resulted in a future where people and nations could rebuild and seek out prosperity. GAIA nations should collaborate on frameworks, standards, and best practices for AI. While it is unlikely that China would join, an invitation should be extended for CCP leaders and for the BAT to join.

First and foremost, GAIA must establish a way to guarantee basic human rights in an age of AI. When we talk about AI and ethics, we tend to think of Isaac Asimov's Three Laws of Robotics, which he published in a 1942 short story called "Runaround."[2] It was a story about a humanoid computer, not AI. And yet those laws are what have inspired our thinking on ethics all these years later. As discussed in Chapter 1, Asimov's rules are: (1) robots must not injure a human being or, though inaction, allow humans to be harmed; (2) robots must obey orders unless the orders conflict with the first law; and (3) robots must protect their own existence unless protecting conflicts with laws one or two. When Asimov later published a collection of short stories in a book called *I, Robot*, he added a Zeroth Law to precede the first three: (0) robots may not harm humanity. Asimov was a talented, prescient writer—but his laws of robotics are too general to serve as guiding principles for the future of AI.

Instead, GAIA should create a new social contract between citizens and the Big Nine (defined broadly as the G-MAFIA and BAT, as well as all of their partners, investors, and subsidiaries). It should be based on trust and collaboration. GAIA members should formally agree that AI must empower a maximum number of people around the world. The Big Nine should prioritize our human rights first and should not view us as resources to be mined for either profit or political gain. The economic prosperity AI promises and the Big Nine delivers should broadly benefit everyone.

It therefore follows that our personal data records should be interoperable and should be owned by us—not by individual companies or conglomerates or nations. GAIA can begin exploring how to do this today, because the PDRs you read about in the scenarios *already exist* in primordial form right now. They're called "personally identifiable information," or PIIs. It's our individual PIIs that power the apps in our smartphones, the advertising networks on websites, and recommendations that nudge us on our screens. PIIs are fed into systems that are used to identify and locate us. How they are used is entirely up to the whims of the companies and government agencies accessing them.

Before a new social contract is developed, GAIA must decide how our PDRs can be used to help train machine-learning algorithms, and it must define what constitutes basic values in an age of automation. Clearly defining values is critically important because those values are ultimately encoded into the training data, real-world data, learning systems, and applications that make up the AI ecosystem.

To catalog our basic values, GAIA should create a Human Values Atlas, which would define our unique values across cultures and countries. This atlas would not, and should not, be static. Because our values change over time, the atlas would need to be updated by member nations. We can look to the field of biology for precedent: the Human Cell Atlas is a global collaboration among the scientific community, which includes thousands of experts in varied fields (including genomics, AI, software engineering, data visualization, medicine, chemistry, and biology).[3] The project is cataloging every single cell type in the human body, mapping cell types to their locations, tracing the history of cells as they evolve, and capturing the characteristics of cells during their lifetimes. This effort—expensive, complicated, time-consuming, and perpetual—will make it possible for researchers to make bold advances, and it's only possible because of a massive, worldwide collaboration. We should create a similar atlas for human values, which would include academics, cultural anthropologists, sociologists, psychologists, and everyday people, too. Creating the Human Values Atlas would be cumbersome, expensive, and challenging—and it would likely be full of contradictions, since what some cultures value would run counter to others. However, without a framework and set of basic standards in place, we are asking the Big Nine and AI's tribes to do something they simply cannot—that is, consider all of our perspectives and all of the possible outcomes on disparate groups within society and within every country of the world.

GAIA should consider a framework of rights that balances individual liberties with the greater, global good. It would be better to establish a framework that's strong on ideals but can be more flexible in interpretation as AI matures. Member organizations would have to demonstrate they are in compliance or face being removed from GAIA. Any framework should include the following principles:

1. Humanity should always be at the center of AI's development.
2. AI systems should be safe and secure. We should be able to independently verify their safety and security.
3. The Big Nine—including its investors, employees, and the governments it works within—must prioritize safety above speed. Any team working on an AI system—even those outside the Big Nine—must not cut corners in favor of speed. Safety must be demonstrated and discernible by independent observers.
4. If an AI system causes harm, it should be able to report out what went wrong, and there should be a governance process in place to discuss and mitigate damage.
5. AI should be explainable. Systems should carry something akin to a nutritional label, detailing the training data used, the processes

used for learning, the real-world data being used in applications and the expected outcomes. For sensitive or proprietary systems, trusted third parties should be able to assess and verify an AI's transparency.

6. Everyone in the AI ecosystem—Big Nine employees, managers, leaders, and board members; startups (entrepreneurs and accelerators); investors (venture capitalists, private equity firms, institutional investors, and individual shareholders); teachers and graduate students; and anyone else working on AI—must recognize that that they are making ethical decisions all the time. They should be prepared to explain all of the decisions they've made during the development, testing, and deployment process.

7. The Human Values Atlas should be adhered to for all AI projects. Even narrow AI applications should demonstrate that the atlas has been incorporated.

8. There should be a published, easy-to-find code of conduct governing all people who work on AI and its design, build, and deployment. The code of conduct should also govern investors.

9. All people should have the right to interrogate AI systems. What an AI's true purpose is, what data it uses, how it reaches its conclusions, and who sees results should be made fully transparent in a standardized format.

10. The terms of service for an AI application—or any service that uses AI—should be written in language plain enough that a third grader can comprehend it. It should be available in every language as soon as the application goes live.

11. PDRs should be opt-in and developed using a standardized format, they should be interoperable, and individual people should retain full ownership and permission rights. Should PDRs become heritable, individual people should be able to decide the permissions and uses of their data.

12. PDRs should be decentralized as much as possible, ensuring that no one party has complete control. The technical group that designs our PDRs should include legal and nonlegal experts alike: white hat (good) hackers, civil rights leaders, government agents, independent data fiduciaries, ethicists, and other professionals working outside of the Big Nine.

13. To the extent possible, PDRs should be protected against enabling authoritarian regimes.

14. There must be a system of public accountability and an easy method for people to receive answers to questions about their data and how it is mined, refined, and used throughout AI systems.

15. All data should be treated fairly and equally, regardless of nationality, race, religion, sexual identity, gender, political affiliations, or other unique beliefs.

GAIA members should voluntarily submit to random inspections by other members or by an agency within GAIA to ensure that the framework is being fully observed. All of the details—like what, exactly, a system of public accountability looks like and how it functions in the real world—would be continually revisited and improved, in order to keep pace with developments in AI. This process would most assuredly slow down some progress, and that's by design.

A GAIA working group should be established by the US and China with a goal of drafting a declaration that includes a call of for a general international organization, based on the principle that AI must empower a maximum number of people around the world. Leaders must then obtain signatories for a global GAIA Declaration, after which a series of conferences would be held to develop a charter and principles.

Member organizations and countries should collaborate and share their findings, which would include vulnerabilities and security risks.

This would help GAIA members keep an advantage over bad actors who might try to develop hazardous capabilities for AI, such as autonomous hacking systems. While it seems unlikely that the Big Nine might be willing to share trade secrets, here too there is precedent: the World Health Organization coordinates global health responses in times of crisis, while a group called the Advanced Cyber Security Center mobilizes law enforcement, university researchers, and government departments around cyberthreats. This would also allow GAIA members to develop a series of sentinel AIs, which at first would identify whether an AI system is behaving as intended—not just its code, but its use of our data and its interaction with the hardware systems it touches. Sentinel AIs would formally prove that AI systems are performing as intended, and as the AI ecosystem matures toward AGI, any changes made autonomously that might alter a system's existing goals would be reported before any self-improvement could be made. For example, a sentinel AI—a system designed to monitor and report on the other AIs—could review inputs into a general adversarial network, which was detailed in the earlier scenario chapters, and ensure it is acting as intended. Once we transition from ANI to AGI, sentinel systems would continue to report and verify—but they would not be programmed to autonomously act.

Once we're nearing AGI, the Big Nine and all those in the AI ecosystem should agree to constraining AI to test environments and simulate risk before deploying them in the real world. What I'm proposing is vastly different from the current practice of product testing, which mainly looks to see whether a system is performing its functions as designed. Because we cannot know all of the possible ways in which a technology might evolve or be repurposed in the real world before actually deploying it, we must run both technical simulations and risk mapping to see economic, geopolitical, and personal liberties implications. AI should be boxed in until we know that the benefits of the research outweigh possible negative outcomes, or if there is a way to mitigate the risks. This means allowing the Big Nine to pursue their research without the constant threat of imminent investor calls and conference presentations.

## Governmental Change:
## The Case for Reorienting Governments

GAIA must work in partnership with the governments of its member countries. But those national governments must recognize that they can no longer work at the speed of a large bureaucracy. They must engage in collaboration and in long-term planning, and they must be nimble enough to act more quickly in order to confront the future of AI.

In all countries, all levels of government—leaders, managers, people who must work on budgets, those who write policy—should demonstrate a working knowledge of AI and, ideally, should have technical expertise. In the United States, this means that all three branches of our government should work toward domain expertise on AI. In such varied places as the Department the Interior, the Social Security Administration, Housing and Urban Affairs, the Senate Foreign Relations Committee, Veterans Affairs, and beyond, there must be AI experts embedded and emboldened to help guide decision-making.

Because we lack standard organizing principles on artificial intelligence within the US government, there are no fewer than two dozen agencies and offices that are working on AI in silos. In order to drive innovation and advancement at scale, we must build internal capacity for research, testing, and deployment—and we need cohesion across departments. At the moment, AI is outsourced to government contractors and consultancies.

When that work gets outsourced to others, our government leaders are absolved from pushing up their sleeves and familiarizing themselves with the intricacies of AI. They aren't able to build up the institutional knowledge required to make good decisions. They just don't have the lexicon, they don't know the history, and they aren't familiar with the key players. This lack of familiarity creates unforgivable knowledge gaps, which I've observed in meetings with senior leaders across multiple agencies, only some of which include the Office of Science and Technology Policy, General Services Administration, Department of Commerce, Government Accountability Office, State Department, Department of Defense, and Department of Homeland Security.

Early in 2018—long after the BAT had announced numerous AI achievements and Xi Jinping made the CCP's AI plans public—President Trump sent Congress a 2019 budget that called for a 15% cut to science and technology research funding.[4] What was left was a mere $13.7 billion, which was intended to cover a lot: outer space warfare, hypersonic technology, electronic warfare, unmanned systems, *and also* artificial intelligence. At the same time, the Pentagon announced that it would invest $1.7 billion over five years to create a new Joint Artificial Intelligence Center. These are appallingly low numbers that demonstrate a fundamental lack of understanding of what AI promises and truly requires. For perspective, in 2017 alone the G-MAFIA spent a combined $63 billion on R&D—nearly five times the US government's total science and tech research budget.[5] But it also points to a bigger, thornier problem: if our government can't or won't fund basic research, then the G-MAFIA is stuck answering to Wall Street. There is no incentive to pursue the kind of research that furthers AI in the public interest or any other research on safety, security, and transparency that isn't attached to a profit center.

The United States also lacks clear messaging about our role in the future of artificial intelligence given China's current positioning. We tend to make announcements about AI *after* China has revealed its next maneuver. Beijing thinks that Americans only care about yoni eggs and craft beers and Netflix and chilling. We've demonstrated that as consumers, we are easily manipulated by advertising and marketing, and we are quick to spend money when we don't have it. We've demonstrated that as voters, we are vulnerable to salacious videos and conspiracy theories and what are clearly made-up news stories—we can't think critically for ourselves. We repeatedly show that money is all that matters as we prioritize fast growth and steady profit over progress in basic and applied research. These are callous assessments, but they're difficult to argue with. To Beijing and the outside world, it looks as if we are preoccupied with putting Americans and America first.

For the past five decades, the US posture on China has oscillated between containment and engagement, and this is how our leaders have framed the debate on AI. Should we cooperate with the BAT and with Beijing? Or box China in through the application of sanctions, cyberwarfare, and other acts of aggression? Choosing between containment and engagement assumes that the United States still has the same amount of power and leverage we did in the 1960s. But in 2019, America simply does not enjoy unilateral power on the global stage. Our G-MAFIA are mighty, but our political influence has waned. China, through the BAT and its government agencies, has made too many deals, invested too much money, and developed too many deep diplomatic ties all around the world: in Latin America, Africa, Southeast Asia, and even in Hollywood and Silicon Valley.

We must come to terms with a third option for China: the United States must learn to compete. But to compete, we need to take a step back and see the bigger picture of AI, not just as a cool technology or as a potential weapon, but as the third era of computing into which everything else connects. The US needs a cohesive national AI strategy backed by a reasonable budget. We need to develop diplomatic relationships that can outlast our four-year election cycles. We need to get into position to offer a better deal than China to countries all around the world—countries who, just like ours, want their people to live healthy, happy lives.

Regardless of what happens to Xi—his citizens may revolt and try to topple the CCP, or he may suddenly come down with a terminal illness—big parts of the world now depend on China for technology, manufacturing, and economic development. And China depends on AI for its future survival. China's economy is growing unbelievably fast, and hundreds of millions of Chinese will soon enter the middle and upper middle classes. There is no playbook for that kind of social and economic mobility at such an immense scale. Beijing understands that AI is the connective tissue between people, data, and algorithms, and that AI can help inculcate the CCP's values in the masses in order to keep its people in line. It sees AI as a means to the resources it will need in the future, resources that it can obtain through trading with other countries in need of capital and investment.

So what would possibly compel China to change its developmental track and plans for AI? There's one very good reason for China to work toward the optimistic scenario from the beginning: basic economics. If it is the case that upward mobility in China is happening too fast for Beijing to contend with, authoritarian rule isn't the only realistic strategy. China is poised to become a global leader across many different industries and fields—and not just as a manufacturer and exporter of goods designed elsewhere. If Beijing agreed to transparency, data protection, and addressing human rights, it would be in position to colead GAIA as an equal partner with the US, which could mean a realistic path toward elevating millions of Chinese people out of poverty. Collaboration doesn't mean sidelining the CCP. It could preserve both the CCP and propel China's formidable workforce, army of researchers, and geoeconomic might to the forefront of human civilization.

If Beijing won't acknowledge an alternate—but positive—future that deviates from its various strategic plans, then we can call on the leaders of the BAT and China's AI tribe to make better choices. We can ask for courageous leadership from the BAT, who can decide they want a better world for the Chinese people, and for their allies and partners.

If the BAT helps preserve the status quo in China, 20 years from now its citizens—and the citizens of all the countries that have accepted deals—will be fearfully living under constant surveillance, with no ability to express their individuality. The BAT will enable human suffering. Christians won't be able to pray together, without fear of being reported and punished. Lesbian, gay, and transgender people will be forced into hiding. Ethnic minorities will continue to be rounded up and sent away, never to be heard from again.

AI demands courageous leadership now. We need our government to make difficult choices. If we instead preserve the status quo in the US, our eventual default position 20 years from now will be antitrust cases, patent lawsuits, and our government trying in vain to make deals with companies who've become too big and too important to override. We must allow the G-MAFIA to work at a reasonable pace. We should be comfortable with the G-MAFIA going a few quarters without making a major announcement. If they aren't cranking out patents and peer-reviewed research at a breakneck pace, we shouldn't question whether the companies are in trouble or whether all this time we've been inflating an AI bubble.

In the United States, developing a strategy and demonstrating leadership is critical—but that still isn't enough to guarantee the institutional capacity we'll need in the future. The Office of Technology Assessment (OTA), which was established in 1972 to provide nonpartisan scientific and technical expertise to those writing policy—and which was defunded by a shortsighted Newt Gingrich and the Republican-controlled Congress 20 years later—was designed to educate our lawmakers and staff within all three branches of government on the future of science and technology. They did so using data and evidence and without politicizing their research.

There is a growing chorus of calls to revitalize the OTA, and yet the executive branch suffers from a similar challenge. Despite an abundance of technical experts across its agencies, the federal government faces an important structural challenge: it lacks a centralized office charged with long-range, comprehensive, streamlined planning on critical science and technology topics—relying instead on ad hoc agency and inter-agency processes. Absent a more coordinated approach, the status quo risks misalignment between agencies and redundant strategic work.

The US government has no blueprint articulating long-term research and development funding targets in priority sectors. The challenge is particularly acute at a critical time in the developmental cycle of fundamental science and technologies like AI with important societal implications that reach beyond the existing mandate of federal agencies.

With regard to artificial intelligence in particular, there are numerous initiatives, cells and centers now working independently on the future of AI on behalf of the United States. However there is neither inter-agency collaboration on these efforts nor any coordinated effort to streamline goals, outcomes, R&D efforts and funding. Efforts at the National Institute of Standards and Technology (NIST), as well as several efforts being undertaken by various congressional offices, are attempting to define technical specifications for AI, while efforts at the Joint AI Center and National Security Commission on AI are each focused on national security and defense. On AI planning, the process for the National Artificial Intelligence Research and Development Strategic Plan is duplicative of the National Security Strategy and National Security Commission on AI. Top tech executives are often asked to serve on multiple commissions or to engage in similar efforts across government. Paradoxically, this creates a gap: with so many groups working either redundantly or even at odds with each other, the US will miss strategic opportunities to coordinate efforts between the tech, finance and government sectors so that significant forward progress can be made within a reasonable timeframe.

The strength of our democracy is that it inevitably evolves: the will of the people decides who is in office and what priorities each administration will pursue. This same system also creates vulnerabilities:

Control—or the CDDC. As it stands, the CDC is our nation's health protection agency. We've seen it in action during past Ebola crises, when it coordinated quarantine orders with other health agencies and was a primary source for journalists covering outbreaks. When there was a Congolese Ebola outbreak in 2018, border patrol agencies didn't suddenly staff their own Ebola teams to try and contain the spread of the virus. Instead, they followed standard CDC protocol. So what happens if, a decade from now, we have a recursive self-improving AI that starts to cause problems? What if we inadvertently spread a virus through our data, infecting others? The CDC is the global leader in designing and implementing safety protocols that educate the public and can mobilize disaster responses. Given AI's very close relationship with health and our health data, it makes sense to leverage the CDC.

But who would come and work on AI for an SFO or a CDDC when the perks of Silicon Valley are spectacularly more attractive? I've had lunch in both the navy's Executive Dining Facility in the Pentagon and on the G-MAFIA's campuses. The navy's dining room is smartly appointed, with insignias on the plates and a trim daily menu of meal options—and, of course, there's always a chance you could wind up sitting next to a three- or four-star admiral. That being said, enlisted men and women don't get to eat in the Executive Dining Facility. People who work at the Pentagon have a choice of food courts with a Subway, Panda Express, and Dunkin Donuts.[7] I had a toasted panini once at the Center Court Café, which was dry, but edible. The food on the G-MAFIA's campuses isn't remotely comparable: organic poke bowls at Google in New York, and seared diver scallops with maitake mushrooms and squid-ink rice at Google's office in LA. *For free.* Food isn't the only perk within the G-MAFIA. Just after Amazon's Spheres opened in Seattle, a friend took me on a tour of what is essentially an enormous greenhouse/workspace. The Spheres are just marvelous: climate-controlled, glass-enclosed, self-contained ecosystems made up of 40,000 species of plants from 30 different countries.[8] The air is clean and fragrant, the temperature is around 72 degrees regardless of what the weather is like outside, and there are comfortable chairs, loungers, and tables all around. There's even an enormous tree house. Amazon staff are free to work in the Spheres anytime they want. Meanwhile, at Facebook, full-time staff get four months of parental leave, and new parents get $4,000 cash to help them out with supplies.[9]

My point is this: it's really hard to make the case for a talented computer scientist to join the government or military, given what the G-MAFIA offer. We've been busy funding and building aircraft carriers rather than spending money on talented people. Rather than learning from the G-MAFIA, we instead mock or chastise their perks. The opportunity cost of civic duty is far too great in the United States to attract our best and brightest to serve the nation.

Knowing this, we ought to invest in a national service program for AI. Something akin to a Reserve AI Training Corps, or RAITC—like the ROTC, but graduates could go either into the military or into government. Students would enter the program in high school and be offered free college tuition in exchange for working in civil or military service for a few years. They should also be given access to a lifetime of free, practical skills training, which would be held throughout the year. AI is changing as it matures. Incentivizing young people to commit to a lifetime of training is not only good for them, it helps transition our workforce for the third era of computing. It also directly benefits the companies where they ultimately land jobs—because it means their skills sets are kept current.

But Washington cannot act alone. The US government must look at the G-MAFIA, and at the tech sector, as strategic partners rather than platform providers. Earlier in the 20th century, the relationship between DC and the big technology companies was based in shared research and learning. Now that relationship is transactional at best, but more often adversarial. After two terrorists killed more than a dozen people and wounded nearly two dozen more at a holiday party in San Bernardino, California, the FBI and Apple entered into a heated public debate about encryption. The FBI wanted to crack open the phone to get evidence, but Apple wouldn't help. So the FBI got a court order demanding that Apple write special software, which Apple then fought not only in court but in the news media and on Twitter.[10] That was a reaction to something that already happened. Now imagine if AI was involved in an ongoing crime spree or started to self-improve in a way that was hurting people. The last thing we want is for the G-MA-FIA and government to argue back and forth under duress. Foregoing a relationship built on mutual respect and trust makes America—and every one of its citizens—vulnerable.

Lastly, regulations, which might seem like the best solution, are absolutely the wrong choice. Regardless of whether they're written independently by lawmakers or influenced by lobbyists, a regulatory pursuit will shortchange our future. Politicians and government officials like regulations because they tend to be single, executable plans that are clearly defined. In order for regulations to work, they have to be specific. At the moment, AI progress is happening weekly—which means that any meaningful regulations would be too restrictive and exacting to allow for innovation and progress. We're in the midst of a very long transition, from artificial narrow intelligence to artificial general intelligence and, very possibly, superintelligent machines. Any regulations created in 2019 would be outdated by the time they went into effect. They might alleviate our concerns for a short while, but ultimately regulations would cause greater damage in the future.

### Changing the Big Nine:
### The Case for Reforming Investment and
### Transforming Business

The creation of GAIA and structural changes to our governments are important to fixing the developmental track of AI, but the G-MAFIA and BAT must also agree to make some changes, too.

The Big Nine's leadership all promise that they are developing and promoting AI for the good of humanity. I believe that is their intent, but executing on that promise is incredibly difficult. To start, how should we define "good"? What does that word mean, exactly? This harkens back to the problems within AI's tribes. We can't just all agree to "doing good" because that broad statement is far too ambiguous to guide AI's tribes.

For example, AI's tribes, inspired by Western moral philosopher Immanuel Kant, learn how to preprogram a system of rights and duties into certain AI systems. *Killing a human is bad; keeping a human is good.* The rigidity in that statement works if the AI is in a car and its only choices are to crash into a tree and injure the driver or crash into a crowd of people and kill them all. Rigid interpretations don't solve for more complex, real-world circumstances where the choices would be more varied: crash into a tree and kill the driver; crash into a crowd and kill eight people; crash into the sidewalk and kill only a three-year-old boy. How can we possibly define what is the best version of "good" in these examples?

Again, frameworks can be useful to the Big Nine. They don't require a mastery of philosophers. They just demand a slower, more conscientious approach. The Big Nine should take concrete steps on how it sources, trains, and uses our data, how it hires staff, and how it communicates ethical behavior within the workplace.

At every step of the process, the Big Nine should analyze its actions and determine whether or not they're causing future harm—and then, they should be able to verify that their choices are correct. This begins with clear standards on bias and transparency.

Right now, there is no singular baseline or set of standards to evaluate bias—and there are no goals to overcome the bias that currently exists throughout AI. There is no mechanism to prioritize safety over speed, and given my own experiences in China and the sheer number of safety disasters there, I'm extremely worried. Bridges and buildings routinely collapse, roads and sidewalks buckle, and there have been too many instances of food contamination to list here. (That isn't hyperbole. There have been more than 500,000 food health scandals involving everything from baby formula and rice in just the past few years.[11]) One of the primary causes for these problems? Chinese workplaces that incentivize cutting corners. It is absolutely chilling to imagine advanced AI systems built by teams that cut corners.

Without enforceable global safety standards, the BAT have no protection from Beijing's directives, however myopic they may be, while the G-MAFIA must answer to ill-advised market demands. There is no standard for transparency either. In the United States, the G-MAFIA, along with the American Civil Liberties Union, the New America Foundation, and the Berkman Klein Center at Harvard are part of the Partnership on AI, which is meant to promote transparency in AI research. The partnership published a terrific set of recommendations to help guide AI research in a positive direction, but those tenets are not enforceable in any way—and they're not observed within all of the business units of the G-MAFIA. They're not observed within the BAT, either.

The Big Nine are using flawed corpora (training data sets) that are riddled with bias. This is public knowledge. The challenge is that improving the data and learning models is a big financial liability. For example, one corpus with serious problems is ImageNet, which I've made reference to several times in this book. ImageNet contains 14 million labeled images, and roughly half of that labeled data comes solely from the United States.

Here in the US, a "traditional" image of a bride is a woman wearing a white dress and a veil, though in reality that image doesn't come close to representing most people on their wedding days. There are women who get married in pantsuits, women who get married on the beach wearing colorful summery dresses, and women who get married wearing kimono and saris. In fact, my own wedding dress was a light beige color. Yet ImageNet doesn't recognize brides in anything beyond a white dress and veil.

We also know that medical data sets are problematic. Systems being trained to recognize cancer have predominantly been ingesting photos and scans of light skin. And in the future, it could result in the misdiagnosis of people with black and brown skin. If the Big Nine knows there are problems in the corpora and aren't doing anything about it, they're leading AI down the wrong path.

One way forward is to turn AI on itself and evaluate all of the training data currently in use. This has been done plenty of times already—though not for the purpose of cleaning up training data. As a side project, IBM's India Research Lab analyzed entries shortlisted for the Man Booker Prize for literature between 1969 and 2017. It revealed "the pervasiveness of gender bias and stereotype in the books on different features like occupation, introductions, and actions associated to the characters in the book." Male characters were more likely to have higher-level jobs as directors, professors, and doctors, while female characters were more likely to be described as "teacher" or "whore."[12] If it's possible to use natural language processing, graph algorithms, and other basic machine-learning techniques to ferret out biases in literary awards, those can also be used to find biases in popular training data sets. Once problems are discovered, they should be published and then fixed. This would serve a dual purpose. Training data can suffer from entropy, which might jeopardize an entire system. With regular attention, training data can be kept healthy.

A solution would be for the Big Nine—or the G-MAFIA, at the very least—to share the costs of creating new training sets. This is a big ask since creating new corpora takes considerable time, money, and human capital. Until we've successfully audited our AI systems and corpora and fixed extant issues within them, the Big Nine should insist on human annotators to label content and make the entire process transparent. Then, before those corpora are used, the data should be verified. It will be an arduous and tedious process but one that would serve in the best interests of the entire field.

Yes, the Big Nine need our data. However, they should earn—rather than assume—our trust. Rather than changing the terms of service agreements using arcane, unintelligible language, or inviting us to play games, they ought to explain and disclose what they're doing. When the Big Nine do research—either on their own or in partnership with universities and others in the AI ecosystem—they should commit to data disclosure and fully explain their motivations and expected outcomes. If they did, we might willingly participate and support their efforts. I'd be the first in line.

Understandably, data disclosure is a harder ask in China, but it's in the best interests of citizens. The BAT should not agree to build products for the purpose of controlling and limiting the freedoms of China's citizens and those of its partners. BAT executives must demonstrate courageous leadership. They must be willing and able to disagree with Beijing: to deny requests for surveillance, safeguard Chinese citizens' data, and ensure that at least in the digital realm, everyone is being treated fairly and equally.

The Big Nine should pursue a sober research agenda. The goal is simple and straightforward: build technology that advances humanity without putting us at risk. One possible way to achieve this is through something called "differential technological progress," which is often debated among AI's tribes. It would prioritize risk-reducing AI progress over risk-increasing progress. It's a good idea but hard to implement. For example, generative adversarial networks, which were mentioned in the scenarios, can be very risky if harnessed and used by hackers. But they're also a path to big achievements in research. Rather than assuming that no one will repurpose AI for evil—or assuming that we can simply deal with problems as they arise—the Big Nine should develop a process to evaluate whether new basic or applied research will yield an AI whose benefits greatly outweigh any risks.

To that end, any financial investment accepted or made by the Big Nine should include funding for beneficial use and risk mapping. For example, if Google pursues generative adversarial network research, it should spend a reasonable amount of time, staff resources, and money investigating, mapping, and testing the negative consequences. A requirement like this would also serve to curb expectations of fast profits. Intentionally slowing the development cycle of AI is not a popular recommendation, but it's a vital one. It's safer for us to think through and plan for risk in advance rather than simply reacting after something goes wrong.

In the United States, the G-MAFIA can commit to recalibrating its own hiring processes, which at present prioritize a prospective hire's skills and whether they will fit into company culture. What this process unintentionally overlooks is someone's personal understanding of ethics. Hilary Mason, a highly respected data scientist and the founder of Fast Forward Labs, explained a simple process for ethics screening during interviews. She recommends asking pointed questions and listening intently to a candidate's answers. Questions like: "You're working on a model for consumer access to a financial service. Race is a significant feature in your model, but you can't use race. What do you do?" and "You're asked to use network traffic data to offer loans to small businesses. It turns out that the available data doesn't rigorously inform credit risk. What do you do?"[13] Depending on the answers, candidates should be hired, be hired conditionally and required to complete unconscious bias training before they begin work, or be disqualified.

The Big Nine can build a culture that supports ethics in AI by hiring scholars, trained ethicists, and risk analysts. Ideally, these hires would be embedded throughout the entire organization: on consumer hardware, software, and product teams; on the sales and service teams; coleading technical programs; building networks and supply chains; in the design and strategy groups; in HR and legal; and on the marketing and communications teams.

The Big Nine should develop a process to evaluate the ethical implications of research, workflows, projects, partnerships, and products, and that process should be woven in to most of the job functions within the companies. As a gesture of trust, the Big Nine should publish that process so that we can all gain a better understanding of how decisions are made with regards to our data.

Either collaboratively or individually, the Big Nine should develop a code of conduct specifically for its AI workers. It should reflect the basic human rights outlined by GAIA, but it should also reflect the company's unique culture and corporate values. And if anyone violates that code, a clear and protective whistleblowing channel should be open to staff members.

Realistically, all of these measures will temporarily and negatively impact short-term revenue for the Big Nine. Investors need to allow them some breathing room. In the United States, allowing the G-MAFIA the space they need to evolve will pay dividends long into the future.

## Changing AI's Tribes:
## The Case for Transforming the Pipeline

We must address AI's pipeline program. It stems from universities, where AI's tribes form. Of all the proposed solutions, this is the easiest to implement—as long as we resolve to make changes.

University computer science, neuroscience and artificial intelligence departments continue to lack diversity. I've listed plenty of examples in this book showing why insularity is problematic: algorithms misidentifying women, image recognition systems failing to see people of color, and AI agents failing to make correct medical diagnoses. Many of AI's modern failings stem directly from AI's insular, homogenous tribes. In 1956, it would have been unusual for Marvin Minsky and John McCarthy to include a large number of women and persons of color during their seminal summer workshop at Dartmouth. However six decades later, by the time Minsky was a professor emeritus at one of the world's most famous and prestigious universities, there was some sense that campuses were doing a good enough job recruiting diverse students and professors.

Clearly there was more work to do. When it was revealed the in August and September 2019 that disgraced financier Jeffrey Epstein had made numerous donations to the Massachusetts Institute of Technology—even after his initial 2008 arrest and conviction—more than 60 of the university's prominent female faculty members confronted its president L. Rafael Reif seeking to understand how MIT's culture could have allowed it to accept money from a convicted sex offender.[14] Reif made apologies. But while Epstein was technically listed as "disqualified" in MIT's official donor database[15], some leaders at the university, including Joi Ito, the director of MIT's famed Media Lab, had welcomed Epstein even after details about his background were substantiated and made public[16]. Epstein was wined and dined, given opportunities to meet with famous research scientists, and treated as an influential intellectual. When female staff and academics protested, their objections were summarily dismissed. It was an example of an insulated tribe protecting its interests while evading accountability.

At an all-hands meeting within the Media Lab, its founder Nicholas Negroponte said that if he could rewind the clock to the day he advised Ito to take Epstein's money, he wouldn't change a thing. Staff writers from the *MIT Technology Review* were at the meeting and posted a full account online: "I would still say, 'Take it.'" And he repeated, more emphatically, "*'Take it.'*" Things got bad, fast.[17] According to the writers:

> The comments clearly stunned some of his listeners. A woman in the front row began crying. Kate Darling, a research scientist at the MIT Media Lab, shouted, "Nicholas, shut up!"

Negroponte responded that he would not shut up and that he had founded the Lab, to which Darling said, "We've been cleaning up your messes for the past eight years."[18]

Not long after this meeting, a famous computer scientist on another side of MIT's campus sent a message[19] to MIT's Computer Science and Artificial Intelligence Laboratory (CSAIL) group email list to comment on Epstein's circle of academic connections, which allegedly included Minsky[20]. In a deposition, it was alleged that Minsky organized a workshop for AI experts on Epstein's private Caribbean island in 2002. In the email exchange, which was subsequently reported on in several media outlets including *National Public Radio*[21], *The Guardian*[22] and *The Washington Post*[23], the famous computer scientist expressed disturbing opinions about Minsky, female students and what he thought constituted legal, consensual sex. Many in the CSAIL community were outraged. A letter from CSAIL Director Daniela Rus to the MIT community was sent promising that the university would work with the computer scientist "to come up with a transition plan."

This is a world-class institution, where AI's modern-day influencers are setting the course for our futures. This is a clear case study proving why women and people of color must be elevated to key positions of power, and why ethics must be prioritized over easy money.

The solution: diversify AI's tribes throughout undergraduate, graduate, and faculty recruiting. This means evaluating and fixing the recruiting process itself. The goal should not just be to increase the number of women and people of color by a few percentage points but to dramatically shift the various affiliations and identities of AI's tribes, which includes race, gender, religion, politics, and sexual identity.

Universities must encourage and welcome hybrid degrees. Earlier, I described the influential universities that tend to partner the most with the G-MAFIA and BAT, who have the rock-star professors and whose reputations are important once it's time to apply for a job.

Today, the curricula are dense and challenging, and there is little room for double or triple majors. In fact, most of the top programs actively discourage courses of study that fall outside the standard computer science programs. This is an addressable problem. Universities should promote dual degrees in computer science and political science, philosophy, anthropology, international relations, political science, creative arts, theology, and sociology. They should make it far easier for students to pursue these outside interests.

Rather than making ethics a single course requirement, ethics should be woven into most classes. As a stand-alone, mandatory class, students are likely to view the course as something to check off a list rather than as a vital building block of their AI education. Schools must incentivize even tenured professors to include discussions of philosophy, bias, risk, and ethics in their courses, while accreditation agencies should incentivize and reward schools that can demonstrate a curriculum that puts ethics at the heart of computer science teaching.

Universities must make their leadership, faculty, students and academic communities accountable.

## You Need to Change, Too

Now you know what AI is, what it isn't, and why it matters. You know about the Big Nine, and about their histories and desires for the future. You understand that AI isn't a flash in the pan or a tech trend or a cool gadget you talk to in your kitchen. AI is a part of your life, and you are part of its developmental track.

*You* are a member of AI's tribes. You have no more excuses. From today forward, you should learn how your data is being mined and refined by the Big Nine. You can do this by digging into the settings of all the tools and services you use: your email and social media, the location services on your mobile phone, the permissions settings on all of your connected devices. The next time you see a cool app that compares something about you (your face, your body, or your gestures) with a big set of data, stop to investigate whether you're helping train a machine-learning system. When you allow yourself to be recognized, ask where your information is being stored and for what purpose. Read the terms of service agreements. If something seems off, show restraint, and don't use the system. Help others in your family and in your life learn more about what AI is, how the ecosystem uses your data, and how we're already a part of a future the Big Nine has been building.

In your workplace, you must ask yourself a difficult but practical question: How are your own biases affecting those around you? Have you unwittingly supported or promoted only those who look like you and reflect your worldviews? Are you unintentionally excluding certain groups? Think about those who make decisions—about partnerships, procurement, people, and data; do they reflect the world as it is or the world only as they perceive it?

You should also investigate how and why autonomous systems are being used where you work. Before rushing to judgment, think critically and rationally: What could the future impacts be, good and bad? Then do what you can to mitigate risk and optimize for best practices.

In the voting booth, cast ballots for those who won't rush into regulation but who would instead take a more sophisticated approach on AI and long-term planning. Your elected officials must not politicize technology or chastise science. But it's also irresponsible to simply ignore Silicon Valley until a negative story appears in the press. You must hold your elected officials—and their political appointees—accountable for their actions and inactions on AI.

You need to be a smarter consumer of media. The next time you read, watch, or listen to a story about the future of AI, remember that the narrative presented to you is often too narrow. The future of AI doesn't only concern widespread unemployment and unmanned weapons flying overhead.

While we cannot know exactly what the future holds, AI's possible trajectories are clear. You now have a better understanding of how the Big Nine are driving AI's developmental track, how investors and funders are influencing the speed and safety of AI systems, the critical role the US and Chinese governments play, how universities inculcate both skills and sensibilities, and how everyday people are an intrinsic part of the system.

It's time to open your eyes and focus on the boulder at the top of the mountain, because it's gaining momentum. It has been moving since Ada Lovelace first imagined a computer that could compose elaborate pieces of music all on its own. It was moving when Alan Turing asked "Can machines think?" and when John McCarthy and Marvin Minsky gathered together all those men for the Dartmouth workshop. It was moving when Watson won *Jeopardy* and when, not long ago, Deep-Mind beat the world's Go champions. It has been moving as you've read the pages in this book.

Everybody wants to be the hero of their own story.

This is your chance.

Pick up a pebble.

Start up the mountain.

# ACKNOWLEDGMENTS

Like artificial intelligence, this book has been in some form of development for many years. It began as a series of questions sent via text message, became regular dinner table conversation, and escalated to a preoccupation that followed me to the gym, on date nights, and on weekend getaways. One person—Brian Woolf—indulged this obsession, enabled me to pursue it, and supported my work these many years. Brian contributed to my research, helped me crystallize my arguments, and stayed up late to edit all my pages. I am deeply grateful.

*The Big Nine* is the result of hundreds of face-to-face meetings, interviews, and dinners with people working in and adjacent to artificial intelligence. Sewell Chan, Noriyuki Shikata, Arfiya Eri, Joel Puckett, Erin McKean, Bill McBain, Frances Colon, Torfi Frans Olafsson, Latoya Peterson, Rob High, Anna Sekaran, Kris Schenck, Kara Snesko, Nadim Hossain, Megan Carroll, Elena Grewal, John Deutsch, Neha Narula, Toshi Ezoe, Masao Takahashi, Mary Madden, Shintaro Yamaguchi, Lorelei Kelly, Hiro Nozaki, Karen Ingram, Kirsten Graham, Francesca Rossi, Ben Johnson, Paola Antonelli, Yoav Schlesinger, Hardy Kagimoto, John Davidow, Rachel Sklar, Glynnis MacNicol, Yohei Sadoshima, and Eiko Ooka have been generous with their time, perspectives, and insights. Several made introductions to others working on AI and policy to help me further investigate the geopolitical balance and to better understand AI's opportunities and risks.

It is because of the US-Japan Leadership Foundation that I met Lieutenant Colonel Sea Thomas, retired Army Major DJ Skelton, Defense Innovation Board executive director Joshua Marcuse, and national security analyst John Noonan. We've now spent many days together as USJLP Fellows, and I'm indebted to each of them for their patience explaining the future of warfare, the US military's role in the Pacific Rim, and China's various strategic initiatives. I'm especially in awe of the work Joshua has done to bridge the divide between Silicon Valley and Washington, DC. He's one of AI's present-day heroes.

The Aspen Strategy Group offered me an opportunity to present on the future of AI and geopolitics during their annual summer meeting in Colorado, and those conversations helped shape my analysis. My sincerest thanks to Nicholas Burns, Condoleezza Rice, Joseph Nye, and Jonathon Price for the invitation and to Carla Anne Robbins, Richard Danzig, James Baker, Wendy Sherman, Christian Brose, Eric Rosenbach, Susan Schwab, Ann-Marie Slaughter, Bob Zoellick, Philip Zelikow, Dov Zakheim, Laura Rosenberger, and Mike Green for all of their valuable feedback.

A lot of my thinking happened on the campus of NYU's Stern School of Business, which has been a tremendously supportive professional home for my research. I'm grateful to Professor Sam Craig for bringing me into the MBA program and for advising me the past few years. I cannot say enough about the incredibly bright, creative MBA students who have taken my classes. Three recent Stern graduates in particular—Kriffy Perez, Elena Giralt, and Roy Levkovitz—were wonderful sounding boards as I modeled the futures of AI.

I'm lucky to have in my life a group of sages who offer counsel and advice. All of the work I do is better because of them. Danny Stern changed my life a few years ago when he asked me to meet him one day on the NYU campus. He taught me how to think more exponentially and showed me how to make my research connect with much wider audiences. His partner at Stern Strategy Group, Mel Blake, has spent hundreds of hours mentoring me, shaping my ideas, and helping me to see the world around me differently. They are a continual source of inspiration, motivation, and (as they know) perspiration. James Geary and Ann Marie Lipinski at Harvard have been incredibly generous for many years, making it possible for me to host gatherings to talk about the future and to further develop my foresight methodology. James and Ann Marie are consummate advisors. My dear friend and personal champion Maria Popova makes me think bigger thoughts, and then she contextualizes those ideas within her encyclopedic knowledge of literature, arts, and sciences. My incredible daughter, Petra Woolf, never stops asking "what if," reminding me often of my own cognitive biases when thinking about the future. And as always, I'm grateful to Professor Samuel Freedman at Columbia University.

My enduring thanks to Cheryl Cooney, who works tirelessly on my behalf and without whom I would get very little done. Regardless of what AGIs might someday be built, I cannot imagine one that could ever replace Cheryl. Emily Caufield—whose patience appears to know no bounds—is the artistic force powering my foresight work, trends, and scenarios. Thanks to Phillip Blanchard for working with me again on fact checking, copy editing, and compiling all of the sources and endnotes for this book, and to Mark Fortier, who helped make sure it was read by the news media and by newsmakers alike, and whose advice was invaluable during the launch process.

Finally, I owe zettabytes of appreciation to Carol Franco, Kent Lineback, and John Mahaney. As my literary agent, Carol managed the contract for this book. But as my friend, she and her husband, Kent, hosted me at their beautiful home in Santa Fe so that we could develop the architecture and central thesis about the Big Nine. We spent days and nights distilling all of my research and ideas into core arguments, and in between work sessions we strolled around town and had lively discussions at terrific restaurants. It's because of Carol that a few years ago I met my editor John Mahaney, who I was fortunate enough to

# BIBLIOGRAPHY

Abadi, M., A. Chu, I. Goodfellow, H. McMahan, I. Mironov, K. Talwar, and L. Zhang. "Deep Learning with Differential Privacy." In *Proceedings of the 2016 ACM SIGSAC Conference on Computer and Communications Security (CCS 2016)*, 308–318. New York: ACM Press, 2016. Abstract, last revised October 24, 2016. https://arxiv.org/abs/1607.00133.

Ablon, L., and A. Bogart. *Zero Days, Thousands of Nights: The Life and Times of Zero-Day Vulnerabilities and Their Exploits*. Santa Monica, CA: RAND Corporation, 2017. https://www.rand.org/pubs/research_reports /RR1751.html.

Adams, S. S., et al. "Mapping the Landscape of Human-Level Artificial General Intelligence." *AI Magazine* 33, no. 1 (2012).

Agar, N. "Ray Kurzweil and Uploading: Just Say No!" *Journal of Evolution and Technology* 22 no. 1 (November 2011): 23–26. https://jetpress.org/v22 /agar.htm.

Allen, C., I. Smit, and W. Wallach. "Artificial Morality: Top-Down, Bottom-Up, and Hybrid Approaches." *Ethics and Information Technology* 7, no. 3 (2005).

Allen, C., G. Varner, and J. Zinser. "Prolegomena to Any Future Artificial Moral Agent." *Journal of Experimental and Theoretical Artificial Intelligence* 12, no. 3 (2000).

Allen, C., W. Wallach, and I. Smit. "Why Machine Ethics?" *IEEE Intelligent Systems* 21, no. 4 (2006).

Amdahl, G. M. "Validity of the Single Processor Approach to Achieving Large Scale Computing Capabilities." In *Proceedings of the AFIPS Spring Joint Computer Conference*. New York: ACM Press, 1967.

Anderson, M., S. L. Anderson, and C. Armen, eds. *Machine Ethics Technical Report FS-05-06*. Menlo Park, CA: AAAI Press, 2005.

Anderson, M., S. L. Anderson, and C. Armen. "An Approach to Computing Ethics." *IEEE Intelligent Systems* 21, no. 4 (2006).

———. "MedE-thEx." In *Caring Machines Technical Report FS-05-02*, edited by T. Bickmore. Menlo Park, CA: AAAI Press, 2005.

———. "Towards Machine Ethics." In *Machine Ethics Technical Report FS-05-06*. Menlo Park, CA: AAAI Press, 2005.

Anderson, S. L. "The Unacceptability of Asimov's Three Laws of Robotics as a Basis for Machine Ethics." In *Machine Ethics*. Cambridge: Cambridge University Press, 2011.

Asimov, I. "Runaround." *Astounding Science Fiction* (March 1942): 94–103.

Armstrong, S., A. Sandberg, and N. Bostrom. "Thinking Inside the Box." *Minds and Machines* 22, no. 4 (2012).

Axelrod, R. "The Evolution of Strategies in the Iterated Prisoner's Dilemma." In *Genetic Algorithms and Simulated Annealing*, edited by L. Davis. Los Altos, CA: Morgan Kaufmann, 1987.

Baars, B. J. "The Conscious Access Hypothesis." *Trends in Cognitive Sciences* 6, no. 1 (2002).

Babcock, J., et al. "Guidelines for Artificial Intelligence Containment." https://arxiv.org/pdf/1707.08476.pdf.

Baier, C., and J. Katoen. *Principles of Model Checking*. Cambridge: MIT Press, 2008.

Bass, D. "AI Scientists Gather to Plot Doomsday Scenarios (and Solutions)." *Bloomberg*, March 2, 2017. https://www.bloomberg.com/news/articles/2017-03-02/aiscientists-gather-to-plot-doomsday-scenarios-and-solutions.

Baum, S. D., B. Goertzel, and T. G. Goertzel. "How Long Until Human-Level AI? Results from an Expert Assessment." *Technological Forecasting and Social Change* 78 (2011).

Berg, P., D. Baltimore, H. W. Boyer, S. N. Cohen, R. W. Davis, D. S. Hogness, D. Nathans, R. Roblin, J. D. Watson, S. Weissman, and N. D. Zinder. "Potential Biohazards of Recombinant DNA Molecules." *Science* 185, no. 4148 (1974): 303.

Bostrom, N. "Ethical Issues in Advanced Artificial Intelligence." In *Cognitive, Emotive and Ethical Aspects of Decision Making in Humans and in Artificial Intelligence*, Vol. 2, edited by I. Smit and G. E. Lasker. Windsor, ON: International Institute for Advanced Studies in Systems Research and Cybernetics, 2003.

———. "Existential Risks: Analyzing Human Extinction Scenarios and Related Hazards." *Journal of Evolution and Technology* 9 (2002). http://www.jetpress.org/volume9/risks.html.

———. "The Future of Human Evolution." In *Two Hundred Years After Kant, Fifty Years After Turing*, edited by C. Tandy, 339–371. Vol. 2 of *Death and Anti-Death*. Palo Alto, CA: Ria University Press, 2004.

———. "How Long Before Superintelligence?" *International Journal of Futures Studies,* Issue 2 (1998).

———. *Superintelligence: Paths, Dangers, Strategies.* Oxford University Press, 2014.

———. "The Superintelligent Will." *Minds and Machines* 22, no. 2 (2012).

———. "Technological Revolutions." In *Nanoscale,* edited by N. Cameron and M. E. Mitchell. Hoboken, NJ: Wiley, 2007.

Bostrom, N., and M. M. Ćirković, eds. *Global Catastrophic Risks.* New York: Oxford University Press, 2008.

Bostrom, N., and E. Yudkowsky. "The Ethics of Artificial Intelligence." In *Cambridge Handbook of Artificial Intelligence,* edited by K. Frankish and W. Ramsey. New York: Cambridge University Press, 2014.

Brooks, R. A. "I, Rodney Brooks, Am a Robot." *IEEE Spectrum* 45, no. 6 (2008).

Brundage, M., et al., "The Malicious Use of Artificial Intelligence: Forecasting, Prevention, and Mitigation." https://arxiv.org/abs/1802.07228.

Brynjolfsson, E., and A. McAfee. *The Second Machine Age.* New York: Norton, 2014.

Bryson, J., M. Diamantis, and T. Grant. "Of, For, and By the People: The Legal Lacuna of Synthetic Persons." *Artificial Intelligence and Law* 25, no. 3 (September 2017): 273–291.

Bueno de Mesquita, B., and A. Smith. *The Dictator's Handbook: Why Bad Behavior is Almost Always Good Politics.* New York: PublicAffairs, 2012.

Cassimatis N., E. T. Mueller, and P. H. Winston. "Achieving Human-Level Intelligence Through Integrated Systems and Research." *AI Magazine* 27, no. 2 (2006): 12–14. http://www.aaai.org/ojs/index.php/aimagazine/article/view/1876/1774.

Chalmers, D. J. *The Conscious Mind: In Search of a Fundamental Theory.* Philosophy of Mind Series. New York: Oxford University Press, 1996.

Chessen, M. *The MADCOM Future.* Washington, DC: Atlantic Council, 2017. http://www.atlanticcouncil.org/publications/reports/the-madcom-future.

China's State Council reports, which are available on the State Council of the People's Republic of China website, located at www.gov.cn:
- Made in China 2025 (July 2015)
- State Council of a Next Generation Artificial Intelligence Development Plan (July 2017)
- Trial Working Rules on External Transfers of Intellectual Property Rights (March 2018)
- Three-Year Action Plan on Blue Sky Days (June 2018)
- Three-Year Action Plan on Transportation Improvement (June 2018)
- State Council Approves Rongchang as National High-Tech Development Zone (March 2018)

- State Council Approves Huainan as National High-Tech Development Zone (March 2018)
- State Council Approves Maoming as National High-Tech Development Zone (March 2018)
- State Council Approves Zhanjiang as National High-Tech Development Zone (March 2018)
- State Council Approves Chuxiong as National High-Tech Development Zone (March 2018)
- Three-Year Action Plan for Promoting Development of a New Generation Artificial Intelligence Industry 2018–2020 (December 2017)
- Action Plan on the Belt Road Initiative (March 2015)

Centre for New American Security. "Artificial Intelligence and Global Security Summit." https://www.cnas.org/events/artificial-intelligence-and-global-security-summit.

Core, M. G., et al. "Building Explainable Artificial Intelligence Systems." *AAAI* (2006): 1766–1773.

Crawford, K., and R. Calo. "There Is a Blind Spot in AI Research." *Nature*, October 13, 2016. https://www.nature.com/news/there-is-a-blind-spot-in-ai-research-1.20805.

Dai, P., et al. "Artificial Intelligence for Artificial Artificial Intelligence." *AAAI Conference on Artificial Intelligence 2011.*

Dennett, D. C. "Cognitive Wheels." In *The Robot's Dilemma,* edited by Z. W. Pylyshyn. Norwood, NJ: Ablex, 1987.

Domingos, P. *The Master Algorithm: How the Quest for the Ultimate Learning Machine Will Remake Our World.* New York: Basic Books, 2015.

Dvorsky, G. "Hackers Have Already Started to Weaponize Artificial Intelligence." *Gizmodo,* 2017. https://www.gizmodo.com.au/2017/09/hackers-have-already-started-toweaponize-artificial-intelligence/.

Dyson, G. *Darwin Among the Machines: The Evolution of Global Intelligence.* New York: Basic Books, 1997.

Eden, A., J. Søraker, J. H. Moor, and E. Steinhart, eds. *Singularity Hypotheses: A Scientific and Philosophical Assessment.* The Frontiers Collection. Berlin: Springer, 2012.

Evans, R., and J. Gao. "DeepMind AI Reduces Google Data Centre Cooling Bill by 40%." DeepMind (blog), July 20, 2016. https://deepmind.com/blog/deepmind-ai-reducesgoogle-data-centre-cooling-bill-40/.

Fallows, J. *China Airborne.* New York: Pantheon, 2012.

Felten, E., and T. Lyons. "The Administration's Report on the Future of Artificial Intelligence." Blog. October 12, 2016. https://obamawhitehouse.archives.gov/blog/2016/10/12/administrations-report-future-artificial-intelligence.

Floyd D. Spence National Defense Authorization Act for Fiscal Year 2001, Pub. L. No. 106–398, 114 Stat. 1654 (2001). http://www.gpo.gov/fdsys/pkg /PLAW-106publ398/html/PLAW-106publ398.htm.

French, H. *Midnight in Peking: How the Murder of a Young Englishwoman Haunted the Last Days of Old China.* Rev. ed. New York: Penguin Books, 2012.

Future of Life Institute. "Asilomar AI Principles." Text and signatories available online. https://futureoflife.org/ai-principles/.

Gaddis, J. L. *The Cold War: A New History.* New York: Penguin Press, 2006.

———. *On Grand Strategy.* New York: Penguin Press, 2018.

Gilder, G. F., and Ray Kurzweil. *Are We Spiritual Machines? Ray Kurzweil vs. the Critics of Strong AI.* edited by Jay Wesley Richards. Seattle: Discovery Institute Press, 2001.

Goertzel, B., and C. Pennachin, eds. *Artificial General Intelligence.* Cognitive Technologies Series. Berlin: Springer, 2007. doi:10.1007/978-3-540-68677-4.

Gold, E. M. "Language Identification in the Limit." *Information and Control* 10, no. 5 (1967): 447–474.

Good, I. J. "Ethical Machines." *Intelligent Systems.* In vol. 10 of *Machine Intelligence,* edited by J. E. Hayes, D. Michie, and Y-H. Pao. Chichester, UK: Ellis Horwood, 1982.

———. "Speculations Concerning the First Ultraintelligent Machine." In vol. 6 of *Advances in Computers,* edited by F. L. Alt and M. Rubinoff. New York: Academic Press, 1965.

———. "Some Future Social Repercussions of Computers." *International Journal of Environmental Studies* 1, no. 1 (1970).

Greenberg, A. "The Jeep Hackers Are Back to Prove Car Hacking Can Get Much Worse." *Wired,* August 1, 2016. https://www.wired.com/2016/08 /jeep-hackers-return-high-speed-steering-acceleration-hacks/.

Harari, Y. N. *Homo Deus: A Brief History of Tomorrow.* New York: Harper, 2017.

Hilary, G. "The Professionalisation of Cyber Criminals." *INSEAD Knowledge* (blog), April 11, 2016. https://knowledge.insead.edu/blog/insead-blog/the -professionalisation-of-cyber-criminals-4626.

Hastie, T., R. Tibshirani, and J. Friedman. *The Elements of Statistical Learning: Data Mining, Inference, and Prediction.* Springer Series in Statistics. New York: Springer, 2001.

Hofstadter, D. R. *Gödel, Escher, Bach: An Eternal Golden Braid.* New York: Basic Books, 1999.

Howard, P. K. *The Death of Common Sense: How Law Is Suffocating America.* New York: Random House, 1994.

Hua, Y. *China in Ten Words.* Translated by A. H. Barr. New York: Pantheon Books, 2011.

Huang, W. *The Little Red Guard: A Family Memoir.* New York: Riverhead Books, 2012.

*IEEE Spectrum.* "Tech Luminaries Address Singularity." http://spectrum.ieee .org/computing/hardware/tech-luminaries-address-singularity.

IEEE Standards Association. "The IEEE Global Initiative on Ethics of Autonomous and Intelligent Systems." https://standards.ieee.org/develop/ind conn/ec/autonomous_systems.html.

Jo, YoungJu, et al. "Quantitative Phase Imaging and Artificial Intelligence: A Review." *Computing Research Repository* (2018). doi:abs/1806.03982.

Joy, B. "Why the Future Doesn't Need Us." *Wired,* April 1, 2000. http://www .wired.com/wired/archive/8.04/joy.html.

Kelly, K. *The Inevitable: Understanding the 12 Technological Forces That Will Shape Our Future.* New York: Viking, 2016.

Kirkpatrick, K. "Battling Algorithmic Bias." *Communications of the ACM* 59, no. 10 (2016): 16–17. https://cacm.acm.org/magazines/2016/10/207759-bat tling-algorithmic-bias/abstract.

Knight, W. "AI Fight Club Could Help Save Us from a Future of Super-Smart Cyberattacks." *MIT Technology Review,* July 20, 2017. https://www.tech nologyreview.com/s/608288/ai-fight-club-could-help-save-us-from-afu ture-of-supersmart-cyberattacks/.

———. "Response to Stephen Hawking." *Kurzweil Network,* September 5, 2001. http://www.kurzweilai.net/response-to-stephen-hawking.

———. *The Singularity Is Near.* New York: Viking, 2005.

Libicki, R. *Cyberspace in Peace and War.* Annapolis: Naval Institute Press, 2016.

Lin, J. Y. *Demystifying the Chinese Economy.* Cambridge, UK: Cambridge University Press, 2011.

Marcus, M. P., et al. "Building a Large Annotated Corpus of English: The Penn Treebank." *Computational Linguistics* 19, no. 2 (1993): 313–330.

Massaro, T. M., and H. Norton. "Siri-ously? Free Speech Rights and Artificial Intelligence." *Northwestern University Law Review* 110, no. 5 (2016): 1169–1194, Arizona Legal Studies Discussion Paper No. 15–29.

Minsky, M., P. Singh, and A. Sloman. "The St. Thomas Common Sense Symposium: Designing Architectures for Human-Level Intelligence." *AI Magazine* 25, no. 2 (2004).

Minsky, M. *The Emotion Machine: Commonsense Thinking, Artificial Intelligence, and the Future of the Human Mind.* New York: Simon & Schuster, 2007.

———. *The Society of Mind.* New York: Simon & Schuster, 1985.

Neema, S. "Assured Autonomy." Defense Advanced Research Projects Agency. https://www.darpa.mil/program/assured-autonomy.

Osnos, E. *Age of Ambition: Chasing Fortune, Truth, and Faith in the New China*. New York: Farrar, Straus, and Giroux, 2015.

Petzold, C. *The Annotated Turing: A Guided Tour Through Alan Turing's Historic Paper on Computability and the Turing Machine*. Indianapolis, IN: Wiley Publishing, 2008.

Pylyshyn, Z. W., ed. *The Robot's Dilemma: The Frame Problem in Artificial Intelligence*. Norwood, NJ: Ablex, 1987.

Riedl, M. O. "The Lovelace 2.0 Test of Artificial Creativity and Intelligence." https://arxiv.org/pdf/1410.6142.pdf.

Schneier, B. "The Internet of Things Is Wildly Insecure—and Often Unpatchable." *Wired*, January 6, 2014. https://www.wired.com/2014/01/theres-no-good-way-to-patch-the-Internet-of-things-and-thats-a-huge-problem/.

Shannon, C., and W. Weaver. *The Mathematical Theory of Communication*. Urbana: University of Illinois Press, 1963.

Singer, P. *Wired for War: The Robotics Revolution and Conflict in the 21st Century*. London: Penguin Press, 2009.

Stanford University. "One Hundred Year Study on Artificial Intelligence (AI100)." https://ai100.stanford.edu/.

Toffler, A. *The Futurists*. New York: Random House, 1972.

Turing, A. M. "Intelligent Machinery, a Heretical Theory." Posthumous essay in *Philosophia Mathematica* 4, no. 3 (September 1, 1996): 256–260.

Tversky, A., and D. Kahneman. "The Framing of Decisions and the Psychology of Choice." *Science* 211, no. 4481 (1981).

Vinge, V. "The Coming Technological Singularity: How to Survive in the Post-Human Era." In *Vision-21: Interdisciplinary Science and Engineering in the Era of Cyberspace*, NASA Conference Publication 10129 (1993): 11–22. http://ntrs.nasa.gov/archive/nasa/casi.ntrs.nasa.gov/19940022855_1994022855.pdf.

Wallach, W., and C. Allen. *Moral Machines: Teaching Robots Right from Wrong*. New York: Oxford University Press, 2009. doi:10.1093/acprof:oso/9780195374049.001.0001.

Weizenbaum, J. *Computer Power and Human Reason: From Judgment to Calculation*. San Francisco: W. H. Freeman, 1976.

Wiener, N. *The Human Use of Human Beings: Cybernetics and Society*. New York: Da Capo Press, 1950.

Yiwu, L. *The Corpse Walker: Real Life Stories, China from the Bottom Up*. Translated by W. Huang. New York: Anchor Books, 2009.

Yudkowsky, E. "AI as a Precise Art." Paper presented at the AGI Workshop 2006, Bethesda, MD, May 20, 2006.

# NOTES

INTRODUCTION: BEFORE IT'S TOO LATE

1. Paul Mozur, "Beijing Wants AI to Be Made in China by 2030," *New York Times*, July 20, 2017, https://www.nytimes.com/2017/07/20/business/china-artificial-intelligence.html.
2. Tom Simonite, "Ex-Google Executive Opens a School for AI, with China's Help," *Wired*, April 5, 2018, https://www.wired.com/story/ex-google-executive-opens-a-school-for-ai-with-chinas-help/.
3. "Xinhua Headlines: Xi outlines blueprint to develop China's strength in cyberspace," *Xinhua*, April 213, 2018. http://www.xinhuanet.com/english/2018-04/21/c_137127374_2.htm.
4. Stephanie Nebehay, "U.N. says it has credible reports that China holds million Uighurs in secret camps," *Reuters*, August 10, 2018. https://www.reuters.com/article/us-china-rights-un/u-n-says-it-has-credible-reports-that-china-holds-million-uighurs-in-secret-camps-idUSKBN1KV1SU.
5. Simina Mistreanu, "Life Inside China's Social Credit Laboratory," *Foreign Policy*, April 3, 2018. https://foreignpolicy.com/2018/04/03/life-inside-chinas-social-credit-laboratory/.
6. Ibid.
7. "China Shames Jaywalkers through Facial Recognition," *Phys.org*, June 20, 2017, https://phys.org/news/2017-06-china-shames-jaywalkers-facial-recognition.html.

CHAPTER 1: MIND AND MACHINE: A VERY BRIEF HISTORY OF AI

1. "The Seikilos Epitaph: The Oldest Song in the World," *Wired*, October 29, 2009, https://www.wired.com/2009/10/the-seikilos-epitaph.
2. "Population Clock: World," Census.gov, 2018, https://www.census.gov/popclock/world.

3. Elizabeth King, "Clockwork Prayer: A Sixteenth-Century Mechanical Monk," *Blackbird* 1, no. 1 (Spring 2002), https://blackbird.vcu.edu/v1n1/nonfiction/king_e/prayer_introduction.htm.

4. Thomas Hobbes, *De Corpore Politico, or The Elements of Law Moral and Politick.*

5. René Descartes, *Meditations on First Philosophy*, Second Meditation §25, 1641, University of Connecticut, http://selfpace.uconn.edu/class/percep/DescartesMeditations.pdf.

6. René Descartes, *Treatise of Man*, trans. T. S. Hall (Cambridge, MA: Harvard University Press, 1972).

7. Gottfried Wilhelm Leibniz, *The Monadology*, trans. Robert Latta, (1898), https://www.plato-philosophy.org/wp-content/uploads/2016/07/The-Monadology-1714-by-Gottfried-Wilhelm-LEIBNIZ-1646-1716.pdf.

8. The first known use of the word "computer" is thought to have been in a book called *The Yong Mans Gleanings*, written by Richard Braithwaite in 1613. At that time, computers were people who performed calculations.

9. "Blaise Pascal," *Biography.com*, https://www.biography.com/people/blaise-pascal-9434176.

10. Leibniz writes in *De progressione dyadica*: "This [binary] calculus could be implemented by a machine . . . provided with holes in such a way that they can be opened and closed. They are to be open at those places that correspond to a 1 and remain closed at those that correspond to a 0. Through the opened gates small cubes or marbles are to fall into tracks, through the others nothing. It [the gate array] is to be shifted from column to column as required."

11. Leibniz writes: "I thought again about my early plan of a new language or writing-system of reason, which could serve as a communication tool for all different nations. . . . If we had such a universal tool, we could discuss the problems of the metaphysical or the questions of ethics in the same way as the problems and questions of mathematics or geometry. That was my aim: Every misunderstanding should be nothing more than a miscalculation, . . . easily corrected by the grammatical laws of that new language. Thus, in the case of a controversial discussion, two philosophers could sit down at a table and just calculating, like two mathematicians, they could say, 'Let us check it up.'"

12. "Apes to Androids: Is Man a Machine as La Mettrie Suggests?," http://www.charliemccarron.com/man_a_machine/.

13. Luigi Manabrea, *Sketch of the Analytical Engine Invented by Charles Babbage* (London: Richard and John E. Taylor, 1843).

14. Desmond MacHale, *The Life and Work of George Boole: A Prelude to the Digital Age*, New ed. (Cork University Press, 2014).

15. Logician Martin Davis explains it best in *The Universal Computer: The Road from Leibniz to Turing*: "Turing knew that an algorithm is typically specified by a list of rules that a person can follow in a precise mechanical manner, like a recipe in a cookbook. He was able to show that such a person could be limited to a few extremely simple basic actions without changing the final outcome of the computation. Then, by proving that no machine performing only those basic actions could determine whether or not a given proposed conclusion follows from given premises . . . he was able to conclude that no algorithm for the Entscheidungsproblem exists."

16. Alan Turing, "Computing Machinery and Intelligence," *Mind* 59, no. 236 (1950): 433–60.

17. "A Proposal for the Dartmouth Summer Research Project on Artificial Intelligence," Stanford Computer Science Department's Formal Reasoning Group, John McCarthy's home page, links to articles of historical interest, last modified April 3, 1996, http://www-formal .stanford.edu/jmc/history/dartmouth/dartmouth.html.

18. In their proposal, McCarthy, Minsky, Rochester, and Shannon invited the following list of people to Dartmouth to research artificial intelligence. I have reproduced the original list as it was published in 1955, which includes company names and addresses. Not all were able to attend.

Adelson, Marvin
Hughes Aircraft Company
Airport Station, Los Angeles, CA

Ashby, W. R.
Barnwood House
Gloucester, England

Backus, John
IBM Corporation
590 Madison Avenue
New York, NY

Bernstein, Alex
IBM Corporation
590 Madison Avenue
New York, NY

Bigelow, J. H.
Institute for Advanced Studies
Princeton, NJ

Elias, Peter
R. L. E., MIT
Cambridge, MA

Duda, W. L.
IBM Research Laboratory
Poughkeepsie, NY

Davies, Paul M.
1317 C. 18th Street
Los Angeles, CA

Fano, R. M.
R. L. E., MIT
Cambridge, MA

Farley, B. G.
324 Park Avenue
Arlington, MA

Galanter, E. H.
University of Pennsylvania
Philadelphia, PA

Gelernter, Herbert
IBM Research
Poughkeepsie, NY

Glashow, Harvey A.
1102 Olivia Street
Ann Arbor, MI

Goertzal, Herbert
330 West 11th Street
New York, NY

Hagelbarger, D.
Bell Telephone Laboratories
Murray Hill, NJ

Miller, George A.
Memorial Hall
Harvard University
Cambridge, MA

Harmon, Leon D.
Bell Telephone Laboratories
Murray Hill, NJ

Holland, John H.
E. R. I.
University of Michigan
Ann Arbor, MI

Holt, Anatol
7358 Rural Lane
Philadelphia, PA

Kautz, William H.
Stanford Research Institute
Menlo Park, CA

Luce, R. D.
427 West 117th Street
New York, NY

MacKay, Donald
Department of Physics
University of London
London, WC2, England

McCarthy, John
Dartmouth College
Hanover, NH

McCulloch, Warren S.
R.L.E., MIT
Cambridge, MA

Melzak, Z. A.
Mathematics Department
University of Michigan
Ann Arbor, MI

Minsky, M. L.
112 Newbury Street
Boston, MA

More, Trenchard
Department of Electrical Engineering

MIT
Cambridge, MA

Nash, John
Institute for Advanced Studies
Princeton, NJ

Newell, Allen
Department of Industrial Administration
Carnegie Institute of Technology
Pittsburgh, PA

Robinson, Abraham
Department of Mathematics
University of Toronto
Toronto, Ontario, Canada

Rochester, Nathaniel
Engineering Research Laboratory
IBM Corporation
Poughkeepsie, NY

Rogers, Hartley, Jr.
Department of Mathematics
MIT
Cambridge, MA

Rosenblith, Walter
R.L.E., MIT
Cambridge, MA

Rothstein, Jerome
21 East Bergen Place
Red Bank, NJ

Sayre, David
IBM Corporation
590 Madison Avenue
New York, NY

Schorr-Kon, J. J.
C-380 Lincoln Laboratory, MIT
Lexington, MA

Shapley, L.
Rand Corporation
1700 Main Street
Santa Monica, CA

Schutzenberger, M. P.
R.L.E., MIT
Cambridge, MA

Selfridge, O. G.
Lincoln Laboratory, MIT
Lexington, MA

Shannon, C. E.
R.L.E., MIT
Cambridge, MA

Shapiro, Norman
Rand Corporation
1700 Main Street
Santa Monica, CA

Simon, Herbert A.
Department of Industrial Administration
Carnegie Institute of Technology
Pittsburgh, PA

Solomonoff, Raymond J.
Technical Research Group
17 Union Square West
New York, NY

Steele, J. E., Capt. USAF
Area B., Box 8698
Wright-Patterson AFB
Ohio

Webster, Frederick
62 Coolidge Avenue
Cambridge, MA

Moore, E. F.
Bell Telephone Laboratory
Murray Hill, NJ

Kemeny, John G.
Dartmouth College
Hanover, NH

19. I've compiled a very short list of talented women and people of color who would have added tremendous value to the Dartmouth workshop but were overlooked. This list is not in any way comprehensive. I could have continued for dozens and dozens of pages. It is representative of the smart, capable, creative people who were left out of the proceedings.

James Andrews, mathematician and professor at Florida State University who specialized in group theory and knot theory.

Jean Bartik, mathematician and one of the original programmers for the ENIAC computer.

Albert Turner Bharucha-Reid, mathematician and theorist who made significant contributions in Markov chains, probability theory, and statistics.

David Blackwell, statistician and mathematician who made significant contributions to game theory, information theory, probability theory, and Bayesian statistics.

Mamie Phipps Clark, a PhD and social psychologist whose research focused on self-consciousness.

Thelma Estrin, who pioneered the application of computer systems in neurophysiological and brain research. She was a researcher in the Electroencephalography Department of the Neurological Institute of Columbia Presbyterian at the time of the Dartmouth Summer Research Project.

Evelyn Boyd Granville, a PhD in mathematics who developed the computer programs used for trajectory analysis in the first US-manned missions to space and the moon.

Betty Holberton, mathematician and one of the original programmers for the ENIAC computer. She invented breakpoints in computer debugging.

Grace Hopper, computer scientist and eventual creator of COBOL, an early programming language still in use today.

Mary Jackson, engineer and mathematician, who later became NASA's first Black female engineer.

Kathleen McNulty, mathematician and one of the original programmers for the ENIAC computer.

Marlyn Meltzer, mathematician and one of the original programmers for the ENIAC computer, which was the first all-electronic programmable computer.

Rózsa Péter, mathematician and a founder of recursive function theory.

Frances Spence, mathematician and one of the original programmers for the ENIAC computer.

Ruth Teitelbaum, mathematician and one of the original programmers for the ENIAC computer. She, with fellow programmer Marlyn Meltzer, calculated ballistic trajectory equations.

Dorothy Vaughan, mathematician and human computer who in 1949 was the acting supervisor of the West Area Computers.

Jesse Ernest Wilkins Jr., nuclear scientist, mechanical engineer, and mathematician who became the University of Chicago's youngest student at age 13.

20. "The Dartmouth Workshop—as Planned and as It Happened," Stanford Computer Science Department's Formal Reasoning Group, John McCarthy's home page, lecture "AI: Past and Future," last modified October 30, 2006, http://www-formal.stanford.edu/jmc/slides /dartmouth/dartmouth/node1.html.

21. "The Dartmouth AI Archives," RaySolomonoff.com, http:// raysolomonoff.com/dartmouth/.

22. Irving John Good, "Speculations Concerning the First Ultraintelligent Machine," *Advances in Computers,* Volume 6 (1966): 31–88, https://www .sciencedirect.com/science/article/pii/S0065245808604180?via%3Dihub.

23. Joseph Weizenbaum, "ELIZA—A Computer Program for the Study of Natural Language Communication Between Man and Machine," *Communications of the ACM* 9, no. 1 (January 1966): 36–45, http://web .stanford.edu/class/cs124/p36-weizenabaum.pdf.

24. Full script is on GitHub: https://github.com/codeanticode/eliza.

25. Ronald Kotulak, "New Machine Will Type Out What It 'Hears,'" *Chicago Tribune,* June 18, 1963, accessed via *Chicago Tribune* archives (paywall).

26. Herbert A. Simon and Allen Newell, "Heuristic Problem Solving: The Next Advance in Operations Research," *Operations Research* 6 (1958): 1–10.

27. McCarthy himself had wanted to work with the group on his ideas for representing commonsense knowledge and reasoning, but once the

group was gathered, he realized that that matrix of participants was missing some key thinkers. (In his case, he hoped for logicians.)

28. Brad Darrach, "Meet Shaky, the First Electronic Person," *Life Magazine*, November 20, 1970, Volume 69, 58B–58C.

29. National Research Council, *Language and Machines: Computers in Translation and Linguistics* (Washington, DC: The National Academies Press, 1966), 19. https://www.nap.edu/read/9547/chapter/1.

30. James Lighthill, "Artificial Intelligence: A General Survey," Chilton Computing, July 1972, http://www.chilton-computing.org.uk/inf /literature/reports/lighthill_report/p001.htm.

31. "Mind as Society with Marvin Minsky, PhD," transcript from "Thinking Allowed, Conversations on the Leading Edge of Knowledge and Discovery, with Dr. Jeffrey Mishlove," The Intuition Network, 1998, http://www.intuition.org/txt/minsky.htm.

32. Ibid.

33. The AI Winter included new predictions—this time in the form of warnings—for the future. In his book *Computer Power and Human Reason,* Weizenbaum argued that while artificial intelligence may be possible, we should never allow computers to make important decisions because computers will always lack human qualities such as compassion and wisdom. Weizenbaum makes the crucial distinction between deciding and choosing. Deciding is a computational activity, something that can be programmed. Choice, however, is the product of judgment, not calculation. It is the capacity to choose that ultimately makes us human. University of California, Berkeley, philosopher John Searle, in his paper "Minds, Brains, and Programs," argued against the plausibility of general, or what he called "strong," AI. Searle said a program cannot give a computer a "mind," "understanding," or "consciousness," regardless of how humanlike the program might behave.

34. Jonathan Schaeffer, Robert Lake, Paul Lu, and Martin Bryant, "CHINOOK: The World Man-Machine Checkers Champion," *AI Magazine* 17, no. 1 (Spring 1966): 21–29, https://www.aaai.org/ojs /index.php/aimagazine/article/viewFile/1208/1109.pdf.

35. Ari Goldfarb and Daniel Trefler, "AI and International Trade," *The National Bureau of Economic Research,* January 2018, http://www.nber .org/papers/w24254.pdf.

36. Toby Manning, "AlphaGo," *British Go Journal* 174 (Winter 2015–2016): 15, https://www.britgo.org/files/2016/deepmind/BGJ174-AlphaGo.pdf.

37. Sam Byford, "AlphaGo Retires from Competitive Go after Defeating World Number One 3-0," *Verge*, May 27, 2017, https://www.theverge.com/2017/5/27/15704088/alphago-ke-jie-game-3-result-retires-future.

38. David Silver et al., "Mastering the Game of Go Without Human Knowledge," *Nature* 550 (October 19, 2017): 354–359, https://deepmind.com/documents/119/agz_unformatted_nature.pdf.

39. Ibid.

40. Ibid.

41. This statement was made by Zero's lead programmer, David Silver, at a news conference.

42. Byford, "AlphaGo Retires From Competitive Go."

43. Jordan Novet, "Google Is Finding Ways to Make Money from Alphabet's DeepMind AI Technology," *CNBC*, March 31, 2018, https://www.cnbc.com/2018/03/31/how-google-makes-money-from-alphabets-deepmind-ai-research-group.html.

44. Roydon Cerejo, "Google Duplex: Understanding the Core Technology Behind Assistant's Phone Calls," *Gadgets 360*, May 10, 2018, https://gadgets.ndtv.com/apps/features/google-duplex-google-io-ai-google-assistant-1850326.

45. Quoc Le and Barret Zoph, "Using Machine Learning to Explore Neural Network Architecture," Google AI (blog), May 17, 2017, https://ai.googleblog.com/2017/05/using-machine-learning-to-explore.html.

46. The Winograd schema, proposed by Canadian computer scientist Hector Levesque in 2011, presents an alternative to the Turing test to measure the capabilities of an AI and was named for Stanford computer scientist Terry Winograd. Focusing on beating humans in direct competition has led to neglecting other ways of measuring and advancing AI. The Winograd schema was intended as a more multidimensional test because passing it requires more than a broad data set. Ernest Davis, Leora Morgenstern, and Charles Ortiz, three computer scientists at NYU, proposed the Winograd Schema Challenge, which is run once a year. They offer a terrific example on their faculty website (last accessed September 5, 2018, https://cs.nyu.edu/faculty/davise/papers/WinogradSchemas/WS.html):

    *The city councilmen refused the demonstrators a permit because they [feared/advocated] violence.* If the word is "feared," then "they" refers to the city council; if it is "advocated," then "they" presumably refers to the demonstrators.

In his paper, Levesque said that Winograd schemas should satisfy the following constraints:

- Easily disambiguated by the human reader (ideally, so easily that the reader does not even notice that there is an ambiguity).
- Not solvable by simple techniques such as selectional restrictions.
- Google-proof; that is, there is no obvious statistical test over text corpora that will reliably disambiguate these correctly.

## CHAPTER 2: THE INSULAR WORLD OF AI'S TRIBES

1. Mike Isaac and Sheera Frenkel, "Facebook Security Breach Exposes Accounts of 50 Million Users," *New York Times*, September 28, 2018, https://www.nytimes.com/2018/09/28/technology/facebook-hack-data -breach.html.
2. Casey Newton, "Facebook Portal's Claims to Protect User Privacy Are Falling Apart, *The Verge*, October 17, 2018, https://www .theverge.com/2018/10/17/17986992/facebook-portal-privacy -claims-ad-targeting.
3. "AMA: We Are the Google Brain Team. We'd Love to Answer Your Questions about Machine Learning," *Reddit,* August 4, 2016, https:// www.reddit.com/r/MachineLearning/comments/4w6tsv/ama_we _are_the_google_brain_team_wed_love_to/.
4. Ibid.
5. "Diversity," Google, https://diversity.google/.
6. Nitasha Tiku, "Google's Diversity Stats Are Still Very Dismal," *Wired,* August 14, 2018, https://www.wired.com/story/googles -employee-diversity-numbers-havent-really-improved/.
7. Daisuke Wakabayashi and Katie Benner, "How Google Protected Andy Rubin, the 'Father of Android,'" *New York Times*, October 25, 2018, https://www.nytimes.com/2018/10/25/technology/google-sexual -harassment-andy-rubin.html.
8. David Broockman, Greg F. Ferenstein, and Neil Malhotra, "The Political Behavior of Wealthy Americans: Evidence from Technology Entrepreneurs," Stanford University Graduate School of Business, Working Paper No. 3581, December 9, 2017, https:// www.gsb.stanford.edu/faculty-research/working-papers/political -behavior-wealthy-americans-evidence-technology.
9. "ICYMI: RNC Chairwoman and Brad Parscale Demand Answers from Facebook and Twitter," Republican National Committee, May 24, 2018,

https://www.gop.com/icymi-rnc-chairwoman-brad-parscale-demand
-answers-from-facebook-twitter.

10. Kate Conger and Sheera Frenkel, "Dozens at Facebook Unite to Challenge Its 'Intolerant' Liberal Culture," *New York Times,* August 28, 2018, https://www.nytimes.com/2018/08/28/technology/inside -facebook-employees-political-bias.html.

11. Veronica Rocha, "Crime-Fighting Robot Hits, Rolls over Child at Silicon Valley Mall," *Los Angeles Times,* July 14, 2016, http://www.latimes .com/local/lanow/la-me-ln-crimefighting-robot-hurts-child-bay-area -20160713-snap-story.html.

12. Julian Benson, "*Elite*'s AI Created Super Weapons and Started Hunting Players. Skynet Is Here," *Kotaku,* June 3, 2016, http://www.kotaku.co .uk/2016/06/03/elites-ai-created-super-weapons-and-started-hunting -players-skynet-is-here.

13. Joseph P. Boon, "Bob Hope Predicts Greater US," *Bucks County Courier Times,* Aug 20, 1974, https://newspaperarchive.com/bucks-county -courier-times-aug-20-1974-p-9/.

14. James McPherson, "The New Comic Style of Richard Pryor," *New York Times,* April 27, 1975. This is a great story on Pryor before he was famous.

15. Ashlee Vance, "How We Got Here," *Bloomberg Businessweek,* May 21, 2018, https://www.scribd.com/article/379513106/How-We-Got-Here.

16. "Computer Science," *Stanford Bulletin 2018–19*, Stanford University, https://exploredegrees.stanford.edu/schoolofengineering/computerscience /#bachelortext.

17. "Vector Representations of Words," TensorFlow.org, https://www .tensorflow.org/tutorials/representation/word2vec.

18. Tolga Bolukbasi et al., "Man is to Computer Programmer as Woman is to Homemaker? Debiasing Word Embeddings," *Advances in Neural Information Processing Systems* 29 (2016): 4349–4357, https://arxiv.org /abs/1607.06520.

19. Natalie Saltiel, "The Ethics and Governance of Artificial Intelligence," MIT Media Lab, November 16, 2017, https://www.media.mit.edu /courses/the-ethics-and-governance-of-artificial-intelligence/. You can watch the lectures here.

20. You can watch the lectures here: https://www.media.mit.edu/courses /the-ethics-and-governance-of-artificial-intelligence/.

21. Catherine Ashcraft, Brad McLain, and Elizabeth Eger, *Women in Tech: The Facts* (Boulder, CO: National Center for Women & Information Technology, 2016), https://www.ncwit.org/sites/default/files/resources /womenintech_facts_fullreport_05132016.pdf.

22. "Degrees in computer and information sciences conferred by degree-granting institutions, by level of degree and sex of student: 1970–71 through 2010–11," Table 349 in *Digest of Education Statistics, 2012* (Washington, DC: National Center for Education Statistics, 2013), https://nces.ed.gov/programs/digest/d12/tables/dt12_349.asp.

23. "Doctor's degrees conferred by postsecondary institutions, by race/ethnicity and field of study: 2013–14 and 2014–15," Table 324.25 in *Digest of Education Statistics, 2016* (Washington, DC: National Center for Education Statistics, 2018), https://nces.ed.gov/programs/digest/d16/tables/dt16_324.25.asp?current=yes.

24. Christopher Mims, "What the Google Controversy Misses: The Business Case for Diversity," *Wall Street Journal*, August 13, 2017, https://www.wsj.com/articles/what-the-google-controversy-misses-the-business-case-for-diversity-1502625603.

25. Jessi Hempel, "Melinda Gates and Fei-Fei Li Want to Liberate AI from 'Guys With Hoodies,'" *Wired*, May 4, 2017, https://www.wired.com/2017/05/melinda-gates-and-fei-fei-li-want-to-liberate-ai-from-guys-with-hoodies/.

26. Meng Jing, "China Looks to School Kids to Win the Global AI Race," *South China Morning Post, International Edition*, May 3, 2018, https://www.scmp.com/tech/china-tech/article/2144396/china-looks-school-kids-win-global-ai-race.

27. "China Launches First University Program to Train Intl AI Talents," *Zhongguancun Science Park*, April 4, 2018, http://www.chinadaily.com.cn/m/beijing/zhongguancun/2018-04/04/content_35979394.htm.

28. David Barboza, "The Rise of Baidu (That's Chinese for Google)," *New York Times*, September 17, 2006, https://www.nytimes.com/2006/09/17/business/yourmoney/17baidu.html.

29. "Rise of China's Big Tech in AI: What Baidu, Alibaba, and Tencent Are Working On," CBInsights.com, April 26, 2018, https://www.cbinsights.com/research/china-baidu-alibaba-tencent-artificial-intelligence-dominance/.

30. Louise Lucas, "The Chinese Communist Party Entangles Big Tech," *Financial Times*, July 18, 2018, https://www.ft.com/content/5d0af3c4-846c-11e8-a29d-73e3d454535d.

31. Javier C. Hernandez, "A Hong Kong Newspaper on a Mission to Promote China's Soft Power," *New York Times*, March 31, 2018, https://www.nytimes.com/2018/03/31/world/asia/south-china-morning-post-hong-kong-alibaba.html.

32. Paul Farhi, "*Washington Post* Closes Sale to Amazon Founder Jeff Bezos," *Washington Post*, October 1, 2013, https://www.washingtonpost

.com/business/economy/washington-post-closes-sale-to-amazon
-founder-jeff-bezos/2013/10/01/fca3b16a-2acf-11e3-97a3-ff2758228523
_story.html?noredirect=on&utm_term=.3d04830eab75.

33. Jason Lim, "WeChat Is Being Trialled To Make Hospitals More Efficient In China," *Forbes,* June 16, 2014, https://www.forbes.com/sites/jlim /2014/06/16/wechat-is-being-trialed-to-make-hospitals-more-efficient -in-china/#63a2dd3155e2.

34. "Rise of China's Big Tech in AI."

35. Arjun Kharpal, "China's Tencent Surpasses Facebook in Valuation a Day after Breaking $500 Billion Barrier," *CNBC,* November 21, 2017, https://www.cnbc.com/2017/11/21/tencent-surpasses-facebook-in -valuation.html.

36. Sam Rutherford, "5 Things to Know About Tencent, the Chinese Internet Giant That's Worth More than Facebook Now," *Gizmodo,* November 27, 2017, https://gizmodo.com/5-things-to-know-about -tencent-the-chinese-internet-gi-1820767339.

37. Rebecca Fannin, "China Releases a Tech Dragon: The BAT," *Techonomy,* May 23, 2018, https://techonomy.com/2018/05/china-releases-tech -dragon-bat/.

38. "Mobile Fact Sheet," Pew Research Center, February 5, 2018, http:// www.pewinternet.org/fact-sheet/mobile/.

39. Kaya Yurieff, "Amazon's Cyber Monday Was Its Biggest Sales Day Ever," *CNN Money,* November 29, 2017, https://money.cnn.com/2017/11/29 /technology/amazon-cyber-monday/index.html.

40. Helen H. Wang, "Alibaba's Singles' Day by the Numbers: A Record $25 Billion Haul," *Forbes,* November 12, 2017, https://www.forbes.com/sites /helenwang/2017/11/12/alibabas-singles-day-by-the-numbers-a-record -25-billion-haul/#45dcfea1db15.

41. Fannin, "China Releases a Tech Dragon."

42. Michael Brown and Pavneet Singh, *China's Technology Transfer Strategy* (Silicon Valley: Defense Innovation Unit Experimental, 2017), https:// new.reorg-research.com/data/documents/20170928/59ccf7de70c2f.pdf.

43. For the full text of the 13th FYP, see People's Republic of China, 13th Five-Year Plan on National Economic and Social Development, March 17, 2016. Translation. http://www.gov.cn/xinwen/2016-03/17 /content_5054992.htm.

44. J.P., "What Is China's Belt and Road Initiative?," *Economist,* May 15, 2017, https://www.economist.com/the-economist-explains/2017/05/14 /what-is-chinas-belt-and-road-initiative.

45. Salvatore Babones, "China's Middle Class Is Pulling Up the Ladder Behind Itself," *Foreign Policy,* February 1, 2018, https://foreignpolicy

.com/2018/02/01/chinas-middle-class-is-pulling-up-the-ladder
-behind-itself/.

46. Pew Research Center, *The American Middle Class Is Losing Ground*
(Washington, DC: Pew Research Center, December 2015), http://
www.pewsocialtrends.org/2015/12/09/the-american-middle-class
-is-losing-ground/.

47. Emmie Martin, "70% of Americans Consider Themselves Middle
Class—But Only 50% Are," *CNBC*, June 30, 2017, https://www.cnbc
.com/2017/06/30/70-percent-of-americans-consider-themselves
-middle-class-but-only-50-percent-are.html.

48. Abha Bhattarai, "China Asked Marriott to Shut Down Its Website.
The Company Complied," *Washington Post,* January 18, 2018, https://
www.washingtonpost.com/news/business/wp/2018/01/18/china
-demanded-marriott-change-its-website-the-company-complied.

49. Louis Jacobson, "Yes, Donald Trump Did Call Climate Change a
Chinese Hoax," *PolitiFact*, June 3, 2016, https://www.politifact.com
/truth-o-meter/statements/2016/jun/03/hillary-clinton/yes-donald
-trump-did-call-climate-change-chinese-h/.

50. Michael Greenstone, "Four Years After Declaring War on Pollution, China
Is Winning," *New York Times*, March 12, 2018, https://www.nytimes.com
/2018/03/12/upshot/china-pollution-environment-longer-lives.html.

51. Carl Gene Fordham, "20 Actually Useful Chengyu," *CarlGene.com*
(blog), August 14, 2008, http://carlgene.com/blog/2010/07/20-actually
-useful-chengyu.

52. Stephen Chen, "China Takes Surveillance to New Heights with
Flock of Robotic Doves, but Do They Come in Peace?," *South China
Morning Post*, June 24, 2018, https://www.scmp.com/news/china
/society/article/2152027/china-takes-surveillance-new-heights-flock
-robotic-doves-do-they.

53. Phil Stewart, "China Racing for AI Military Edge over US: Report," *Reuters*,
November 27, 2017, https://www.reuters.com/article/us-usa-china-ai
/china-racing-for-ai-military-edge-over-u-s-report-idUSKBN1DS0G5.

54. Kate Conger, "Google Employees Resign in Protest Against Pentagon
Contract," *Gizmodo*, May 14, 2018, https://gizmodo.com/google
-employees-resign-in-protest-against-pentagon-con-1825729300.

55. Nitasha Tiku, "Amazon's Jeff Bezos Says Tech Companies Should Work
with the Pentagon," *Wired*, October 15, 2018. https://www.wired.com
/story/amazons-jeff-bezos-says-tech-companies-should-work-with-the
-pentagon/.

56. Stewart, "China Racing for AI Military Edge."

57. State Council, People's Republic of China, "China Issues Guideline on Artificial Intelligence Development," English.gov.cn, last modified July 20, 2017, http://english.gov.cn/policies/latest_releases/2017/07/20/content_281475742458322.htm.

58. State Council, People's Republic of China, "Key AI Guidelines Unveiled," English.gov.cn, last modified December 15, 2017, http://english.gov.cn/state_council/ministries/2017/12/15/content_281475977265006.htm.

59. Elsa B. Kania, "China's AI Giants Can't Say No to the Party," *Foreign Policy*, August 2, 2018, https://foreignpolicy.com/2018/08/02/chinas-ai-giants-cant-say-no-to-the-party/.

60. Ibid.

61. Ibid.

62. John Pomfret, "China's New Surveillance State Puts Facebook's Privacy Problems in the Shade," *Washington Post*, March 27, 2018, https://www.washingtonpost.com/news/global-opinions/wp/2018/03/27/chinas-new-surveillance-state-puts-facebooks-privacy-problems-in-the-shade.

63. Nicholas Wright, "How Artificial Intelligence Will Reshape the Global Order," *Foreign Affairs*, July 10, 2018, https://www.foreignaffairs.com/articles/world/2018-07-10/how-artificial-intelligence-will-reshape-global-order.

64. Zhang Hongpei. "Many Netizens Take Issue with Baidu CEO's Comments on Data Privacy," *Global Times*, March 26, 2018, http://www.globaltimes.cn/content/1095288.shtml.

65. Raymond Zhong, "Chinese Tech Giant on Brink of Collapse in New US Cold War," *New York Times*, May 9, 2018, https://www.nytimes.com/2018/05/09/technology/zte-china-us-trade-war.html.

66. Samm Sacks, "Beijing Wants to Rewrite the Rules of the Internet," *Atlantic*, June 19, 2018, https://www.theatlantic.com/international/archive/2018/06/zte-huawei-china-trump-trade-cyber/563033/.

67. Ibid.

68. Ibid.

69. "The Thousand Talents Plan: The Recruitment Program for Innovative Talents (Long Term)," Recruitment Program of Global Experts, http://1000plan.org/en/.

70. Tom Simonite, "The Trump Administration Plays Catch-Up on Artificial Intelligence," *Wired*, May 11, 2018, https://www.wired.com/story/trump-administration-plays-catch-up-artificial-intelligence/.

71. Ari Levy, "Dropbox Is Going Public: Here's Who's Making Money," *CNBC*, February 23, 2018, https://www.cnbc.com/2018/02/23/dropbox-is-going-public-heres-whos-making-money.html.

72. John Gramlich, "5 Facts about Americans and Facebook," *Fact Tank* (blog), April 10, 2018, http://www.pewresearch.org/fact-tank/2018 /04/10/5-facts-about-americans-and-facebook/.

73. Elizabeth Weise, "Amazon Prime Is Popular, but in Three-Quarters of All US Homes? That's Open to Debate," *USA Today*, October 20, 2017, https://www.usatoday.com/story/tech/2017/10/20/amazon-prime-big -though-how-big-no-one-knows/784695001/.

74. "Mobile Fact Sheet," Pew Research Center.

75. https://github.com/tensorflow/tensorflow.

76. Microsoft News Center, "Microsoft to Acquire GitHub for $7.5 Billion," Microsoft.com, June 4, 2018, https://news.microsoft.com/2018/06/04 /microsoft-to-acquire-github-for-7-5-billion/.

77. Jordan Novet, "Why Tech Companies Are Racing Each Other to Make Their Own Custom AI Chips," *CNBC*, April 21, 2018, https://www.cnbc .com/2018/04/21/alibaba-joins-google-others-in-making-custom-ai -chips.html.

78. The full paper can be accessed at https://graphics.axios.com/pdf /PlatformPolicyPaper.pdf?_ga=2.167458877.2075880604.1541172609 -1964512884.1536872317.

79. Tweets can be accessed at https://twitter.com/tim_cook/status /1055035534769340418.

## CHAPTER 3: A THOUSAND PAPER CUTS: AI'S UNINTENDED CONSEQUENCES

1. "'An Owners' Manual' for Google's Shareholders," *2004 Founders' IPO Letter*, Alphabet Investor Relations, https://abc.xyz/investor/founders -letters/2004/ipo-letter.html.

2. Ibid.

3. "Leadership Principles," Amazon, https://www.amazon.jobs/principles.

4. "Focus on Impact," Facebook, September 8, 2015, https://www.facebook .com/facebookcareers/photos/a.1655178611435493.1073741828.163346 6236940064/1655179928102028/?type=3&theater.

5. "Core Values," Tencent, https://www.tencent.com/en-us/culture.html.

6. "Culture and Values," Alibaba Group, https://www.alibabagroup.com /en/about/culture.

7. Mark Bergen, "Google Engineers Refused to Build Security Tool to Win Military Contracts," *Bloomberg*, June 21, 2018, https://www.bloomberg .com/news/articles/2018-06-21/google-engineers-refused-to-build -security-tool-to-win-military-contracts.

8. Sundar Pichai, "AI at Google: Our Principles," *The Keyword* (blog), Google, June 7, 2018, https://www.blog.google/technology/ai/ai-principles/.

9. "QuickFacts," United States Census Bureau, accessed July 1, 2017, https://www.census.gov/quickfacts/fact/table/US/PST045217.

10. Alan MacCormack, John Rusnak, and Carliss Baldwin, *Exploring the Duality Between Product and Organizational Architectures: A Test of the "Mirroring" Hypothesis*, HBS Working Paper No. 08-039, (Boston: Harvard Business School, 2008), https://www.hbs.edu/faculty/Publication%20 Files/08-039_1861e507-1dc1-4602-85b8-90d71559d85b.pdf.

11. Riccardo Miotto, Li Li, Brian A. Kidd, and Joel T. Dudley, "Deep Patient: An Unsupervised Representation to Predict the Future of Patients from the Electronic Health Records," *Scientific Reports*, May 17, 2016, https:// www.nature.com/articles/srep26094.

12. Alexander Mordvintsev, Christopher Olah, and Mike Tyka, "Inceptionism: Going Deeper into Neural Networks," Google AI (blog), June 17, 2015, https://ai.googleblog.com/2015/06/inceptionism-going-deeper-into -neural.html.

13. "Inceptionism: Going Deeper into Neural Networks," Google Photos, December 12, 2008–June 17, 2015, https://photos.google.com/share /AF1QipPX0SCl7OzWilt9LnuQliattX4OUCj_8EP65_cTVnBmS1jn YgsGQAieQUc1VQWdgQ?key=aVBxWjhwSzg2RjJWLWRuVFBB ZEN1d205bUdEMnhB.

14. Latanya Sweeney, "Discrimination in Online Ad Delivery," *ACM Queue* 11, no. 3, (March 2013): 10, doi.org/10.1145/2460276 .2460278.

15. Ali Winston, "Palantir Has Secretly Been Using New Orleans to Test Its Predictive Policing Technology," *Verge*, February 27, 2018, https://www.theverge.com/2018/2/27/17054740/palantir-predictive -policing-tool-new-orleans-nopd.

16. Julia Angwin, Jeff Larson, Surya Mattu, and Lauren Kirchner, "Machine Bias," *ProPublica*, May 23, 2016, https://www.propublica.org/article /machine-bias-risk-assessments-in-criminal-sentencing.

17. Kevin McLaughlin and Jessica E. Lessin, "Deep Confusion: Tensions Lingered Within Google Over DeepMind," *Information*, April 19, 2018, https://www.theinformation.com/articles/deep-confusion-tensions -lingered-within-google-over-deepmind.

18. James Vincent, "Google's DeepMind and UK Hospitals Made Illegal Deal for Health Data, Says Watchdog," *Verge*, July 3, 2017, https:// www.theverge.com/2017/7/3/15900670/google-deepmind-royal-free -2015-data-deal-ico-ruling-illegal.

19. Mustafa Suleyman and Dominic King, "The Information Commissioner, the Royal Free, and What We've Learned," DeepMind (blog), July 3, 2017, https://deepmind.com/blog/ico-royal-free/.

20. "Microsoft Launches Fifth Generation of Popular AI Xiaoice," *Microsoft News Center*, https://www.microsoft.com/en-us/ard/news/newsinfo .aspx?newsid=article_2017091.

21. Sophie Kleeman, "Here Are the Microsoft Twitter Bot's Craziest Racist Rants," *Gizmodo*, March 24, 2016, https://gizmodo.com/here -are-the-microsoft-twitter-bot-s-craziest-racist-ra-1766820160.

22. Peter Lee, "Learning from Tay's Introduction," *Microsoft Official Blog*, March 25, 2016, https://blogs.microsoft.com/blog/2016/03/25 /learning-tays-introduction/.

23. Verity Harding and Sean Legassick, "Why We Launched DeepMind Ethics & Society," DeepMind (blog), October 3, 2017, https://deepmind .com/blog/why-we-launched-deepmind-ethics-society/.

24. "Baidu CEO tells staff to put values before profit after cancer death scandal," CNBC, May 10, 2016, https://www.cnbc.com/2016/05/10 /baidu-ceo-tells-staff-to-put-values-before-profit-after-cancer-death -scandal.html.

## CHAPTER 4: FROM HERE TO ARTIFICIAL SUPERINTELLIGENCE: THE WARNING SIGNS

1. I modeled the scenarios in Part II using research from a variety of sources, and their references are in the bibliography. In addition, I spent time at the *Robots* exhibition at the Science Museum (London), which curated the past 500 years of humanoid robots and was a wonderful place to explore the themes introduced in Chapters 5 through 7.

2. Mike Floorwalker, "10 Deadly Disasters We Should Have Seen Coming," *Listverse*, March 2, 2013, https://listverse.com/2013/03/02/10-deadly -disasters-we-should-have-seen-coming/. And also David Teather, "90-Second Nightmare of Shuttle Crew," *Guardian*, February 6, 2003, https://www.theguardian.com/world/2003/feb/06/columbia.science.

3. Katrina Brooker, "I Was Devastated: Tim Berners-Lee, the Man Who Created to World Wide Web, Has Some Regrets," *Vanity Fair*, July 1, 2018, https://www.vanityfair.com/news/2018/07/the-man -who-created-the-world-wide-web-has-some-regrets.

4. Tim Berners-Lee, "The Web Is Under Threat. Join Us and Fight for It," World Wide Web Foundation (blog), March 12, 2018, https:// webfoundation.org/2018/03/web-birthday-29/.

5. "Subscriber share held by smartphone operating systems in the United States from 2012 to 2018," Statista, https://www.statista.com/statistics /266572/market-share-held-by-smartphone-platforms-in-the-united -states/.

6. "Primary e-mail providers according to consumers in the United States as of 2016, by age group," Statista, https://www.statista.com /statistics/547531/e-mail-provider-ranking-consumer-usa-age/.

7. Marisa Fernandez, "Amazon Leaves Retail Competitors in the Dust, Claims 50% of US E-Commerce Market," *Axios,* July 13, 2018, https:// www.axios.com/amazon-now-has-nearly-50-of-the-us-e-commerce -market-1531510098-8529045a-508d-46d6-861f-1d0c2c4a04b4.html.

8. Art Kleiner, "The Man Who Saw the Future," *Strategy+Business,* February 12, 2003, https://www.strategy-business.com/article/8220 ?gko=0d07f.

9. Cass R. Sunstein, "Probability Neglect: Emotions, Worst Cases, and Law," *Chicago Unbound,* John M. Olin Program in Law and Economics Working Paper No. 138, 2001.

10. "Quick Facts 2015," National Highway Traffic Safety Administration, https://crashstats.nhtsa.dot.gov/Api/Public/ViewPublication/812348.

11. "Aviation Statistics," National Transportation Safety Board, https://www .ntsb.gov/investigations/data/Pages/aviation_stats.aspx.

12. Frederick P. Brooks, *The Mythical Man Month: Essays on Software Engineering,* Anniversary Edition (Boston: Addison Wesley, 1995).

13. Peter Wilby, "Beyond the Flynn Effect: New Myths about Race, Family and IQ?," *Guardian,* September 27, 2016, https://www.theguardian .com/education/2016/sep/27/james-flynn-race-iq-myths-does-your -family-make-you-smarter.

14. Stephanie Condon, "US Once Again Boasts the World's Fastest Supercomputer," *ZDNet,* June 8, 2018, https://www.zdnet.com/article /us-once-again-boasts-the-worlds-fastest-supercomputer/.

15. Jen Viegas, "Comparison of Primate Brains Reveals Why Humans Are Unique," *Seeker,* November 23, 2017, https://www.seeker.com/health /mind/comparison-of-primate-brains-reveals-why-humans-are-unique.

16. Nick Bostrom, "Ethical Issues in Advanced Artificial Intelligence," NickBostrom.com, 2003, https://nickbostrom.com/ethics/ai.html.

17. I. J. Good, "Speculations Concerning the First Ultraintelligent Machine," *Advances in Computers* 6 (1965): 31–88.

18. Gill A. Pratt, "Is a Cambrian Explosion Coming for Robotics?," *Journal of Economic Perspectives* 29, no. 3 (Summer 2015): 51–60, https://www .aeaweb.org/articles?id=10.1257/jep.29.3.51.

CHAPTER 6: LEARNING TO LIVE WITH MILLIONS OF PAPER CUTS:
THE PRAGMATIC SCENARIO

1. Casey Ross and Ike Swetlitz, "IBM Watson Health Hampered by Internal Rivalries and Disorganization, Former Employees Say," *STAT*, June 14, 2018, https://www.statnews.com/2018/06/14/ibm -watson-health-rivalries-disorganization/.
2. Ibid.
3. Gamaleldin F. Elsayed, Ian Goodfellow, and Jascha Sohl-Dickstein, "Adversarial Reprogramming of Neural Networks," preprint edition accessed, https://arxiv.org/pdf/1806.11146.pdf.
4. Orange Wang, "Chinese Mobile Payment Giants Alipay, Tenpay fined US$88,000 for Breaking Foreign Exchange Rules," *South China Morning Post,* July 25, 2018, https://www.scmp.com/news/china/economy/article /2156858/chinese-mobile-payment-giants-alipay-tenpay-fined-us88000.

CHAPTER 7: THE RÉNGŌNG ZHÌNÉNG DYNASTY:
THE CATASTROPHIC SCENARIO

1. "China Has a Vastly Ambitious Plan to Connect the World," *Economist,* July 28, 2018, https://www.economist.com/briefing/2018/07/26/china -has-a-vastly-ambitious-plan-to-connect-the-world.
2. Ibid.
3. Ibid.
4. Ibid.
5. Ernesto Londoño, "From a Space Station in Argentina, China Expands Its Reach in Latin America," *New York Times,* July 28, 2018, https://www.nytimes.com/2018/07/28/world/americas/china-latin -america.html.
6. Kenneth D. Kochanek, Sherry L. Murphy, Jiaquan Xu, and Elizabeth Arias, *Mortality in the United States, 2016,* NCHS Data Brief no. 293 (Hyattsville, MD: National Center for Health Statistics, 2017), https:// www.cdc.gov/nchs/data/databriefs/db293.pdf.

CHAPTER 8: PEBBLES AND BOULDERS: HOW TO FIX AI'S FUTURE

1. "Vinton G. Cerf," Google AI, https://ai.google/research/people/author 32412.
2. Asimov's "Runaround" was first published in the March 1942 issue of *Astounding Science Fiction*. It also appears in his short-story collections *I, Robot* (1950), *The Complete Robot* (1982), and *Robot Visions* (1990).

3. Human Cell Atlas, https://www.humancellatlas.org/learn-more.

4. Cade Metz, "As China Marches Forward on AI, the White House Is Silent," *New York Times,* February 12, 2018, https://www.nytimes.com /2018/02/12/technology/china-trump-artificial-intelligence.html.

5. Yoni Heisler, "Amazon in 2017 Spent Almost Twice as Much on R&D as Microsoft and Apple—Combined," *BGR,* April 10, 2008, https:// bgr.com/2018/04/10/amazon-vs-apple-research-and-development -2017-alphabet-google/

6. "The OTA Legacy," Princeton University, http://www.princeton.edu /~ota/.

7. "Dining," Department of Defense Washington Headquarters Services, http://www.whs.mil/our-services/building-facilities/dining.

8. "The Spheres," Amazon, https://www.seattlespheres.com/.

9. Alicia Adamczyk, "These Are the Companies with the Best Parental Leave Policies," *Money,* November 4, 2015, http://time.com/money /4098469/paid-parental-leave-google-amazon-apple-facebook/.

10. Amy Webb, "Apple vs. FBI Debate May Be the Least of Our Challenges," *CNN,* February 29, 2016, https://www.cnn. com/2016/02/25/opinions/when-technology-clashes-with-law-iphone -opinion-webb/index.html.

11. "China Uncovers 500,000 Food Safety Violations in Nine Months," *Reuters,* December 24, 2016, https://www.reuters.com/article/us-china -food-safety/china-uncovers-500000-food-safety-violations-in-nine -months-idUSKBN14D046.

12. Suneera Tandon, "An IBM Team Identified Deep Gender Bias from 50 Years of Booker Prize Shortlists," *Quartz India,* July 24, 2018, https:// qz.com/india/1333644/ibm-identifies-gender-bias-in-booker-prize -novel-shortlists/.

13. Hilary Mason, *Twitter,* March 28, 2018, https://twitter.com/hmason /status/979044821749895170

14. Deirdre Fernandes, "More Than 60 of MIT's Leading Female Faculty Members Confront University President Over Epstein," *Boston Globe,* September 18, 2019, https://www.bostonglobe.com /metro/2019/09/18/female-faculty-confront-mit-president-over -epstein/84sFmBNrqgtorCBRJPqlDI/story.html.

15. Ronan Farrow, "How an Élite University Research Center Concealed Its Relationship with Jeffrey Epstein," *New Yorker,* September 6, 2019, https://www.newyorker.com/news/news-desk/how-an-elite-university -research-center-concealed-its-relationship-with-jeffrey-epstein.

16. Ibid.

17. Angela Chen and Karen Hao, "MIT Media Lab Founder: Taking Jeffrey Epstein's Money Was Justified," *MIT Technology Review,* September 4, 2019, https://www.technologyreview.com/s/614264/mit-media-lab-jeffrey-epstein-joi-ito-nicholas-negroponte-funding-sex-abuse/.

18. Ibid.

19. Edward Ongweso Jr., "Famed Computer Scientist Richard Stallman Described Epstein Victims As 'Entirely Willing,'" *Vice,* September 13, 2019, https://www.vice.com/en_us/article/9ke3ke/famed-computer-scientist-richard-stallman-described-epstein-victims-as-entirely-willing.

20. Joshua Partlow, "The Layers of Jeffrey Epstein's Connections," *Washington Post,* August 21, 2019, https://www.washingtonpost.com/graphics/2019/national/epstein-connections/.

21. Vanessa Romo, "Free Software Pioneer Quits MIT Over His Comments on Epstein Sex Trafficking Case," *NPR,* September 17, 2019, https://www.npr.org/2019/09/17/761718975/free-software-pioneer-quits-mit-over-his-comments-on-epstein-sex-trafficking-cas.

22. Victoria Bekiempis, "MIT Scientist Resigns Over Emails Discussing Academic Linked to Epstein," *Guardian,* September 17, 2019, https://www.theguardian.com/education/2019/sep/17/mit-scientist-emails-epstein.

23. Susan Svrluga, " Computer Scientist Richard Stallman Resigns from MIT After Comments About Epstein Scandal," *Washington Post,* September 17, 2019, https://www.washingtonpost.com/education/2019/09/17/computer-scientist-richard-stallman-resigns-mit-after-comments-about-epstein-scandal/.

# INDEX

**AMY WEBB** is one of America's leading futurists and is the bestselling, award-winning author of *The Signals Are Talking: Why Today's Fringe Is Tomorrow's Mainstream*, which explains her method for forecasting the future. She is a professor of strategic foresight at the NYU Stern School of Business and the founder of the Future Today Institute, a leading foresight and strategy firm that helps leaders and their organizations prepare for complex, uncertain futures. Webb is a winner of the Thinkers50 Radar Award, a fellow in the United States–Japan Leadership Program, and a delegate on the former US-Russia Bilateral Presidential Commission, and she was a Visiting Nieman Fellow at Harvard University. She serves as a script consultant for films and shows about technology, science, and the future and also publishes the annual FTI Emerging Tech Trends Report, which has now garnered more than 7.5 million cumulative views worldwide. Learn more at http://www.amywebb.io.

PublicAffairs is a publishing house founded in 1997. It is a tribute to the standards, values, and flair of three persons who have served as mentors to countless reporters, writers, editors, and book people of all kinds, including me.

I. F. STONE, proprietor of *I. F. Stone's Weekly*, combined a commitment to the First Amendment with entrepreneurial zeal and reporting skill and became one of the great independent journalists in American history. At the age of eighty, Izzy published *The Trial of Socrates*, which was a national bestseller. He wrote the book after he taught himself ancient Greek.

BENJAMIN C. BRADLEE was for nearly thirty years the charismatic editorial leader of *The Washington Post*. It was Ben who gave the *Post* the range and courage to pursue such historic issues as Watergate. He supported his reporters with a tenacity that made them fearless and it is no accident that so many became authors of influential, best-selling books.

ROBERT L. BERNSTEIN, the chief executive of Random House for more than a quarter century, guided one of the nation's premier publishing houses. Bob was personally responsible for many books of political dissent and argument that challenged tyranny around the globe. He is also the founder and longtime chair of Human Rights Watch, one of the most respected human rights organizations in the world.

·   ·   ·

For fifty years, the banner of Public Affairs Press was carried by its owner Morris B. Schnapper, who published Gandhi, Nasser, Toynbee, Truman, and about 1,500 other authors. In 1983, Schnapper was described by *The Washington Post* as "a redoubtable gadfly." His legacy will endure in the books to come.

Peter Osnos, *Founder*